Gilbert And Sullivan

Also By Michael Ffinch

Voices Round A Star
The Beckwalker
Selected Poems
Westmorland Poems
Simon's Garden
The Dame School at Raisbeck
A Portrait of The Howgills and the Upper Eden Valley
A Portrait of Kendal and the Kent Valley
A Portrait of Penrith and the East Fellside
G.K. Chesterton
Cardinal Newman : The Second Spring

Michael Ffinch

GILBERT AND
SULLIVAN

Weidenfeld and Nicolson · London

Copyright © 1993 by Michael Ffinch
First published in Great Britain in 1993
by George Weidenfeld and Nicolson Limited,
Orion House, 5 Upper St Martin's Lane, London
WC2H 9EA

British Library Cataloguing in Publication Data is
available

ISBN 0 297 81236 X

Typeset by Keyspools Ltd, Golborne, Lancs
Printed by Butler & Tanner Ltd, Frome, Somerset

Contents

Contents

To my daughter Lucy

Illustrations

Acknowledgement is made to the D'Oyly Carte Archive for: 4, 5, 6, 7, 8, 9, 10, 11, 12, and 13 above; and for 14 and 15 to the Theatre Museum (reproduced by kind permission of the Board of Trustees of the Victoria and Albert Museum).

Introduction

One of my earliest childhood memories, at the age of three, is of a performance of *The Yeomen of the Guard* given in Nottinghamshire by the Boots' Operatic Society at Lowdham Grange Borstal Institution where my father was the Deputy Governor. My mother, I am sure, added an attractiveness to the chorus, and the few privileged Borstal inmates brought in to swell the troop of Beefeaters or the crowd of castle-folk must surely have decided to 'go straight' from that moment, but it was neither their presence on the stage, nor Gilbert's words, nor indeed Sullivan's music, that captured my imagination. No, it was the set that did that. The backcloth had been painted by an exceptionally fine German artist who had recently come to live in the village, and, I believe, he and his family were being fully supported there after they had fled from the Nazis. Faced with the prospect of depicting an English castle, the artist had decided to use the keep of Nottingham Castle as his model, something accessible and close at hand, rather than the Tower of London which he had never seen. I had recently been taken to see the castle myself, and the effect of finding it so magnificently recreated before me was thrilling.

I recall that moment not only because it gives me, however tenuously, some justification for being the author of this book, but also because it is an illustration of the kind of licence in production that Gilbert himself would have loathed – though he would most certainly have applauded the artist's desire for accuracy – for Gilbert was meticulously exact in all things and would allow no one to 'improve' upon his own rigid idea of how his opera should be staged; even Sullivan had learnt to remain silent on that score. Gilbert had spent many hours at the Tower of London making sketches in the course of his work for *The Yeomen of the Guard*, and in preparation for the earlier opera, HMS *Pinafore*, he had taken Sullivan to spend a day at Portsmouth to such effect that there was, as Lord Jellicoe confirmed, 'not a rope wrong' in the rigging of the vessel Gilbert recreated on the stage.

As will be made abundantly clear during the course of my narrative, Gilbert's eye for detail made him a very hard task-master. He did not suffer fools gladly, but he was scrupulously fair, and his honesty was of such a high order that he was upset if he found it in the slightest way lacking in others. He was a gentleman at the time when to be such meant something; his success in the theatre coincided exactly with the rising tide of England's greatness, the years of the growth of Empire. His first success with Sullivan, *Trial by Jury*, came in 1875, the year after Disraeli had come to power confirming a time of happy assurance in the twin 'virtues' of imperialism and patriotism, and the blinkered national pride, the jingoism, that these nurtured. Moreover, people knew where they stood in society, and if they 'forgot' they were soon reminded of it. All this with its attendant hypocrisy came as grist to Gilbert's satirical mill, but his satire had nothing of waspishness about it, neither did he choose to use the razor-sharp cutting-edge of Pope or Swift; rather it was the absurdity of a situation that attracted him, and he invited his audiences to share in his sense of fun, so that when they crowded to the Gilbert and Sullivan operas they were able to applaud loudly, though the author was as often as not making them laugh at themselves.

In the course of my endeavours I have come to accept Gilbert as our greatest writer of comic verse, and it is no surprise that snatches from his operas take up much more space in *The Oxford Dictionary of Quotations*, than those of his obvious rivals for the comic bays, Lear and Carroll. Spurred on by this confidence, in relating the operas I have, I hope, quoted enough of Gilbert's verse to give the full flavour of his achievement, and my only regret is that Sullivan's perfectly matching music must remain unheard. Short of issuing an audio tape to go with the book, there is no way of avoiding this; much is the pity.

Now that the Gilbert and Sullivan operas have come out of copyright, there will no doubt be many weird interpretations, and directors' fads and fancies, and, above all, their names will probably eclipse Gilbert's own in the publicity, but this book is intended to give the operas just as Gilbert meant them to be, and as the D'Oyly Carte Company for so many years faithfully performed them, so that they seemed to be as set in their ways as the Nö or Kabuki traditions of Japan. Perhaps the English could never have been expected to be such slaves for long, but there is surely irony in the thought that for so many people the best loved of all Gilbert and Sullivan's operas, *The Mikado*, has a Japanese setting. Japanese? Get away! It's as English as the rest!

Michael Ffinch
Dodding Green
1992

Acknowledgements

I should like to thank the D'Oyly Carte Archive for permission to reproduce their photographs. Also, Macmillan & Co., New York, for permission to use extracts from Sir William Gilbert's and Sir Arthur Sullivan's letters and diaries originally published by Cassell & Company Limited in *Sir Arthur Sullivan* by Herbert Sullivan and Newman Flower, and *The Gilbert and Sullivan Book* by Leslie Baily. I should also like to thank Methuen & Company Limited for permission to use extracts from Gilbert's letters and diaries published in *Gilbert. His Life and Strife* by Hesketh Pearson. I wish to acknowledge the help of the Bodleian Library; the British Library; and the Cumbria County Library, as well as that of many other people, particularly Mr Graeme Soffe, Miss Judy Medrington, Mr and Mrs Matthew Fullerton, Dr and Mrs Roger Baxter, Mr Andrew Maynard, Miss Lucy Ffinch, Mr Peter George, Mr Lawrence James, Mr and Mrs Gordon Stuart, Mrs Veronica Ffinch, Dr and Mrs Christopher Tinker, Mr and Mrs Richard Thomas, Dr Lawrence Catlow, Mr and Mrs Francis Shaw, Mr and Mrs John Robotham, Mr Alexander Ffinch, Mr Martin Blake, Mr Oswald Tatt, the Society of Authors, Mr and Mrs Martin Gardner, Mrs Elspeth Griffiths, the archivist and librarian of Sedbergh School, for permission to consult the early back numbers of *Punch*, and R. F. G. Hollett and Son, Anne Fitzsimmons, Ewen Kerr, and the Harrogate Bookshop for supplying the essential books.

I also wish to thank Christopher Falkus and Hilary Laurie of Weidenfeld and Nicolson, and especially Rosemary Legge, my editor, for the care and interest taken in this book, and, finally, my wife Patricia, for her support during its creation.

Part 1

No Englishman
Unmoved

I

An Unequal Beginning

ᘓ 1836–1867 ᘒ

In 1838, barely a year after Queen Victoria had succeeded to the throne, William Gilbert, a young naval surgeon who had retired early, and his Scottish wife, Anne, left England on a tour of Germany and Italy. They had decided to take with them their small son, also called William, and his nurse. One day during their stay in Naples the nurse was wheeling little Bab, as the child was affectionately called by the family, in his pram when she was met by two seemingly innocuous Neapolitans who assured her that as a matter of urgency the child's parents wished their offspring returned to them at once. What was more, these two swift-footed gentlemen had been instructed to take the boy with them. The nurse was either gullible in the extreme or so sweetly overcome by Latin charm that she handed her charge over without alarm. That is how the author of *The Pirates of Penzance* was kidnapped by brigands at the age of two!

William Schwenck Gilbert had been born in London on 18 November 1836 at his grandfather's house, No. 17 Southampton Street, just off the Strand. His grandfather, described as a tea-merchant and the last man in London to wear Hessian boots and a pigtail, had known Dr Johnson and his circle which included Goldsmith, Reynolds, and Garrick. In one sense young Gilbert was destined to spend much of his future life in the vicinity of his birthplace, since it was no distance from both the Opera Comique, situated on the corner where the Strand met Holywell Street, and the site of the future Savoy Theatre on the Embankment. It was along these streets rising gently up from the Thames or running parallel with it that he would pace anxiously on many a first night, only returning to the theatre for the final curtain.

Although Gilbert himself claimed some lineal affinity with the great Elizabethan explorer Sir Humphrey Gilbert, it is impossible to substantiate the claim. What is known is that William Gilbert's immediate ancestors were of yeoman stock and had lived off the land at Shipton Bellinger, a few miles west of Andover on the Hamphire–Wiltshire border. Gilbert's great-grandfather had moved to London and established a grocery business on the south side of the Thames. His son evidently developed the business further and not only purchased the house in Southampton Street, but also owned property at Hammersmith. There was sufficient money to provide liberally for his family and he appointed as trustees John Samuel and Mary Schwenck, the latter being young William's great-aunt and godmother, from whom at his christening at St Paul's church, Covent Garden on 11 January 1837, he took his second name, a name he grew to loathe intensely, especially as his family tended to address him by it. He would always be known to his sisters' children as Uncle Schwenck.

Gilbert's mother, Anne Morris, was the daughter of a Scottish medical practitioner, and although she was to bear her husband four children – there were three daughters younger than William: Jane, Maud and Florence – the marriage was not happy, and she parted from her husband when Gilbert was nineteen. William Gilbert senior must have been an exceedingly difficult man to live with, even for someone more long-suffering than Anne Morris turned out to be. Born in 1804, he had retired from the navy at the early age of twenty-five on inheriting a comfortable private income. By all accounts the home he provided for his young family at No. 4 Portland Place, Hammersmith, was finely furnished and well staffed, but much time was spent abroad, and so it is not entirely surprising that young Gilbert's first formal education at the age of seven was at a school in Boulogne: throughout his life he could converse and write in fluent French.

When he was thirteen Gilbert entered Great Ealing School, a school with the reputation for 'getting boys on'. Among its pupils at different times were John Henry Newman, Thomas Henry Huxley, William Makepeace Thackeray and Frederick Marryat, the author of *Mr Midshipman Easy* and *The Children of the New Forest*. Unlike Newman who was the most brilliant pupil the master, Dr George Nicholas, had ever known, Gilbert, though clever enough, was idle. As he himself explained: 'It was soon discovered that he could work so quickly that this natural tendency to idleness was no handicap to his abilities.'[1] However, he was on occasion competitive and carried off several prizes. Among his memorable activities were drawing and acting; not only did he act himself, but he also stage-managed and painted the backcloths. The term stage-manager at the time denoting what later came to be called a producer, and, even later, a director. In a melodrama about the Gunpowder Plot Gilbert played the part of Guy Fawkes. 'Rehearsals were noisy, and recalcitrant members of the cast were dealt with in physical combat. The stage-manager discovered that when an actor was knocked down he usually calmed down and did as he was told.'[2]

So fired was Gilbert's enthusiasm for the theatre that in 1851 at the age of fifteen he made a bid to leave school and go on the stage professionally. He sought out the actor-manager Charles Kean at the Princess's Theatre in Oxford Street. It was unfortunate for Gilbert that Kean was on friendly enough terms with Mr Gilbert senior to recognise the young thespian and sent him packing back to Ealing. Perhaps Kean saw much of the father in the boy, for, as the father was to write: 'From my earliest childhood the ridiculous has thrust itself into every action of my life. I have been haunted through my whole existence by the absurd.'[3] Not that young Gilbert's vaulting ambition was absurd exactly, though decidedly hot-headed. Nevertheless, one cannot help wondering what might have happened had Gilbert succeeded in his quest, as the nine-year-old Ellen Terry was to do only four years later when she played Mamillius in Kean's production of *The Winter's Tale*. Not only would he have participated in the best Shakespearian productions of the time, but he might also have developed a love for the bard's language, something he affected to dislike intensely for the rest of his life. 'I don't think Shakespeare rollicking,' he confided to George Grossmith.[4]

Back at school, Gilbert carried on much as before, but in 1852 he contracted typhoid fever so badly that he had to be taken away to recuperate in France. As a result of the fever his hair began to fall out and it was thought wise to shave his head completely. Fully recovering, however, and after another year at the school as head boy, he entered King's College, London, where he read General Literature and Science with the intention of going on to Oxford. Within weeks of Gilbert's arrival news reached England that Turkey had declared war on Russia, and the following spring Lord Raglan, in command of 'the finest army that has ever left our shores',[5] sailed for the Black Sea. These events were to have an immediate and lasting effect on Gilbert.

The outbreak of the Crimean War would have had little effect on the choristers of the Chapel Royal, except possibly on one boy who joined them during Easter Week of 1854: a particularly striking-looking little twelve-year-old of part-Irish, part-Italian descent, called Arthur Sullivan, whose father was the bandmaster at the Royal Military College at Sandhurst. Sullivan had seen many soldiers and so proficient had he been at playing wind instruments that his father had allowed him to rehearse with the band.

Thomas Sullivan had been fortunate to go to Sandhurst in the first place. 'The change drew me out of the awful life of sameness. It was like the coming of a new day.'[6] The old day had been difficult; Sullivan had struggled to bring up a young family on the guinea a week he could earn with his clarinet in the orchestra pit of the Surrey Theatre in Blackfriars Road, Lambeth, where at that time grand opera was being performed. After the final curtain he would hurry home and work far into the night copying out orchestra parts in order to supplement his income. Not that he had far to go, since the house the Sullivans lived in, No. 8 Bolwell Terrace, was within easy walking distance of the theatre, and led off Lambeth Walk. The terrace had been completed in 1838 and the small two-storey houses, with basements and iron palings, were considered modern and desirable; for No. 8 Sullivan paid £20 a year. He was one of the original tenants and he was thirty-three years old when he took it on.

Sullivan's wife, Maria Clementina Coghlan, was, as her name suggests, also partly Irish, but she had strong Italian connections: her mother was a member of the Righi family and, like her husband, had music in her blood. A graduate of a Catholic convent school in Hampstead, she was, prior to her marriage, employed as an assistant at a young ladies' seminary run by her parents. Her life with Thomas Sullivan was blissfully happy and was to remain so in spite of many financial difficulties in the early years. The couple's first child, Frederic, was born a little less than two years after the marriage, and on 13 May 1842 came Arthur Seymour, when his mother was thirty-one years old. It looked for a time as though the financial strain might continue: after Frederic's birth Maria had put him out to a nurse and taken work as a governess in order to make ends meet. Then in 1845, when little Arthur was three, came the move to Camberley.

'Sullivan is one of the most remarkable people we have ever had here. He is what we have lacked – a real musician,'[7] wrote the Colonel about his new bandmaster. As far as Thomas Sullivan himself was concerned the change had brought him closer to the military life his father had known so well though he had not exactly chosen a military career. As Arthur Sullivan, his grandson, remembered:

He was an impoverished young squire, much given to steeplechasing. One day he won a noteworthy steeplechase, and riding homewards he stopped at a little village inn to celebrate the event. This he did, as was the wine-bibbing custom of those days, somewhat too freely. At that time every able-bodied man was being pressed into the King's service. There happened to be a recruiting sergeant in the inn, who pressed the King's shilling into my grandfather's hand. The next morning when he awoke from his heavy sleep he discovered he had enlisted. There was no help for it. Unfortunately, he had just married the handsome daughter of a well-to-do farmer, but the farmer absolutely declined to buy his discharge, and having no money himself, there was nothing to be done but to submit to the inevitable. He was immediately ordered off for foreign service.[8]

The foreign service was the Peninsula campaign, and Sullivan, the hard-living Irishman from County Cork, 'behaved with distinction at Vittoria, Salamanca, and Badajos',[9] rising to the rank of sergeant. After Waterloo he was sent to St Helena as a member of the garrison appointed to guard the exiled Emperor. There his wife and young family joined him, living in the regimental quarters close to Longwood where Napoleon lived. The harmless mischief Napoleon did get up to at Longwood consisted of handing out sweets and cakes to the children on the island; in particular he grew fond of two little girls, the daughter of the Countess Montholon, whose husband was in exile also, and Elizabeth Sullivan, who would one day enter the religious life and end up as the Mother Superior of a convent at Bruges. Reminiscences of this strange posting to St Helena were well known to the Sullivan family. On the day Thomas Sullivan's younger brother John was born, a British soldier had been sentenced to the 'cat' for rudeness to the Emperor: Arthur Sullivan's own version has it that the man was drunk on duty. It was said that Napoleon himself intervened and asked that the man should be reprieved so that Mrs Sullivan might bring her child into the world undisturbed by the cries of the miscreant. So the soldier was taken down from the triangle and let off, eternally grateful for the timely arrival of John

Sullivan! Sergeant Sullivan's last days were spent as a Chelsea Pensioner, where he must have regaled his companions with tales about the strange happenings after 5 May 1821, when Napoleon had died, and Sullivan had found himself sitting through the night with an old 'Brown Bess' in his hand, guarding the heart of the emperor which had been placed in a basin of water with a lamp on a table beside it for fear of its being eaten by rats!

Arthur Sullivan remained at home until he was eight years old; by which time he had composed his first anthem, 'By the Waters of Babylon', and become proficient in playing most of the intruments in his father's band. He seems to have had little difficulty with the flute, clarinet, alt-horn, French horn, cornet, trombone and euphonium. 'I gradually learnt the peculiarities of each, and found out where it was strong and where it was weak; what it could do and what it was unable to do. In this way I learnt the best possible way how to write for an orchestra. I regularly attended the daily practices, in which I was always able to take part – although I was not, of course, allowed to play in public.'[10] Nevertheless, he lacked the embouchure to play the oboe, and the intricacies of the bassoon proved too tricky. In spite of the precocious musical talent his son displayed Thomas Sullivan did not at this time consider a musical career advisable. It was important that an all-round education should be given, and so Arthur was sent away to a private academy run by William Gordon Plees, at No. 20 Albert Terrace, Bishop's Road, Bayswater. Here the boy remained until he was twelve. As the years progressed young Sullivan began to take his life into his own hands: he became determined to enter the Chapel Royal as a chorister and set about the slow process of breaking down his father's resistance. Letter after letter reiterated his ambition. Purcell had been a chorister, he pleaded. Yes, replied his father, but Beethoven had not. 'It means everything to me',[11] the boy insisted. Eventually, with Mr Plees's backing and obvious powers of persuasion, Thomas Sullivan gave way, and Arthur was allowed to seek admission. Arthur wrote home,

I went to see Sir George Smart (the organist at the Chapel Royal) yesterday afternoon. He is a funny old gentleman. He read your letter, patted me on the head, and told me that I must go to Mr Helmore of Onslow Square, Brompton. I and Mr Plees went there, and found that he had gone to live in Cheyne Row. When we got there he was not in, and would not be back until seven, so Mr Plees took me to a coffee shop and we had a cup of coffee and a roll each. Then we went back to Mr H's. He tried my voice and said it was very clear. Asked me some of the Catechism. He seemed very pleased with me.[12]

Thomas Helmore, Master of the Chapel Royal, was pleased indeed. 'Little Sullivan has called here this evening. I like his appearance and manner. His voice is good, and if arrangements can be made to obviate the difficulty of his age being greater that that of the probationers in general, I shall be glad to give him a trial. I shall speak about A.S. to the Sub-Dean tomorrow, and, if he approves of his admission, I will write early next week to his father.'[13]

Helmore was anxious to have the rule of entry waved in Sullivan's case not so much because of the boy's voice, which was certainly excellent, but because of his remarkable musical knowledge. In the event there was no difficulty and only two days after his admission, dressed in the fine gold-braided red jacket and white neckerchief of a chorister, with his father present, Sullivan sang the solo in 'Blessed Is He', an anthem by James Nares, at one time organist at the Chapel. It was not long before Helmore was applying the word 'genius' to his newest arrival, and accounts of Arthur's progress were relayed back to Sandhurst.

'Arthur sang a very elaborate solo in Church today. His expression was beautiful, it brought the tears very near my eyes (although the music itself was rubbish), but as I was immediately to enter the pulpit I was obliged to restrain myself,'[14] Helmore informed Maria Sullivan. The boy was chosen to sing solo on all important occasions, particularly when the nine boys of the choir visited the royal palaces. When the little Duke of Albany, the Queen's eighth child, was christened, Sullivan sang the solo in Michael Costa's anthem 'Suffer little children to come unto me'. Prince Albert was so impressed he gave the 'first chorister' half a sovereign. In fact, with the adulation of his tutors and with his anthem, 'O Israel', published by Novello when he was barely thirteen, there seemed very little musically this prodigious youth could not do.

For Gilbert, the progress of the Crimean War was a call to arms, and he decided to cram himself for the highly competitive examination for a commission in the Royal Artillery. Any idea he might have had of going on to Oxford for further study was forgotten; he would, however, take his BA at King's and then hopefully move on to the

Field of Mars. The examination was to be held round about Christmas-time in 1856, but there was a problem with regard to his age.

'The limit of age was twenty,' Gilbert recalled, 'and as at the date of examination I should have been six weeks over age, I applied for and obtained from Lord Panmure, the then Secretary of State for War, a dispensation for this excess, and worked away with a will.'[15] Yet it was all to no avail: the war came to rather an abrupt and unexpected end, and no more officers were required; the examination was indefinitely postponed. The disappointment Gilbert felt was to have a positive result in the future. As he himself expressed it: 'Among the blessings of peace may be reckoned certain comedies, operas, farces, and extravaganzas which, if the war had lasted another six weeks, would in all probability never have been written.'[16]

Nevertheless he was determined to be a soldier of some sort, and, although he would not make the army his profession, he served for almost twenty years as an officer, firstly as ensign in the 5th West Yorkshire Militia, whose headquarters were at Knaresborough, and secondly in the Royal Aberdeenshire Militia, a regiment in which he rose to the rank of Captain. The Education Department was in Gilbert's eyes 'an ill-organized and ill-governed office',[17] but he was to spend the next four years there, though he described himself as 'one of the worst bargains any Government ever made'.[18] His salary was £120 a year and it seemed this might remain the situation had he not quite unexpectedly inherited a legacy of £300 from an aunt. In one of his few autobiographical fragments Gilbert explains how he used the money: 'I resolved to emancipate myself from the detestable thraldom of this baleful office; and on the happiest day of my life I sent in my resignation. With £100 I paid my call to the Bar, with another £100 I obtained access to a conveyancer's chambers, and with the third £100 I furnished a set of chambers of my own, and began life afresh as a barrister-at-law.'[19]

Gilbert's first chambers were in Clement's Inn, but it was not long before he had moved to Pump Court, Temple, where he shared rooms with two colleagues. Neither was this his final move, for his last chambers were at No. 1 Verulam Buildings, Gray's Inn. His four years at the Bar proved to be a disastrous failure, and it is surprising in view of the torrent of words that flowed into print at this time that he lacked one of the essential qualities of a barrister, the ability to express himself clearly in public. 'I was always a clumsy and inefficient speaker,' he admitted. 'Moreover, an unconquerable nervousness prevented me from doing justice to myself or my unfortunate clients.'[20] So clumsy had he been on one occasion that an old woman whom he was defending on a pick-pocketing charge took off one of her heavy boots in the dock and hurled it at his head as a reward for his effort on her behalf.

During his first two years at the Bar Gilbert earned only £25, a quarter of what he would earn in four years; though he had 'an appetite fresh and hearty', he was indeed 'as many young barristers are, An impecunious party.'[21] However, these lean years were fruitful in other respects, for it was during this time also that he began his literary career, dispatching stories and articles to magazines, most of which were returned with the editor's compliments; until in 1861 *Fun* was launched, a new magazine which became a ready vehicle for Gilbert's particular brand of humour. It was in the pages of *Fun* that the best of what later was known as the Bab Ballads made their first appearance suitably embellished by Gilbert's drawings of grotesque figures with enlarged ears, imbecilic eyes and distended noses reminiscent of Edward Lear's illustrations for *The Book of Nonsense*. Yet there was something distinctive about the ballads and several of them were rich mines from which Gilbert later took characters and plots for his operas. One such was the ballad of 'Captain Reece' who as commander of HMS *Mantelpiece* tried to make the members of his crew as comfortable as possible.

> A feather bed had every man.
> Warm slippers and hot-water can,
> Brown windsor from the captain's store,
> A valet, too, to every four.[22]

On hot days the captain would hand round ice creams on trays and the sailors were encouraged to read *The Times* and the *Saturday Review*. But there were more possible comforts, as the captain's coxswain suggested:

> You have a daughter, Captain Reece,
> Ten female cousins and a niece,
> A ma, if what I'm told is true,
> Six sisters, and an aunt or two.
>
> Now, somehow, sir, it seems to me,
> More friendly-like we all should be,

> If you united of 'em to
> Unmarried members of the crew.
>
> If you'd ameliorate our life,
> Let each select from them a wife
> And as for nervous me, old pal,
> Give me your own enchanting gal![23]

However, one snag threatened to thwart this ingenious plan: the captain's daughter had been promised to an earl and the other ladies 'To peers of various degree'. Nevertheless, the captain did not hesitate to do his duty towards his men for:

> ... what are dukes and viscounts to
> The happiness of all my crew?[24]

and furthermore he himself was willing to marry the coxswain's widowed mother who long had loved him from afar: 'She washes for you, Captain R.'[25]

Here, as will easily be recognised, is the germ of HMS *Pinafore*, and some of the themes included in that and the other Gilbert librettos. The topsy-turvy world of reversed roles, the mocking of class divisions at the expense of the nobility, the pomposity of office, and the absurd fruits of an unbalanced sense of duty.

Gilbert contributed to *Fun* on and off for almost ten years and in 1869 he collected his ballads together in a volume published by John Camden Hotten of Piccadi¹ly, because, as Gilbert expressed it in his preface, they had 'achieved a certain popularity among a special class of readers'.[26] In the same way that Dickens had chosen to use his family's childhood nickname Boz in the title of his first collection of descriptive sketches, so Gilbert chose his 'Bab' for his collection of ballads of 'Much sound and little sense'.[27] A good choice in either instance for both books were successes and each led to greater things.

The musical progress of Arthur Sullivan had continued to be spectacular. In 1856 when he was fourteen and the youngest of seventeen entrants he had won the first Mendelssohn Scholarship which took him to the Royal Academy of Music. 'I could not suppress the tears that accompanied my prayer to the Almighty for his goodness',[28] wrote his father on hearing the news, and in his letter of thanks to Helmore he predicted even greater things, 'should the

Almighty spare him'.[29] Although the scholarship instituted by the singer Jenny Lind and her husband was ostensibly only for one year, because of Sullivan's industry at composition and his general popularity among staff and pupils alike it was extended and he was sent out to Leipzig to continue his studies. He remained there for two and a half years; the Grieg brothers and Carl Rosa were among his fellow-students. It was during his time at Leipzig that Sullivan composed music which would soon make his name even better known when he returned home, in particular his music to Shakespeare's *The Tempest* which was to bring him the friendship of Charles Dickens, for at the piece's second performance at the Crystal Palace in April 1862 Dickens stopped the composer outside the artist's room and enthusiastically revealed his admiration declaring, 'I don't pretend to know much about music, but I know I have been listening to a very great work.'[30] The friendship had one far-reaching effect since it was through Dickens that Sullivan came to meet Rossini.

Nevertheless, it would have been difficult for Sullivan to support himself from composition alone, and he not only taught at this time, but he also took organ lessons from George Cooper, the assistant organist at St Paul's Cathedral, which enabled him to accept the post of organist at St Michael's, Chester Square, a post he held for eight years. Sullivan's choral training enabled him to organise a lively choir at the church; the tenors and basses being drawn from the policemen at the station at Cottage Row nearby: certainly a foretaste of things to come!

'To see the way he kept the constables at the boiling-point of enthusiasm as well as on the brink of laughter,' wrote one who attended the choir practices. 'The organist's good spirits were infectious, and though, as Mr Gilbert said in after years," taking one consideration with another, a policeman's life is not a happy one," I am sure the able-bodied of St Michael's were during rehearsal as cheerful as all the birds in the air. They could not help it, neither could their chief help it, so ebullient was his good nature and so everlasting his charm.'[31] Sullivan himself was full of admiration for his singers: there had been a ready supply of sopranos and contraltos but he had been at his wits' end for the men's parts until he had hit on the idea of the police. 'The Chief Superintendent threw himself heartily into my scheme,' he recalled, 'and capital fellows they were. However tired they might be when they came off duty, they never missed a practice.'[32] On another occasion he described one of those practices as giving the police 'a long grind'.[33]

Sullivan's teaching was not restricted to music, although through his friend George Grove he became Professor of Pianoforte and Ballad singing at the Crystal Palace School of Art. He also returned to the Chapel Royal to teach the choristers the ordinary curriculum, in other words the 3 Rs. However, he never enjoyed the experience. 'I hated teaching and nothing on earth would ever have made me a good teacher. The first guineas that I gave up for the work that I wanted to do were those that came from giving lessons,'[34] he wrote. With many irons already in the fire his health, which would never be robust, began to suffer. 'I am sorry to hear you have not been well,' wrote Jenny Lind. 'Do you give too many lessons, together with too much – sleep (oh!) and too much indigestible food? (Oh! oh!) You don't doubt but that only the desire of seeing you shake off all that does not belong to a gifted nature dictates these seemingly harsh words from your true friend.'[35]

The great success of *The Tempest* spurred Sullivan on to set six of Shakespeare's songs, each of which he sold to a publisher for five guineas; their popularity led to the setting of 'Orpheus With His Lute' from *Henry VIII*, one of Sullivan's most famous settings for which he received ten guineas. It was Grove, at whose house in Sydenham Sullivan often stayed, who persuaded him that this method of publishing was foolish, and that rather than selling the songs outright he should demand a royalty on each copy sold and retain the copyright. 'My next song "Will He Come?" went to Messrs Boosey, on the understanding that I was to have a royalty on every copy sold. And oh the difference to me! I did very well with "Will He Come?" and never afterwards sold a song outright.'[36] This upturn in his fortune meant that during the 1860s Sullivan composed many songs destined to become exceedingly popular. Writing at what amounted to fever-pitch he was capable of composing several songs in the course of a few hours. In one day he was said to have produced 'Sweethearts', 'Looking Back', 'Once Again' and 'Let Me Dream Again'! 'I have worked lika a horse this last week,' he informed his mother from Sydenham, 'and have got over a great deal of ground. Mr Grove and I write on till two every morning, and then have a cigarette and go to bed.'[37] Neither were songs his only interest, for it was at this time also that Sullivan's interest in opera was aroused.

The Italian Michael Costa, whose anthem the boy Sullivan had sung at the royal christening, had become a close friend and was now the controller of Covent Garden. Through his encouragement Sullivan began to attend as many performances, and more particularly rehearsals, at Covent Garden as he could manage, and eventually Costa offered him the post of organist at the Opera House, and this in turn led to Sullivan's commission to write a ballet. *L'Ile Enchanté* was the result, but it was not a success and Sullivan decided that perhaps after all the opera house was not for him, though he slaved away setting the libretto of *The Sapphire Necklace* for his friend Chorley, Besides, a visit to Ireland in 1863 would result in his first symphony, the 'Irish Symphony', as it was later called. He informed his mother from Belfast,

it is true I am not working much, but I shall feel the practical results when I return to London. My life is a lazy one, as I do little else but lie on the grass (if it is fine), or lie in the drawing-room, reading and playing, but I already feel my ideas assuming a newer and fresher colour. I shall be able to work like a horse on my return. Why, the other night as I was jolting home from Holestone through the wind and rain on an open jaunting car, the whole first movement of a symphony came into my head with a real fresh flavour about it – besides scraps of the other movements.[38]

George Grove, who was twenty-six years older than Sullivan, had begun his career as a civil engineer. For some years he had lived in the West Indies where he had been responsible for erecting lighthouses. On his return to England he fostered his interest in music, becoming successively Secretary to the Society of Arts and the Crystal Palace Company: it had been through his influence that the performance of Sullivan's *The Tempest* had been organised. However, Grove's talents were far-reaching, and he is well-known particularly for his editing work; not only did he help compile *Smith's Dictionary of the Bible*, but also his own *Dictionary of Music and Musicians*. The latter, of course, is still in print, though much extended from the original four volumes published between 1879 and 1889 while its editor was Director of the Royal College of Music.

Grove first met Sullivan, 'an engaging looking young man' just back from Leipzig, at a concert in St James's Hall. The two struck up an immediate friendship destined to last for life. Sullivan engaged Grove in a long discussion of Schumann's music, about which Grove knew next to nothing, and through the young man's enthusiasm and powers of persuasion Schumann's Symphony in B Flat was soon played at the Crystal Palace.

Sullivan was one of those who in the most charming manner sought to ingratiate himself to those he thought might be useful to him. 'He always wanted to make an impression, and, what is more, always succeeded in doing so,' wrote Clara Barnett who had studied at Leipzig with him. 'Whenever some distinguished persons came for the Gewandhaus concerts or to visit the Conservatorium, Sullivan always contrived to be on hand to render some little service which brought him to their notice and formed an entering wedge to their acquaintance, and in this way he got into personal touch with most of the celebrities, while the rest of us only worshipped at a distance.'[39] It was, Clara Barnett thought, Sullivan's natural instinct that eventually brought him so close to the Royal Family. He was a natural courtier; which did not prevent him from being a very lovable person. Yet, it will be remembered, Sullivan had been first noticed at court when he had sung at the royal christening, but in 1863 when his song 'Bride from the North' celebrated the arrival of the Danish Princess Alexandra he was further appreciated, and the Wedding March he composed for the marriage of the Princess to the Prince of Wales was played up and down the country. Through these compositions Sullivan was soon on intimate terms with the Prince himself, but more particularly with his brother Prince Alfred, the Duke of Edinburgh and Saxe-Coburg-Gotha, the Queen's second son, an amateur composer of some talent and a competent violinist with a wide knowledge of music: here was another lasting friendship.

However, no one was closer to Sullivan than Grove at this time, and it was through him that he met the Scott Russell family. John Scott Russell, the illustrious engineer responsible with Brunel for building the liner the *Great Eastern*, was one of the directors of the Crystal Palace Company: he had three beautiful daughters and two of them, Rachel and Louise (Scott Russell), formed a particular friendship with Sullivan. In fact, it is probable that both girls were in love with him, although it was Rachel with whom Sullivan himself became romantically attached, and for a while she dominated his life, attempting to organise every aspect of it, since she knew that unless his life could be more stable there would be no chance whatever of her father approving a marriage, even if Sullivan had really wished it. Certainly Rachel did most of the running, and without her parents' knowledge she and Sullivan became engaged.

'If you are ready to marry me next year then well and good,' she wrote. 'I will tell Mama and Papa when you see the project clear before you without a doubt – clear of debt – and then there will be no reasonable objection. I will try and not fret, and keep up my courage. My father doats so on me that I think it will be a fearful blow to him.'[40]

There was to be no marriage, to Rachel or anyone else, neither did Sullivan feel ready to be tied down. Had he married Rachel he would never have been able to continue in the free and easy manner he enjoyed. 'I cannot think how you can go on living the life you do, going to miserable sickly London parties, smoking half the night through, and then getting up seedy and limp and unfit for any honest work,' she fretted. For Rachel, 'honest work' could only consist of composing serious music: grand opera, symphonies, sacred cantatas; she would never have imagined herself as the wife of the composer of *Trial by Jury*! No, for her the future was serious: 'I want you to write an opera – such an opera – and I feel it must be done this winter – a grand and vigorous work,'[41] she was insisting during the summer of 1866.

Nevertheless Sullivan was soon to need Rachel's comforting hand, for in the third week of September his father died suddenly after only a few days' sickness. 'Oh, it is so hard, it is so terribly hard to think that I shall never see his dear face again, or hear his cheery voice saying, "God bless you, my boy!"'[42] Sullivan wrote to his friend Nina Lehmann. His father had been the mainstay of his life up till now, his sternest critic, but always ready with positive advice. Sullivan knew what sacrifices both his parents had made on his behalf, but it was to his father that he more often turned. In spite of his own busy musical life – he had moved from Sandhurst to the Royal Military School of Music at Kneller Hall in 1857 – Thomas Sullivan had made himself available to his son and was full of encouragement. At an inconvenient time he had hurried to catch the train to Birmingham in order to be present at the first performance of *Kenilworth*, the cantata Arthur had composed for the festival there. 'You will never have another opportunity of hearing the work performed in such a magnificent style again. It is a great event in my life, and one that I should like you to witness.'[43] Such a request could not be ignored.

A few days before he died he had again offered encouragement when he learnt how Arthur was finding it difficult to fulfil a commission for the Norwich Festival: weeks had passed and nothing worthwhile had come; he was on the edge of despair; he quite thought he would have to give up the attempt. 'Don't give it up,' his father had exhorted. 'Something will probably occur which will put new vigour and fresh thought into you.'[44] It did, but it was the last thing either of his sons would have wished. Within a week after his father's funeral in the fullness of his grief Sullivan had completed his overture *In Memoriam*. Music could express what he felt unable to do with words, not even to his mother, for another two years.

On 26 July 1867 *Fun* advertised that the burlesque *Robinson Crusoe or the Injun Bride and the Injured Wife* was ready for sale at the magazine's office: among its six authors was W. S. Gilbert, a regular contributor. The piece had been performed at the Theatre Royal, the Haymarket, some three weeks earlier, and the proceeds of the sale of the text were now for the benefit of the widowed mother of the late Paul Gray. Gray had also worked for the magazine and with H. J. Byron, the first editor, and Thomas Hood, his successor, had become Gilbert's close friend. The man Gilbert referred to as 'poor Tom Hood' should not be confused with his more illustrious father, the poet of the same name, though also an editor, and friend of Lamb, Hazlitt and de Quincey. However, Hood the younger achieved some notoriety as editor not only of *Fun* but also *Tom Hood's Comic Annual* begun in 1867.

There was nothing striking about Gilbert's contribution to the Crusoe burlesque, but it was not his first venture in this field. Towards the end of the previous year the same theatre had presented his *Dulcamara; or the Little Duck and the Great Quack*, billed as a 'new and original extravaganza'. An 'extravaganza' it might be, but there was nothing 'new' or 'original' about it: the plot had been lifted from Donizetti's *L'Elixir d' amore* and the style was not recognisably Gilbert's. The piece had taken him barely ten days to dash off, and it was in rehearsal for a week, but speed had been essential, as Gilbert explained: the lessee of the theatre had asked the dramatist Tom Robertson if he knew anyone who could write a Christmas piece in a fortnight!

After the first performance the author took a dozen of his friends out to dinner; it had never entered his head that the performance would be a failure, neither was it, though in later life such foolhardiness evaded him. 'I have since learned something about the risks inseparable from a "first night" and I would as soon invite friends to supper after an amputation at the hip-joint.'[45] However, the burlesque had been appreciated, largely owing to Frank Matthews's 'excellent impersonation' of Dr Dulcamara, but in the hurry of production no terms of payment had been discussed, as Gilbert recalled.

I modestly hoped that, as the piece had been a success, £30 would not be considered an excessive price for the London right. Mr Emden, the acting manager, looked rather surprised, and, as I thought, disappointed. However, he wrote a cheque, asked for a receipt, and, when he had got it he said: 'Now take a bit of advice from an old stager who knows what he is talking about: never sell so good a piece as this for £30 again.'[46]

Gilbert never did, and from that time onwards somehow he was able to keep his head above water, which was just as well because he was soon to ask Lucy Agnes Turner, a very young girl with whom he was infatuated, to be his wife.

Lucy, the daughter of an Indian Army officer, was still only seventeen when she married Gilbert at St Mary Abbot's Church, Kensington, on 6 August 1867. She was exceptionally pretty with fair hair, blue eyes and a petite figure. Gilbert called her his little 'Kitten' – Kitty – and she answered to that name for the rest of his life. The marriage, though childless, was destined to be very happy, and Kitty seems to have known exactly how to please her husband, supporting his wildest whims and soothing his moods; quite remarkably, through the years she remained unaffected by jealousy at his attachment to other women, which she realised was inevitable in the theatre, largely playful and no real threat to her own position.

The couple's first Kensington home was No. 28 Eldon Road, but before long they moved to No. 8 Essex Villas. To support his young wife Gilbert worked away at his theatrical ventures with great gusto.

Dulcamara had been followed by another burlesque of a Donizetti opera: this time *La Figlia del Regimento* was the target. Gilbert's *La Vivandiere; or True to the Corps* opened on 6 July 1867 at the Queen's Theatre in Long Acre, and ran for 120 nights bringing its author more notoriety.

Gilbert always acknowledged how much he revered the theatrical innovations of T. W. Robertson: 'It is entirely to him that I owe my introduction to stage work,'[47] he said. Robertson had virtually invented stage management, an unknown art before his time; he brought life and spontaneity to his productions. Gilbert made a point of attending many of his rehearsals and noticed how Robertson by taking upon himself every detail of the production was able to bring variety and nature to a scene, by breaking it up with all sorts of little incidents and delicate byplay. Born into a theatrical family from Lincoln, the eldest of the twenty-two children of an actor, Tom Robertson had acted as a child, but it was as a dramatist that he made his name and his play *David Garrick*, performed at the Haymarket in 1864, brought him considerable notice. Soon Robertson's 'cup-and-saucer drama' typified in such plays as *Society*, *Ours* and *Caste*, seen at the Prince of Wales Theatre, established his reputation. Sadly for Gilbert, after a few years of fame Robertson died suddenly in 1871 leaving a permanent mark on the theatre upon which Gilbert was able to build, but not living long enough to share in the success of his protégé. It was Robertson's youngest sister. Madge, who, with her future husband William Kendal, would help further Gilbert's career by playing with great brilliance the leading parts in his plays, particularly *The Palace of Truth* and *Pygmalion and Galatea*, at the Haymarket, regarded as the leading playhouse in London at the time.

It was a chance meeting in Bond Street with F.C. (Francis Cowley) Burnand, the future editor of *Punch*, that brought Sullivan into the world of operetta. Burnand was looking for a composer for his burlesque of J.Maddison Morton's popular one-act farce *Box and Cox* which had been first performed in London in 1847. As the burlesque was only to be presented before friends at a musical supper party, with the parts played chiefly by amateurs, there would be no fee attached. Sullivan agreed and dashed off the music at great speed, thinking little more of it. However, it was immediately seen that the piece had merit and it was performed once or twice again privately before Burnand decided on a repeat performance in aid of a fund that *Punch* was organising for the families of deceased members of the staff. The result was another successful performance at the Adelphi Theatre in the Strand, with the *Punch* artist George du Maurier singing the leading part, and Sullivan himself at the piano. The audience was wild with enthusiasm, with the result that the piece was transported to Manchester before returning to London for a longer run. What made *Cox and Box; or The Long Lost Brothers*, Burnand's version with the heroes' names reversed, different from other burlesques was its lack of crudity; here was a burlesque worthy of the Victorian sense of decency, and the music was tuneful and lively. The obvious producers for the peice were the German Reeds. Thomas

German Reed and his wife Priscilla Horton, both actors, had established themselves at the Royal Gallery of Illustration in Waterloo Place, Lower Regent Street, a theatre which specialised in the kind of humorous sketches any respectable family could go to without experiencing the vulgar or suggestive allusions, the 'French sauciness', usually associated with burlesque. As was said of them, the German Reeds 'made a triumph of legitimate comedy'. *Cox and Box* opened at the Gallery and ran for three hundred performances!

The plot is typical enough. The action takes place in a boarding house run by an old military campaigner, Bouncer, who has let the same room to two lodgers: Cox, a hatter, who works during the day, and Box, a printer, who works at night. All goes smoothly until Cox is given a day off and then the fun begins. Bouncer attempts to control the situation by bursting into military songs to delay things whenever the two are about to meet: but all in vain. Cox and Box do meet and find they have much in common: not only do they share the same room, but they discover they are both involved in different ways with the same girl, Penelope Ann. Box is being sued for breach of promise, and Cox is about to marry her. A duel seems inevitable, pistols are called for; then Bouncer produces a letter he should have given Cox; it is from Penelope Ann announcing that she is breaking off the engagement to marry a man called Knox! Both relieved, Cox and Box decide to make the best of it, and the 'triumviretta in one act' comes to a happy finale with the two discovering they are in fact long-lost brothers, since neither has a strawberry mark on his left arm!

Among those who reviewed this happy piece was the theatre critic of *Fun*: 'Mr Sullivan's music is, in many places, of too high a class for the grotesquely absurd plot to which it is wedded,' Gilbert wrote. 'It is very funny, here and there, and grand or graceful where it is not funny; but the grand and graceful have, we think, too large a share of the honours themselves.'[49] There seemed only one remedy for any further collaboration: either Sullivan must match his music to the text more closely, or the text should be of a higher and more subtle tone. Only time would tell.

As for Sullivan himself, he was completely taken by surprise at his success and, spurred on by Burnand and the German Reeds, he agreed to set the libretto of a more ambitious project, the comic opera *The Contrabandista*, a tale of Spanish brigandage. Although as with *Cox and Box* it took him only a few days to compose the music Sullivan felt pleased with it, and even Rachel was more than approving. 'I think the

Contrabandista music too lovely all through,'[50] she wrote excitedly. Fully expecting a further boost to their fortunes, the German Reeds decided to launch the opera at the St George's Hall in Langham Place, which was raised to the dignity of the St George's Opera House. An orchestra of forty musicians was employed and some of the best singers, but there was trouble ahead: the bass withdrew after a few rehearsals and it was decided the soprano was too weak. They must search about for a better soprano. One of those auditioned had 'a fine voice with rather a coarse Italian style of singing'. She was short and fat, but, as German Reed informed Sullivan, this could be compensated for. The lady was not pretty, 'but with paint and bismuth might be made to look decent'.[51] Not 'decent' enough perhaps, but the opening night, 18 December 1867, was a modest success: there were several musical encores, 'and both composer and author were called to the footlights at the conclusion of the performance'. The critics were respectful of Sullivan's music, considering it gay, tripping, and humorous, without at any point degenerating into burlesque. In spite of all endeavour *The Contrabandista* failed to pay its way and only ran for a few weeks before it was withdrawn. Sullivan hung on to the score and the opera was revived many years later with the title *The Chieftain*.

Sullivan was disappointed by this comparative failure, but was forced to accept the situation, seeing it as an omen that perhaps after all his true vocation did not lie in the direction of comedy. Besides, he had been engaged in much else that pointed along a more serious path. Early that same autumn, soon after his appointment as Professor of Composition at the Royal Academy of Music, he had accompanied Grove to Vienna with the purpose of tracing some Schubert manuscripts, there being very little of that composer's work obtainable in England. Having arranged to visit C. A. Spina, the music publisher, on their arrival, all that the shop had was placed at their disposal and Herr Spina personally regaled them with cigars; but more importantly he had also arranged an introduction with Dr Schneider, a relative of Schubert's, from whom they were able to obtain the scores of two symphonies, the C Major and the C Minor, and an overture, *Die Freunde von Salamanca*. The old frail clerk in the shop, Doppler, fascinated them. He had known Beethoven and Schubert well, he told them. 'Beethoven wore a green and Polish coat with frogs on it – and when in the shop generally leant against a wooden pillar by the counter, whilst Czerny, Siegfried and Stradler sat on a leather sofa. They wrote down their conversation on a slate as Beethoven was stone deaf.'[52]

What Grove most wished to discover was the music for *Rosamunde*. Spina's shop provided no sign of it, and the two Englishmen decided to leave Vienna for Prague. On their last day they returned to Schneider's house to say goodbye. As Grove recalled:

The doctor was civility itself; and again he had recourse to the cupboard, and showed us some treasures which had escaped us before. I again turned the conversation to the *Rosamunde* music; he believed that he had at one time possessed a copy of the sketch of it all. Might I go to the cupboard and look for myself? Certainly, if I had no objection to being smothered in dust. In I went; and after some search, during which my companion kept the doctor engaged in conversation, I found, at the bottom of a cupboard, and in its farthest corner, a bundle of music-books two feet high, carefully tied round, and black with the undisturbed dust of half a century. These were the part books of the whole of the music for *Rosamunde*, tied up after the second performance in December 1823, and probably never disturbed since.[53]

The link with Beethoven and Schubert gave Sullivan an added confidence, but the visit was to influence him in other ways: the Vienna they were visiting was the city of the Strausses, and at the time the waltz was all the rage. Quite by chance another Strauss – a viola player – had travelled on the same boat from England. 'We fraternised and sat on the deck together, and suffered agonies in company – so that was quite jolly,'[54] Sullivan wrote. During the same journey Grove and he spent time at Baden in the company of Clara Schumann, then at Munich, and Salzburg where they visited the Mozartium. As Sullivan wrote in the Visitors' Book, the curator asked if he was the composer of whom he had often read in the musical papers. Sullivan modestly owned that he did occasionally write a little music. Then on leaving Vienna the two had travelled on to Prague and finally Leipzig, where *In Memoriam* was performed at the Gewandhaus as part of a concert in which Rubenstein had played his own Concerto in D Minor. 'Everyone of note came and congratulated me,' Sullivan informed his mother, 'and I think it has laid a firm foundation for a good reputation in Germany. Next Monday the Symphony is to be tried, and then I leave for Paris.'[55]

The journey to Paris was broken at Dresden, where Sullivan had hoped to see his old tutor Dr Rietz. Rietz was unfortunately away, but he attended a performance of Wagner's *Rienzi* which he found a great disappointment – 'a mixture of Weber, Verdi, and a touch of Meyerbeer. The whole very commonplace, vulgar and uninteresting.'[56]

2

The Gods Grown Old

⤳ 1867–1875 ⤳

The 1860s were to witness a revival of popular interest in the theatre. Suddenly the theatre became respectable; even the Queen approved and in the previous few years had been a frequent visitor to the Princess's Theatre for the lavish Charles Kean productions. But old prejudices die hard and for decades the public had thought of the stage as something low and degrading. Perhaps Dickens had not helped; the kind of private theatre he described few people would have wished to visit, where the principal patrons were 'dirty boys, low copying-clerks in attorneys' offices, capacious-headed youths from city counting houses; Jews, whose business as lenders of fancy dresses, is a sure passport to the amateur stage; shop-boys, who now and then mistake their masters' money for their own; and a choice miscellany of idle vagabonds.'[1] Actresses had been thought of as little more than whores. It was no doubt true that in the past the two professions had often worked in close proximity, the predominantly male audiences providing ready clients for 'girls of a certain class'; but in the October of 1860 a definite change was felt. It was noted that in the winter season all the theatres in London from Her Majesty's to the Soho were open at the same time, something unheard of before. Soon it was estimated that in the course of a day as many as 15,000 might attend some kind of theatrical performance.

There was much on offer, anything from the serious productions of Shakespeare by Samuel Phelps at the Sadler's Wells Theatre, to Astley's, now renamed the Theatre Royal, Westminster, where in a stage adaptation of Lord Byron's *Mazeppa* the American actress, Adah Isaacs Menken, caused a sensation by appearing, 'in a state of virtual nudity while bound to the back of a wild horse'.[2] Horses had appeared in other productions, and Kean himself playing the part of Bolingbroke had ridden on to the stage to be greeted by a cheering crowd in his production of *Richard II*.

The rise in demand meant a rise in standards; what might have satisfied in the past was now considered second-rate. There was a need for new serious drama, though few, if any, authors to provide it; serious opera was available, not only at Her Majesty's but also at the Royal Italian Opera at Covent Garden: Gounod's *Faust* received London performances at both theatres in 1864. Giuseppe Mario and Adelina Patti made their debuts, and photography helped to make such singers better known. *The Illustrated London News* which had been founded in 1842 was by now including photographs as well as sketches and was anxious to publish reviews of opera, ballet and stage plays. Opera began to have a wider and wider appeal during the following years, while burlesques of serious productions provided lively humour.

This was the time also that saw the emergence of the music hall as a popular place of entertainment. The halls had their origin in the rowdy taverns on the fringes of central London and had developed from the Catch and Glee clubs by which a publican might keep better order and boost trade. Soon rooms were being specially converted or built for the purpose with a small stage and curtains, and a chairman appointed, often the landlord himself, to introduce the performers. However, the idea, though working class in origin, was seen to have promise for a more sophisitcated audience; for some time there had been Song and Supper rooms such as Evans's, in King Street, Covent Garden, where gentlemen might dine and be entertained at one and the same time. Among the first music halls de luxe, both opening in 1861, were the Oxford Music Hall, managed by Charles Morton, 'the father of the Halls', who had earlier run musical entertainments as landlord of the Canterbury Arms; and the London Pavilion in Tichborne Street which grew from the roofed-in stableyard of the Black Horse Coaching Inn. Before long the music halls were becoming serious rivals to the theatres in popularity, and often staged burlesques of the burlesques. It was into this quickly expanding business of newly built theatres or refurbished old ones and the rising music halls that Gilbert had already made his mark.

On Boxing Day 1867 the Lyceum Theatre's grand comic Christmas pantomime was entitled *Harlequin and Jenny Wren: or Fortunatus and the Water of Life, the Three Bears, the Three Gifts, the*

Three Wishes, and the Little Man who woo'd the Little Maid. Gilbert had taken four days to write it and it was in rehearsal for three weeks. Among its attractions was the 'Finette Troupe' who had travelled over from France. They made a shaky start, as Gilbert recalled. 'They looked white – a dirty white – after the Channel crossing. Hats, cloaks, wraps were cast off – and eventually, I am bound to add, their dresses also, and in their petticoats, they went through their business with extraordinary spirit. The rehearsals were a wild scramble.'[3] There were more problems with the scenery; it did not arrive on time, and the fish ballet was played in a forest scene instead of the crystal fountain! Gilbert was paid £60 for his effort, but he had to wait for the money.

During the same autumn the Prince of Wales Theatre had presented his farce *Allow Me to Explain*, a piece adapted from the French. The plot turned upon Cadderby's annuity of £300 a year being dependent on the life of Mr John Smith, whom he has never seen. The Royalty Theatre had also produced another Gilbert farce, *Highly Improbable*, the action of which takes place at a croquet party where the six daughters of the local MP dress up as professional men, in order to 'drive away' a friend of their father who is up from the country and for whom the father has political ambitions. The friend turns the tables on the girls and finally marries the eldest.

In the following March the Royalty, now the New Royalty, staged Gilbert's whimsical parody on the *Bohemian Girl* with the title *The Merry Zingara; or the Tipsy Gipsy and the Pipsy Wipsy*. The printed text announced the author as a member of the 'Dramatic Authors' Society'.

Gilbert would have been well aware at this time of the busy building activity at the east end of the Strand where John Hollingshead was overseeing the resurrection of the Gaiety Theatre on the site of the earlier Strand Musick Hall which had closed down at the end of 1866. Hollingshead was anxious to establish a permanent company of the finest actors and to encourage authors. The theatre was scheduled to open for the Christmas season on 21 December 1868, and Hollingshead had commissioned Gilbert to produce a suitable piece as one of the three items for the occasion. The result was the operatic extravaganza *Robert the Devil; or the Nun, the Dun, and the Son of a Gun*, a burlesque of Mayerbeer's opera, which came last on the bill.

As the theatre was swarming with workmen up to the last minute

Gilbert had been unable to rehearse the cast on the stage there; rehearsals had taken place at Astley's, and the actors had had to move from place to place in order to rehearse certain scenes with the ballet or the chorus. There was no dress rehearsal, the actors only seeing their costumes on the day of the performance. Neither had things gone smoothly for the scenery owing to Grieve's paintroom in Macklin Street being gutted by fire, so a second set of backdrops had to be prepared at great speed in a windswept, leaking oil-cloth factory in Camberwell. Nevertheless the theatre and production were ready on the night, though the workmen refused to leave the building they had so long attended and occupied the first two rows of the gallery, insisting that they deserved to be allowed to be there. Hollingshead was inclined to agree with them and they were allowed to stay, while those who had actually bought the seats were found places elsewhere.

The whole evening was a resounding success, as the *Daily Telegraph* related the following morning. 'The programme comprised a sparkling one-act operetta, called *The Two Harlequins*, composed by M. E. Jonas; a comedy-drama in three acts adapted from *L'Escamoteur*, and re-named *On the Cards*; and a new operatic extravaganza by Mr W. S. Gilbert, giving a fresh version of the old legend of Robert le Diable.'[4] The music for *Robert the Devil* had been selected and arranged by M. Kettenus, the musical director whom Hollingshead had coaxed from the Royal Opera; it was drawn from popular composers, from Mayerbeer naturally, but also Auber, Herold, Bellini, Hervé and Offenbach. The part of Robert of Normandy, the wicked father of William the Conqueror, was played by Miss E. Farren, the famous Nellie Farren, who through the following years remained one of the Gaiety's chief attractions, the principal of 'principal boys', appearing as Aladdin during the Christmas season in 1870.

The audience, as the *Daily Telegraph* went on to describe, 'proved enthusiastic in their appreciation of all the exertions which had been so strenuously made to secure their comfort and ensure their amusement'.[5] Tom Robertson was there to see his sister Madge play the part of Florence Ethelward in *On the Cards*; Dion Boucicault, the Irish dramatist and actor; Mr and Mrs George Grossmith, whose son, also named George, would play such an important part in Gilbert and Sullivan's lives; and Gilbert's friend Tom Hood, together with many who later became leading names in the theatre and journalism. Charles Dickens had written to say he was sorry not to be able to attend because he was in Glasgow on one of his reading tours. Among the audience also was Arthur Sullivan, but on that occasion he was not destined to meet the author of *Robert the Devil*. One can only assume that he laughed heartily at the fun as Gilbert fitted his absurd words to well-known tunes, the sort of words Sullivan would often find so frustrating to set to music in the future.

> If you intend to stay with us, before you've been a day with us,
> You'll learn the proper way with us, of saying what you say to us.
> Each speech should have a pun in it, with very foolish fun in it,
> And if you can't bring one in it – you'd better stay away.[6]

It was through the composer Frederic Clay that Gilbert did eventually meet Sullivan early in the autumn of 1869 at the Royal Gallery of Illustration. After their brief time at the St George's Hall the German Reeds had moved back to No. 14 Regent Street and had commissioned Clay to set Gilbert's one-act operetta *Ages Ago*, of interest chiefly because Gilbert employed a device he would later use again in *Ruddigore*: characters from portraits coming out of their frames to take part in the action.

Clay was one of Sullivan's closest friends, described as 'a genial, wandering soul, and a slave to music'.[7] He was older than Sullivan by two years, but had studied at Leipzig at the same time, after giving up a post at the Treasury to concentrate on his music, a move he felt able to make only after his father, a Member of Parliament, had died. Something of a bohemian, he had introduced Sullivan to a wide circle of like-minded people. He is best known as the composer of three songs, popular in their day: 'I'll sing thee songs of Araby', 'The Sands of Dee' and 'She wandered down the mountain side', but he composed many operas and collaborated with Gilbert on several occasions.

If the account of the famous meeting is accurate, the composer of the recently successful oratorio *The Prodigal Son* might have thought the author of the *The Bab Ballads* an odd sort of fish, had he not known something of Gilbert's work and manner already. Perhaps he was not then too surprised when Gilbert addressed him with:

I am very pleased to meet you, Mr Sullivan, because you will be able to settle a question which has arisen between Mr Clay and myself. My contention is that when a musician, who is master of many instruments, has a musical theme to express, he can express it as perfectly upon the simple tetrachord of Mercury (in which there are, as we all know, no diatonic intervals whatever) as upon the more elaborate disdiapason (with the familiar four tetrachords and the redundant note) which, I need not remind you, embraces in its simple consonance all the single, double and inverted chords.[8]

Gilbert was trying it on. Sullivan asked him to repeat the question and then said he would have to reflect upon such a 'nice point' before giving a definite answer. Gilbert never did receive an answer, neither did he really expect one, since he had merely quoted a speech from *The Palace of Truth*, the three-act 'fairy comedy' on which he was currently working; the musical terms had been lifted from an article in the *Encyclopaedia Britannica*.

Once the contact had been made German Reed was swift to make use of it, if at all possible. Soon after *Ages Ago* had ended its short run he wrote to Sullivan with a suggestion. 'Gilbert is doing a comic one-act entertainment for me – soprano, contralto, tenor, baritone and basso. Would you like to compose the music? If so on what terms? Reply at once as I want to set the piece going without loss of time.'[9]

German Reed was unsuccessful. Sullivan had other ventures; if he were to write an opera it would be something big. Rachel hoped for another symphony or a concerto, but there was the possibility of a grand opera. 'Tell me of Queen Isobel', she wrote. 'You will get it played if you will write it in Italian, and it is quite worth making a present sacrifice to show that an English composer can write opera.'[10]

Italian! That would count Gilbert out anyway, but nevertheless, 'Queen Isobel' came to nothing. No, it was Hollingshead at the Gaiety and not the German Reeds who brought the two together in the autumn of 1871 for the 'entirely original Grotesque Opera: *Thespis*,' which opened for the Christmas season with Nellie Farren playing one of the leading roles together with the actor John Laurence Toole, and Frederick Sullivan, Arthur's brother, playing others. It ran for sixty-four performances, a modest success.

Thespis: or The Gods Grown Old, is set in ancient Greece; its central theme revolves upon how a group of Thessalonian actors led by their stage-manager, Thespis, ascend Mount Olympus to celebrate the wedding of two of their number and come across the Gods who are now dispirited and despondent, and dwell among the ruins of the temple. Only Mercury among them has any sparkle left, but even he complains:

> Oh, I'm the celestial drudge,
>   From morning to night I must stop at it,
> On errands all day I must trudge,
>   And I stick to my work till I drop at it!
> In summer I get up at one
>   (As a good-natured donkey I'm ranked for it),
> Then I go and I light up the sun,
>   And Phoebus Apollo gets thanked for it![11]

Such stuff is recognisably Gilbertian, as is the absurdity that Mercury has had to visit earth to obtain cosmetics and hair-dyes so the 'immortal' gods can disguise their ages! Mercury was played by Nellie Farren dressed in a tightly fitting shining silver costume, and there were also 'large numbers of shapely ladies in tights', in the chorus, a feature for which the Gaiety became famous, in an age when prudery could even put veils round piano legs. Sullivan was himself impressed by the production. 'I have rarely seen anything so beautifully put upon the stage,'[12] he informed his mother.

As the plot developed the Gods agree at Thespis's suggestion to change places with the actors for a year, so they can visit earth to find out why they have grown so unpopular, but when the year is up the actors have made such a mess of the job that the Gods are needed back; the actors are banished back to earth, where with Jupiter's curse upon them they are destined to become 'eminent tragedians,/ Whom no one ever goes to see!'

> Heres's a pretty tale for future Iliads and Odyssies.
> Mortals are about to personate the gods and goddesses.
> Now to set the world in order, we will work in unity.
> Jupiter's perplexity is Thespis's opportunity.[13]

The text of *Thespis* has always been available, but apart from two passages Sullivan's score remains unknown, and is still missing. Thus there is no way of telling what the piece was like. Certainly Gilbert's humour is immediately recognisable, not only in the clever absurdity of the plot, but also in the dialogue and lyrics. For example, at the moment when the Gods are discussing the downturn in devotion:

JUPITER. The sacrifices and votive offerings have fallen off terribly of late. Why, I can remember the time when people offered us human sacrifices – no mistake about it – human sacrifices! Think of that!

DIANA.   Ah! Those good old days!
JUPITER.   Then it fell off to oxen, pigs and sheep.
APOLLO.   Well, there are worse things than oxen, pigs and sheep.
JUPITER.   So I've found to my cost. My dear sir – between ourselves, it's dropped off from one thing to another until it has positively dwindled down to preserved Australian beef! What do you think of that?
APOLLO: I don't like it at all.[14]

The part of Thespis himself was taken by John Laurence Toole who had only recently joined the Gaiety company, though he had made his mark some years earlier as Bob Cratchit in an adaptation of Dickens's *A Christmas Carol*. Gilbert had given Thespis a song about the railway which was a precursor of his later patter songs:

> I once knew a chap who discharged a function
> On the North South East West Diddlesex junction,
> He was conspicuous exceeding,
> For his affable ways and his easy breeding . . . .

In typical topsy-turvy fashion, in the manner of Captain Reece to his crew, this Chairman of Directors of the railway set out to be as generous to his employees as possible.

> He tipped the guards with bran-new fivers,
> And sang little songs to the engine-drivers.
>
> Each Christmas day he gave each stoker
> A silver shovel and a golden poker,
> He'd button-hole flowers for the ticket sorters,
> And rich Bath-buns for the outside porters,
> He'd mount the clerks on his first-class hunters,
> And he built little villas for the road-side shunters,
> And if they were fond of pigeon shooting,
> He'd ask them down to his place at Tooting.[15]

Perhaps the audience saw that Gilbert's song had been at the expense of the Duke of Sutherland, an inveterate railway enthusiast with an insatiable passion for driving engines. One can only wish Sullivan's setting of this lyric had survived.

It has always been thought that the standard of singing in the production might have been poor because the character parts were all played by actors and not singers. However, the critic of the *Standard* found the music excellent and considered that Gilbert had given the composer all he could desire. Yet Sullivan for his part was disappointed; as far as he was concerned few of the cast could sing at all and those who made some pretence at it could hardly compass more than six notes. 'The first night I had a great reception, but the music went badly,' he wrote, 'and the singer sang half a tone sharp, so that the enthusiasm of the audience did not sustain itself towards me.'[16] Sullivan does not betray the singer by naming him or her, but he decided the best course was to leave the song out of the subsequent performances. Even if he did feel somewhat let down in his own department his admiration for Gilbert as a producer was firmly established; the chorus had come alive under his direction; and Sullivan had noticed how strict his partner could be as he drilled the cast, also his ability to keep the upper hand with the principals. 'Why should I stand here? I'm not a chorus girl' complained one senior member of the cast. 'No, madam, your voice is not strong enough or no doubt you would be,'[17] was Gilbert's cutting reply!

On the first night *Thespis* had been the chief attraction, but, as was the custom at the time, it was only one of the pieces on offer, and the audience was also entertained by H.J. Byron's *Dearer Than Life*. Pieces by the two greatest humorists of the day on the same night and 'No Fees', so the Gaiety prided itself, 'for Booking, Programmes, or Cloak Rooms!'

Apart from the incidental music for two of Shakespeare's plays, *The Merchant of Venice* and *The Merry Wives of Windsor*, the former commissioned by the Prince's Theatre, Manchester, Sullivan wrote nothing for the theatre for the next four years. In 1872 Rachel Scott Russell married; it was three years since Sullivan and she had broken off their engagement, though the years since had been painful.

'Let us wander again hand in hand under the shadow of green trees, and cast away all this bitter pain. I have never been happy for an hour since we parted in that little room, and I ache for a little happiness,'[18] she had pleaded soon after they separated. In one of her last letters she wrote:

I can have no other ending, even in the future and your young life shall not be dimmed by the nurture of a hope which will never be fulfilled. I hear you are changed and ill. God help you, and give you strength to bear it all. You have others to work for, and your beautiful genius to work for, and neither I, nor any other woman on God's earth is worth wasting one's life for. With all my heart I thank you for the past which has given a colour to my life.[19]

Rachel destroyed all the letters she had received from Sullivan, but allowed him to keep hers to him, though she would have preferred him to have burnt them. Her married life out in India with her husband, William Henn Holmes, produced two daughters, but her own life came to a sad end through cholera at the age of thirty-seven.

It was typhoid, not cholera, which had gripped the mind of the nation and Sullivan's in particular while *Thespis* had been in rehearsal. The Prince of Wales had contracted the disease while on a visit to Lord Londesborough's estate at the end of October 1872; by the end of the next month there seemed little hope of recovery as the patient lay delirious in his room at Sandringham. The physicians issued bulletins each day and during the crisis as many as five up-to-date reports were given. The telegraph buzzed the news to an anxious people prompting the excited couplet from the poet laureate:

> Across the wires, the electric message came:
> 'He is no better, he is much the same.'

The prayers of the Queen and her family were answered and the Prince recovered slowly. National thanks were given formally for this happy deliverance in St Paul's Cathedral on 27 February 1873, and 1 May was designated 'Thanksgiving Day'. At the celebration concert given at the Crystal Palace on that day about 30,000 people attended, with members of the Royal Family including the Princess Louise, the Duke of Edinburgh, the Prince and Princess of Teck, and the Duke of Cambridge. The London contingent of the Handel Festival Choir with a vast orchestra performed Sullivan's Festival 'Te Deum' composed specially for the occasion: yet another moment of royal recognition for this 'musical genius of the Queen's kingdom'.

The Queen had already requested a complete set of Sullivan's works and had sent him some of the songs and melodies her adored Albert had composed. Sullivan arranged these so that the Queen could play them for her own pleasure. The close link with the Queen and her family strengthened. When Sullivan's oratorio *The Light of the World* was performed at the Birmingham Festival, the Duke of Edinburgh, who had travelled up for the occasion, declared it a triumph. Some time later the Queen herself heard the piece in London and knew it was 'destined to uplift British music'.[20] Another to sing the oratorio's praises was Gounod, who declared it a master-piece. Nevertheless, as with so much Sullivan composed, *The Light of the World* had been dashed off at great speed, the entire score having taken less than a month. Yet it is not *The Light of the World* that is remembered of the music Sullivan wrote in the years between *Thespis* and his next Gilbertian venture, *Trial by Jury*, so much as a hymn he had published in the previous year. For inclusion in Novello's *The Hymnery* he had contributed twelve hymns, and Hymn No. 476 was 'Onward Christian Soldiers'.

On the night of 25 March 1875 the Royalty Theatre in Dean Street, Soho, presented Offenbach's operetta *La Perichole* with 'little, pretty, fiery' Madame Selina Dolaro, wife of the musical director, in the title role; also in the cast was Frederick Sullivan. As a 'curtain-raiser' there was a short play by Charles Collette with the eye-catching, but difficult-to-pronounce title, *Crypto-conchoidsyphonostomata*. Happily the play, in which the author himself played the lead, had the alternative title *While It's to Be Had*. Then after *Perichole* came 'a novel and entirely original Dramatic Cantata', *Trial by Jury*, with music by A. Sullivan and book by W.S. Gilbert.

Gilbert's *Trial by Jury* had appeared in a very much slighter form as an 'operetta' in the pages of *Fun* some years back, in the issue dated 11 April 1868; but he had expanded the idea considerably as a libretto for Sullivan's old friend from Leipzig days, Carl Rosa, as a suitable vehicle for the talents of Rosa's wife, Perepa. Owing to the untimely death of Madame Rosa, the plan was to be shelved, so that when D'Oyly Carte suggested to Gilbert that he might write a short 'after-piece' to follow *La Perichole* Gilbert told him he had the book already written, and produced it from his pocket. D'Oyly Carte was impressed by what he read, but thought that Sullivan, not Rosa, would be the preferable composer. Sullivan was soon made acquainted with the idea, as he recalled.

Gilbert came to my rooms and read it through to me in a perturbed sort of way with a gradual crescendo of indignation, in the manner of a man considerably disappointed with what he had written. As soon as he had come to the last word he closed up the manuscript violently, apparently uncon-scious of the fact that he had achieved his purpose, inasmuch as I was screaming with laughter the whole time:[21]

The result was that Sullivan readily agreed to set the words and, composing with his accustomed haste, had the music ready in three weeks, the time it took Gilbert to rehearse the company, and on the opening night conducted his own orchestration.

Trial by Jury was an immediate success and continued to run long after *La Perichole* had been replaced by Lecocq's *La Fille de Madame Angot*. Gilbert had drawn upon his experience as a barrister to recreate a typical British court of justice; it has been thought that he had the Clerkenwell Sessions in mind. The fact that the curtain rose upon such a realistic set with the lawyers correctly dressed added to the absurdity of the action as the plot unfolded. Parody is always most successful when it keeps its original closely in mind and exactness in set and costume, something learnt from Tom Robertson, would be the hallmark of future Gilbertian productions, particularly with regard to legal, naval and military dress.

The case under consideration in *Trial by Jury* is the breach of promise of marriage brought by Angelina against Edwin, the 'ruffianly defendant'. The barristers, attorneys and jurymen are assembled in court at ten o'clock in the morning awaiting the entrance of the judge. The usher addresses the jury telling them to put aside all prejudice and 'with stern judicial frame of mind', free from bias, they must try the case. He reminds them that the plaintiff is a 'broken-hearted bride' and must be heard, whereas when the defendant speaks upon the other side they need not take any notice of him! Edwin enters and explains that he quite simply had become 'another's love-sick boy' no matter how much in love he had been with Angelina in the past. The jurymen are inclined to sympathise with his dilemma; they had all been young once, as they explain in chorus:

> Oh, I was like that when a lad!
>   A shocking young scamp and a rover,
> I behaved like a regular cad;
>   But that sort of thing is all over.[22]

However, they are all now respectable, shining with virtue, and therefore haven't a scrap of sympathy with the defendant!

The usher then orders the court to rise as the judge enters to the kind of reception usually reserved for a conquering hero. The judge, in a manner which would become common to many of Gilbert's chief characters, outlines his career in a seemingly innocent, self-descriptive, confessional ditty, as though prompted by some inner compulsion to speak the truth. This was something Gilbert had learnt, of course, from Shakespeare and other dramatists, and it was inherited as a common feature in opera. In *Trial by Jury* the judge's revelation only serves to disrobe him and expose his unsuitability to be a judge at all, particularly of a matrimonial case. When he had first been called to the Bar, he says, he had found the going tough and he feared he might never succeed until he resorted to a desperate measure.

> In Westminster Hall I danced a dance,
>   Like a semi-despondent fury;
> For I thought I should never hit on a chance
>   Of addressing a British Jury –
> But I soon got tired of the third class journeys,
>   And the dinners of bread and water:
> So I fell in love with a rich attorney's
>   Elderly, ugly daughter.
>
> The rich attorney, he jumped for joy,
>   And replied to my fond professions:
> 'You shall reap the reward for your pluck, my boy,
>   At the Bailey and Middlesex Sessions.
> You'll soon get used to her looks,' said he,
>   'And a very nice girl you'll find her!
> She may very well pass for forty-three
>   In the dusk, with a light behind her!'[23]

The attorney proved as good as his word and furthered his son-in-law's career to the extent that he became 'as rich as the Gurneys' but he soon found his wife a burden, or, as he expresses it, an incubus, and threw her over. The rich attorney tried vainly to disparage his character, but that is as far as the judge will tell: he is now ready to try the case.

After the jury has been sworn in by taking to their knees and disappearing from view, the chorus of bridesmaids enters to announce the arrival of the plaintiff. The judge immediately has an eye for the first bridesmaid and sends her a note via the usher, which she reads, kisses rapturously, and places in her bosom. Then Angelina enters and is so stunningly beautiful that the judge transfers his attention to her; the usher retrieves the note from the first bridesmaid and hands it to Angelina who in the same manner kisses it rapturously and places it in her bosom.

The counsel for the plaintiff says that he approaches the painful case with a sense of deep emotion, for he had never thought a man could be so base as to deceive a girl in such a manner.

> See my interesting client,
>   Victim of a heartless wile!
> See the traitor all defiant
>   Wear a supercilious smile!
> Sweetly smiled my client on him
> Coyly wooed and gently won him.
>
> Swiftly fled each honeyed hour
>   Spent with this unmanly male!
> Camberwell became a bower,
>   Peckham an Arcadian Vale,
> Breathing concentrated otto! –
> An existence à la Watteau.
>
> Picture, then, my client naming,
>   and insisting on the day:
> Picture him excuses framing –
>   Going from her far away;
> Double criminal to do so,
> For the maid had bought her trousseau![24]

Helped fondly into the witness-box by counsel, Angelina seems likely to faint and is comforted by the foreman and the judge while all shake their fists at the defendant with 'Oh perjured monster, atone, atone'. Angelina jumps up on to the bench, sits down by the judge and falls sobbing on his breast. Water from far Cologne is called for by counsel and once again the defendant is harangued by all. Edwin then pleads his cause and comes up with what seems a possible solution:

> But this I am ready to say,
>   If it will appease their sorrow,
> I'll marry this lady today,
>   And I'll marry the other tomorrow![25]

To marry two wives at once is Burglaree, counsel advises, certainly considered a very serious crime in the reign of James the Second. Angelina will have none of that and once more declares her love for

Edwin and embracing him rapturously pleads that when damages are being assessed the fact that she worships and madly adores him should be remembered. Edwin repels her, furiously insisting that life with him would be hellish.

> I smoke like a furnace – I'm always in liquor,
>   A ruffian – a bully – a sot;
> I'm sure I should thrash her, perhaps I should kick her
>   I am such a very bad lot!
> I'm not prepossessing, as you may be guessing,
>   She couldn't endure me a day;
> Recall my professing, when you are assessing
>   The damages Edwin must pay![26]

The judge decides that if the question is one of liquor the right course is to make the defendant tipsy and see if he would thrash and kick. All except Edwin object to this, with the result that the judge loses his patience and begins to toss his books and papers about.

> All the legal furies seize you!
> No proposal seems to please you,
> I can't stop up here all day,
> I must shortly go away.
> Barristers and you attorneys,
> Set out on your homeward journeys;
> Gentle, simple-minded usher,
> Get you, if you like to Russher;
> Put your briefs upon the shelf,
> I will marry her myself![27]

Rather than inviting the whole court back to his house, No. 511 Eaton Square for breakfast, as he had done in Gilbert's original *Fun* operetta sketch, the judge comes down from the bench to the floor of the court to embrace Angelina who experiences joy unbounded, while the judge delcares that though his law may be fudge, he is certainly a good judge of beauty, and all agree.

No one was more happy about the instantaneous success of *Trial by Jury* than Richard D'Oyly Carte. Not only were the audiences still crowding into the theatre nine months after the opening, but also the partnership of Gilbert and Sullivan was being talked about with enthusiasm, Gilbert's words were relished and 'Sullivan's tuneful numbers were carried away to be murdered and mutilated in every drawing-room and every kitchen throughout the length and breadth of town from Bow to Belgravia.'[28]

Although D'Oyly Carte was not the first to bring the two men together he could certainly take much of the credit for the present venture. As with any success, perhaps, there were difficulties, clashes of personality and petty jealousies to contend with; chief of these, it seems, was the resentment felt by Selina Dolaro at the popularity of Nellie Bromley, the tall and very pretty actress with a winsome manner, who played the part of Angelina. There could not be two prima donnas on the Royalty stage in any one night, in Dolaro's opinion, and as she was the daughter of the leader of the orchestra and playing the main part in what should have been the major attraction of the evening, a three-act, not to say French, comic opera, Nellie Bromley must be the one to go. Whatever the circumstances, Nellie Bromley was replaced after a month by Linda Verner, one of Dolaro's closest friends.

Nevertheless if the presence of Nellie Bromley had caused a stir on the night of 25 March, so for a different reason had that of Frederick Sullivan who played the part of the judge, an especially brilliant performance by all accounts. As the critic of the *Daily Telegraph* noted, Sullivan, by 'a blending of official dignity, condescension and, at the right moment, extravagant humour, made the character of the judge stand out with all requisite prominence, and added much to the interest of the piece'.[29] Gilbert had evidently expanded the judge's part with Frederick Sullivan in mind, and Arthur had composed the music for 'When first, my friends, I was called to the Bar', knowing well his brother's range, but he could hardly have known that he was giving him one of the best-known comic songs in the language.

Another to make his mark in *Trial by Jury* was the comic actor William Penley who was a member of the jury on the opening night, but soon rose to foreman of the jury and brought the house down with the one-liner in answer to the judge.

JUDGE [to Jury]. How say you is she not designed for capture?

FOREMAN [after consulting with the Jury]. We've but one word, my lord, and that is – Rapture.[30]

Penley's serious, rather pathetic facial expressions and gestures were as much part of his attraction as the solemnity of his voice, an invaluable asset for any comic, as we have seen in our own time in the cases of Frankie Howerd and Rowan Atkinson. Penley's other great moment came when Angelina was being comforted after reeling in the witness-box; the foreman kisses her saying: 'Just like a father I wish to be.' In the opinion of some who were present Penley's performance caused as much laughter as all the rest of the cast put together. Of course, he went on to greater things, later creating the part of Lord Fancourt Babberley in Brandon Thomas's *Charley's Aunt* which ran for 1,466 performances after its opening at the Royalty in 1892.

Such a comic discovery was grist to D'Oyly Carte's mill. As this entrepreneur comes more and more to influence the careers of Gilbert and Sullivan it is as well to know more about him.

Richard D'Oyly Carte, D'Oyly being his second Christian name, had been born in Soho on 3 May 1844, the son of a competent flautist, also called Richard, who was one of the partners of the firm Rudall, Rose and Carte, wood-wind instrument makers, in Charing Cross. D'Oyly Carte's mother was Elizabeth Jones, from a Welsh branch of the ancient Norman D'Oyly family. She was the daughter of a clergyman who for many years was attached to the Chapel Royal, Whitehall. What the reverend gentleman thought of his future son-in-law's elopement with Eliza can only be imagined, but he is said to have had a cosmopolitan outlook and to have been well-acquainted with the Parisian professional class, advantages which might have helped absorb the shock.

Richard D'Oyly Carte joined his father's firm after his education at University College School and graduating from London University. Rudall, Rose and Carte was fortunate in having the sole agency for the Belgian musical-intrument maker, Adolphe Sax, the inventor of the saxophone, but in spite of the firm's undoubted prospects young Richard decided to launch out on his own, and before long set himself up as an operatic and concert agent with small premisis in Craig's Court, near his father's shop at Charing Cross. Besides his agency work D'Oyly Carte was soon also acting as business manager for various operatic enterprises, which is how he came to be at the Royalty Theatre in 1875.

D'Oyly Carte was himself very musical, though hardly in Sullivan's class, and he had composed many songs and set the librettos of several operettas including *Happy Hampstead*. However, he was sensible enough to realise his creative talent lay more in the direction of organisation and the management of others. It is thought he had first seen the potential of Gilbert and Sullivan when he had attended a performance of *Thespis*, which was why he had been so keen to suggest Sullivan rather than Costa as the composer for *Trial by Jury*. What was special, perhaps unique even, about these two was the way they matched each other – so perfectly in fact that, as *The Times* critic had noticed on the opening night of *Trial by Jury*, 'It seems, as in the great Wagnerian operas, as though poem and music had proceeded simultaneously from one and the same brain.'[31] Gilbert's words were surely difficult to set; they could never be subservient to the music, but Sullivan was able to do more than merely set them, he was able to take the words and relish them, enjoy their humour and enrich them with humorous music. Perhaps that was the secret: the two men in an unusual way shared an identical sense of humour. One thing was certain in D'Oyly Carte's mind: there must be another Gilbert and Sullivan opera to follow *Trial by Jury*. Why not revive *Thespis*? It would have to be rewritten and the music revised. Would the two agree? Carte was excited at the prospect.

3

A Dealer in Magic and Spells

᪥ 1875–1878 ᪥

In October 1875 Gilbert agreed to D'Oyly Carte's proposal that *Thespis* should be revived at the Criterion Theatre for the Christmas season in return for a fee of two guineas each per performance for Sullivan and himself, and a guaranteed run of a hundred performances on condition that they also reworked the dialogue, lyrics and music. Sullivan for his part was also happy at the idea, but stipulated that a hundred guineas should be paid in advance on delivery of the revised work, and that the proposed performances should be restricted to London and run continuously. Carte agreed, but a month afterwards nothing had happened.

'I have heard no more about *Thespis*,' Gilbert informed Sullivan. 'It is astonishing how quickly these capitalists dry up under the magic influence of the words "cash down".'[1]

Cash was the problem, and Carte was not in a position to raise the sum, neither was Gilbert or Sullivan prepared to put pen to paper until the agreed advance was paid. In the event the project was dropped.

Trial by Jury, however, continued to draw the crowd and so the relationship with Carte was not unduly hurt by his failure to raise the necessary capital. In fact Gilbert agreed to Carte's request on behalf of Selina Dolaro to transfer the operetta to another London venue for fifty performances. By arrangement with Charles Morton, the manager of the Opera Comique, *Trial by Jury* opened there on 10 January 1876 with Fred Sullivan and Penley in their original parts, and Clara Vesey as Angelina.

At this time Gilbert and Sullivan were losing money which was rightfully theirs, though there was precious little they could have done about it owing to the lack of copyright laws relating to America. An unauthorised production of *Trial by Jury* had opened at the Eagle Theatre in New York on 15 November 1875, and the audience was able to purchase a pirated edition of the libretto. Perhaps it was this Gilbert had in mind when he wrote to Carte, 'It's a pity, but the piece has been so be-devilled that I have lost interest in it.'[2] There were other matters on his mind: on 17 December his 'entirely original Fairy Play' in three acts, *Broken Hearts*, written for the actor-manager, John Hare, had opened at the Court Theatre, and he was already working on another play, *The Vagabond*, for the actor, Edward Askew Southern. When Carl Rosa suggested to Gilbert that Sullivan and he should write an opera for his company Gilbert said he was too busy, but might consider the project after 1 January the following year.

'After that date I shall be quite ready to undertake a two-act comic opera for you, and I will undertake to get it practically finished – that is to say, I will have supplied Sullivan with the principal number by 1 February. I hope this will meet your views – as I should be very sorry not to be associated with the new work. If you say "yes" I will arrange to undertake no other work until March.'[3]

For some unknown reason Carl Rosa did not follow the matter up; it has been suggested he thought there might after all be more profit from Italian operas than from untried English ones, even if they should be composed by Arthur Sullivan.

Gilbert was certainly not a man to turn down work should it come his way, but he wished to make sure the terms were favourable. Both Sullivan and he had been prepared to revise *Thespis* and receive two guineas per performance, as has been seen. When it became obvious to Charles Morton at the Opera Comique that *Trial by Jury* was a continuing success he made a proposal for another opera from the pair. This time the terms should be four guineas each per performance, they replied, and £105 paid in advance. Other stipulations were that the full control of production should rest with them, the choice of subject, whether the piece should be two-act or three-act, the selection of a suitable company and the rehearsals.

When it was rumoured what Morton was up to D'Oyly Carte was offended. Surely, he had first call? Gilbert was quick to remind him that although Sullivan and he had agreed to give him an opera he had not fulfilled the conditions laid down. The plan had been that work on the revision of *Thespis* should begin on 1 March 1876.

I wrote to you on that day to say I was ready to begin. But you left my note unanswered for a week, and then wrote to say that there was a hitch somewhere. And then it turned out that you were going to close the theatre for a few weeks and reopen perhaps with a revived comedy, perhaps with a revived opera; but in any case our little one act 'Bouffe' [*Trial by Jury*] was to constitute the whole substantial attraction.

Now this won't do for either Sullivan or myself. If we're to be business-like, you must be businesslike too. Give us a fair chance at a good theatre, and comply with our conditions precedent, and we'll work like Trojans. But we can't hold ourselves at your disposal whenever you want us.[4]

Sullivan was in France at the time and Gilbert did not know when he was expected to return, but he was writing on behalf of them both. It is interesting to note that Gilbert was wary of Carte even at this early stage in his dealings with him. Although exceedingly generous by nature, Gilbert was astute about financial matters, meticulously careful about contracts and agreements at all times; particularly he had the artist's natural distrust of middle-men, those who might profit unduly from their labour, and in his mind, at this period at any rate, Carte was little more than that; what is more he had already shown himself to be unreliable.

In fact Gilbert's next operatic venture had nothing to do with either Carte or Sullivan, but was written for Frederic Clay with whom he had collaborated before in *Ages Ago*. This new three-act comic opera, *Princess Toto*, was in the process of creation before the production of *Trial by Jury*; when it was eventually performed at the Strand Theatre on 2 October 1876 after a trial run earlier in the summer at the Theatre Royal, Nottingham, it was described as 'ambitiously comic and not funny'. Gilbert had persuaded Penley and several from the cast of *Trial by Jury* to appear in the new piece, but he had not personally supervised the rehearsals, and he seemed anxious that no one should assume that he had. He insisted:

I want to disclaim all responsibility for the stage-management. Without the smallest desire to deprecate the production, I should like you to understand that it is Clay's property and that he has thought proper to produce it without consulting me either as to caste [*sic*], rehearsals or stage-management. I don't mean to imply that it will be any the worse for my not having had anything to do with it – but, at the same time, I don't want to be saddled with a responsibility to which I have no claim.[5]

During the summer of 1876 Sullivan was in the company of Sir Coutts and Lady Lindsay at Cadenabbia on Lake Como.

'The heat is so great as to make it almost impossible to do anything but sit about without movement in a chair until the evening,'[6] he informed his mother. There was nothing unexpected about the heat – on the journey they had stopped at Paris to buy suits made of batiste 'very light and very cool' – but it was slightly unusual in those days for an English party to visit Italy in the midst of summer. Sullivan saw it as an advantage that he could relish 'the magnificence of the foliage and the beautiful colours and lights, which can only be seen at this time of the year'. Besides on the journey he had been to Milan at last! At the Conservatoire the director, Mazzucato, had welcomed him with great warmth, and accompanied his guest to the station on his departure. He had met Ricordi, Verdi's publisher, and Visetti, who was kindness itself, and 'almost more gratified than myself at the success of my visit'.

Yet it was the early morning bathing and the cool, fresh evenings at Cadenabbia that made the deeper impression when Sullivan and his friends would saunter out a little after a day sitting on a stone covered-in balcony in rocking chairs, 'sometimes going through the exertion of reading a novel'. On some evenings they preferred to be paddled about in a flat-bottomed boat.

Then it is delicious, and absolutely lovely. The stillness of the water, the brilliant moon, throwing its glittering light on the lake, and making a long trail of little diamonds, the mountains all round looking grave and calm, little boats filled with men and women, some of them with mandolines and singing popular melodies, and the light from the villages and towns dotted round the lake contribute to form a scene which is enchanting, and unlike anything one has dreamed of.[7]

Such idleness must not be allowed to continue. By way of Geneva, Cologne and Paris Sullivan returned to England. In Cologne Cathedral he was moved to tears by the boys' voices heard faintly in the distance and then more loudly singing all the while as they moved through the building though on a closer hearing 'the music was weak and the boys' voices execrable!'[8]

There was much to return for. Sullivan was now conductor of the Glasgow Orpheus Choir, a post which, though rewarding, meant tiring travel and he often felt 'knocked up'. Rehearsals for concerts during the day and the concerts themselves in the evening. Concerts at Glasgow, Greenock, Perth, Dundee and then Glasgow again, all in one week. It was sometimes difficult to rest.

'There's a wretched creature on the floor above me who plays the piano a little. He, or she, has been playing my hymn tunes all this afternoon. I hope they don't do it out of compliment to me, for they put their own harmony which, to say the least of it, isn't as good as mine.'[9]

Of course it was a compliment, no matter how irritating. He would soon be used to such moments, and while in Germany many years later even the Kaiser would join the throng of flatterers by singing snatches from *The Mikado*.

Two important moments of a different kind came during 1876. In June Sullivan received an honorary doctorate of music from Cambridge University. This honour was conferred, in the words of Professor Macfarren: 'as an assurance that your highest productions are appreciated'. His 'highest productions'? The professor had hardly been thinking of *Trial by Jury*, at least Sullivan hoped he had not.

'Now I am dressed in a black silk gown and a trencher hat, and am going to dine in the hall of my own College.'[10] His mother would be impressed: after dinner at Trinity, there was to be a party in his honour given by the Master, Dr Thornton.

The second honour at this time was his appointment in May as the Principal of the newly founded National Training School of Music. The school had been the brain-child of the Duke of Edinburgh, but he had wisely involved his brother as patron and had brought the Prince and Sullivan together to discuss the subject of encouraging English musicians, particularly young performers. Sullivan's attitude was that he would not give English concerts performed by foreigners if he could possibly help it, so it was essential to foster the talent of young British musicians. The school received the Prince of Wales's full support and was a successful venture from the start; it emerged in time as the Royal College of Music.

During the winter of 1876–7 Sullivan was busier than ever. He could not help noticing his concert audiences had swelled; he was in even greater demand to compose pieces for choirs and festivals, and his creative imagination did not let him down. He visited Scotland yet again and was snowed up in the Highlands; the trains were slow, cold and comfortless, and he drove in 'wretched horse-cabs through weather that forced cold into his bones'.[11] Then in the early weeks of the new year, suddenly, with the cruellest force, tragedy struck the Sullivan family.

Soon after Christmas Sullivan learnt that his brother had fallen seriously ill. He hurried to his bedside to offer what comfort he could to the sick man, and to console his mother, Fred's wife and the children. Thirty-nine was too young to die. As he sat watching by his brother's bed he sketched out the notes for a song, the words by Adelaide Procter he had long treasured since first finding them in the pages of *Household Words*.

> Seated one day at the organ,
>   I was weary and ill at ease,
> And my fingers wandered idly
>   Over the noisy keys.

'The Lost Chord'; so Sullivan named his song. 'But I struck one chord of music./Like the sound of a great Amen.'

From start to finish the words were set as his brother slumbered, struggling for life, but all the while growing weaker and weaker. On 18 January the end came peacefully. Sullivan felt quite unable to compose anything else for months.

Fred Sullivan's death came as a blow to Gilbert also. As his performance in *Trial by Jury* had made such a major contribution towards the opera's success, it had been assumed that Fred would play a leading part in any future venture. Besides, to have Arthur Sullivan's brother on the stage made a firm link between the actors and the author and composer, and his good nature and sense of humour had added to the enjoyment of production. Certainly Gilbert had created the character of Dr Daly, the love-sick Vicar of Ploverleigh, in *The Sorcerer*, the libretto he was preparing for D'Oyly Carte, with Fred in mind. Now the piece would be performed without him.

D'Oyly Carte himself had been exceedingly active. Realising that he could only fulfil his dream of setting up a permanent opera company if he sought financial backing, he had approached four men connected in some way with the music profession: the music publisher Frank Chappell, who had brought out *Trial by Jury*, and George Metzler also a publisher; John Collard, the piano-maker; and Edward Bailey, whose business interests included the water-sprinklers that through the summer months controlled the dust in the London streets. Each put up capital of £500 and became a director of the Comedy Opera Company. It seemed at the time a happy enough arrangement, so the new opera from Gilbert and Sullivan was formally commissioned in July and the company arranged to pay them each an advance of £200 on delivery.

D'Oyly Carte's purpose was made clear from the outset: it was intended to establish 'permanently in London a theatre which shall have for its staple entertainment light opera of a legitimate kind, by English authors and composers'.[12] The more pronounced forms of *opéra bouffe* and burlesque were now decidedly unpopular; it was now the right time to launch a legitimate musical-dramatic undertaking. The very successful production of *Prés St Gervais* at the Criterion Theatre was proof that the public would flock to see a really good entertainment; but Lecocq, the composer of *Prés St Gervais*, was a Frenchman. Just look on the piano in any drawing-room: it was piled with songs by an Englishman, Arthur Sullivan. Carte insisted:

I believe there is in England no lack of appreciation of native talent and no lack of efficient artists. I also believe that the causes of the failure of what is known as English opera have been – first, that to perform grand opera grand singers are required, whereas any grand English singers that appear are drafted at once to an Italian stage; and secondly, what is more important, the utter feebleness and absurdity of the plots and books. My plan is to obtain the services of the most distinguished composers of the day to write the music, for a series of light and amusing but interesting 'comedy operas', for the interpretation of which I have secured the refusal of an excellent West-end theatre, and propose to produce, in the first instance, a new 'opera comique', by Messrs. W. S. Gilbert and Arthur Sullivan.[13]

Carte's plan had not been restricted to Gilbert and Sullivan only, for he had also approached Burnand, Alfred Cellier, brother of François, James Albery and Frederic Clay. In fact, when *The Sorcerer* opened at the Opera Comique on 17 November it was preceded by a curtain-raiser by Cellier, *Dora's Dream*, with words by Arthur Cecil, but it was a revival and not a specially commissioned piece.

The central theme of *The Sorcerer; or the Elixir of Love* was one of Gilbert's favourites: the love-potion. There was no originality in the theme, since it was also used in various ways by Wagner, Auber and particularly Donizetti, on whose *L'Elixir d'amore* Gilbert had, it will be remembered, based his burlesque *Dulcamara*. Notwithstanding this fact *The Sorcerer* was billed as an 'entirely new and Original

Comic Opera'. In fact, Gilbert had adapted the libretto from one of his own short stories which had appeared in the previous Christmas number of the *Graphic* magazine.

The action of the two-act opera takes place at Ploverleigh outside the Elizabethan mansion of Sir Marmaduke Pointdextre, whose son, Alexis, an officer of the Grenadier Guards, is to be betrothed that day to Aline, the daughter of Lady Arabella Sangazure, a Lady of Ancient Lineage. In Act I at mid-day a chorus of villagers brings a mood of joy at such a happy event; however, Mrs Partlet, a widowed pew-opener, and her daughter, Constance, introduce a contrary mood, for Constance is in love with the elderly Vicar of Ploverleigh, Dr Daly. The revelation of this fact astonishes Mrs Partlet as Dr Daly himself enters and the audience learns how he has long given up all hope of finding satisfaction in love. Though the air is charged with amatory numbers, soft madrigals, and dreamy lovers' lays, it is foolish to arouse 'the aching memory of the old, old days'.

> Time was when Love and I were well acquainted.
>> Time was when we walked hand in hand,
> A saintly youth, with worldly thought untainted –
>> None better-loved than I in all the land!
> Time was, when maidens of the noblest station,
>> Forsaking even military men,
> Would gaze upon me, rapt in adoration –
>> Ah me, I was a fair young curate then!
>
> Had I a headache? sighed the maids assembled,
>> Had I a cold? welled forth the silent tear;
> Did I look pale? then half a parish trembled;
>> And when I coughed all thought the end was near
> I had no care – no jealous doubts hung o'er me –
>> For I was loved beyond all other men.
> Fled gilded dukes and belted earls before me –
>> Ah me, I was a pale young curate then.[14]

Mrs Partlet attempts to draw Dr Daly's attention towards Constance, but although he is struck by the girl's undoubted comeliness the time has passed for such things. After mother and daughter have left the Vicar admits: 'Time was when this old heart would have throbbed in double-time at the sight of such a fairy form! But tush! I am puling!'[15]

Sir Marmaduke and Alexis appear and the father admits that fifty years ago he and Lady Sangazure were in love! Aline arrives with a chorus of girls, soon followed by her mother. Alexis and Aline are immediately drawn to each other, but it is also quite obvious the ardour between the two former lovers is in no way abated. As they admit in asides they are still 'Wild with adoration!' and 'Mad with fascination'. Soon Alexis and Aline are left alone and Alexis is so ecstatic at his own deep feelings of love that he wishes everybody in Ploverleigh to share them; as he says, to steep the whole village up to its lips in love, and couple them in matrimony without distinction of age, rank or fortune. It is a cause Alexis has espoused for a long time: men and women should be coupled in matrimony without distinction of rank.

'I have lectured on the subject at Mechanics' Institutes, and the mechanics were unanimous in favour of my views. I have preached in workhouses, beershops, and Lunatic Asylums, and I have been received with enthusiasm. I have addressed navvies on the advantages that would accrue to them if they married wealthy ladies of rank, and not a navvy dissented!'[16]

There must be some means to this end: a love-philtre is the answer. Fortunately, the man to supply it is in a nearby tent.

John Wellington Wells, of J.W. Wells & Co., the old-established family sorcerers, whose premises are at No.70 St Mary Axe, London, is the central character of the opera, and one of Gilbert's liveliest. Wells can provide anything in the way of magic and spells, in blessings and curses, prophecies, witches and knells.

> If you want a proud foe to 'make tracks',
> If you'd melt a rich uncle in wax,
> You've but to look in
> On our resident Djinn,
> Number seventy, Simmery Axe![17]

In Wells's Skeltonic patter-song Gilbert gives of his best and it has justly remained popular. Particularly memorable is Wells's account of the remarkable accomplishments of the firm's prophet, 'a very small prophet, a prophet/Who brings us unbounded returns',

> For he can prophesy
> With the wink of an eye
> Peep with security
> Into futurity,

Sum up your history,
Clear up a Mystery,
Humour proclivity
For a nativity, for a nativity;
He has answers oracular,
Bogies spectacular.
Tetrapods tragical,
Mirrors so magical,
Facts astronomical,
Solemn or comical,
And, if you want it, he
Makes a reduction on taking a quantity.[18]

What Alexis requires is a quantity of the firm's Patent Oxy-Hydrogen Love-at-first-sight Philtre. Wells hastily produces some in a phial, but advises that if a quantity is required then it might be better to take it in the wood, so that it could be drawn off as required. There are four-and-a-half and nine gallon casks available, 'also in pipes and hogsheads for laying down', and 10 per cent is deducted for prompt cash. Alexis replies that perhaps he should mention he is a member of the Army and Navy Stores: Wells immediately offers a 25 per cent deduction!

Aline enters carrying a large teapot and Wells drops the potion into it; the stage grows dark and with a grim incantation, amid flashes and the laughter of fiends, Wells with the assistance of Mrs Partlet administers the mysterious brew to all except Alexis, Aline and himself. The effect is immediate, in vain the villagers struggle against the potion's power, and at the end of the act they fall insensible to the stage.

Act 2 takes place twelve hours later, at midnight. Now the full effect of the potion is revealed: all the villagers are in love and wish to be married, and Constance, no longer attracted by Dr Daly, has fallen for the deaf old notary who had come to record Alexis and Aline's betrothal.

I know not why I love him so;
 It is enchantment, surely!
He's dry and snuffy, deaf and slow,
 Ill-tempered, weak and poorly!
He's ugly, and absurdly dressed,
 And sixty-seven nearly,

> He's everything that I detest,
> But if the truth must be confessed.
> I love him very dearly![19]

Worse is to come. Sir Marmaduke and Mrs Partlet are in love; Lady Sangazure falls for Wells, who only manages to evade the situation by claiming that he is already engaged to a girl from a Pacific island. Then Aline, at first refusing Alexis's request that she take the potion, does so and immediately falls in love with Dr Daly. Matters have clearly got out of hand. Alexis learns from Wells that there is only one way out of the tangle: someone must offer himself as a sacrifice to Ahrimanes, the evil one. Alexis offers himself since Aline now despises him, but Dr Daly intervenes to explain that Aline only drank the potion at Alexis's insistence; she had been hurrying to find him when she happened to meet Daly – the result was inevitable.

'But fear nothing from me – I will be no man's rival,' the Vicar insists. 'I shall quit the country at once – and bury my sorrow in the congenial gloom of a Colonial Bishopric.'[20]

Eventually all decide that Wells himself should be sacrificed as he has caused the chaos.

> So be it! I submit! My fate is sealed.
> To public execration thus I yield!
> Be happy all – leave me to my despair –
> I go – it matters not with whom – or where![21]

A gong sounds. All quit their present partners, and rejoin their old lovers. Sir Marmaduke leaves Mrs Partlet, and goes to Lady Sangazure. Aline leaves Dr Daly, and goes to Alexis. Dr Daly leaves Aline, and goes to Constance. The notary leaves Constance, and goes to Mrs Partlet. All the villagers make a corresponding change. All embrace and begin a joyful dance prior to joining Sir Marmaduke for a feast at the mansion, while John Wellington Wells, like Don Giovanni, slowly sinks through a trap in the centre of the stage amid flickering tongues of red fire.

D'Oyly Carte might have hoped to establish his newly founded company at a more spacious theatre than the Opera Comique, but he was able to rent the place on reasonable terms. Situated in Wych Street at the junction of the Strand and Holywell Street, and standing back to back with the old Globe Theatre whose front was in

Newcastle Street – the two theatres being nicknamed the 'Rickety Twins' because they were so hastily erected and ramshackle – the Opera Comique was approached by an underground passage, so any audience had to show enthusiasm to be there at all. Nevertheless, the theatre was a suitable choice from another point of view, since it had long been associated with foreign theatrical companies: the Comédie Française had been there during the Franco-Prussian War. The fact that it was now to be the bastion of Englishness added an ironic twist. So English did the Opera Comique become that two members of the chorus for *The Sorcerer* changed their names from the Italian names they had assumed when they became singers!

Gilbert, and Sullivan to a lesser extent, had a very definite idea as to what kind of performance they wanted. For a start they did not wish to employ only well-established singers, those who had made their way in Italian opera. No, Gilbert wanted people who could act as well, if not better, than they could sing, to take people with natural talent and mould them into the kind of performer required. All important in Gilbert's view was the delivery of the spoken words in the dialogue: in no way should any performer attempt to force humour into the words; this was comedy and not farce, the humour was there already. As he had insisted in October 1877 while he was rehearsing the actors for his comedy *Engaged*, which would run for 105 performances at the Haymarket concurrently with *The Sorcerer*, it was absolutely essential to deliver the words with 'the most perfect earnestness and gravity throughout. There should be no exaggeration in costume, make-up, or demeanour; and the characters, one and all, should appear to believe, throughout, in the perfect sincerity of their words and actions. Directly the actors show that they are conscious of the absurdity of their utterances the piece begins to drag.'[22]

The fact that *Trial by Jury* had been so successfully performed by relatively unknown people, gave Gilbert the confidence to look about for suitable performers to join the new company regardless of reputation. The result was that only Mrs Howard Paul, who played the part of Lady Sangazure, was an established figure, and she had been signed up by D'Oyly Carte. Mrs Howard Paul had her own travelling entertainment company and, in agreeing to appear in the opera, stipulated that a young actor in her troupe should also take part. This was Rutland Barrington who played the part of Dr Daly, a happy choice, for he soon made his name and remained with Gilbert and Sullivan for many years, taking the leading parts that naturally might have gone to Fred Sullivan.

The part of John Wellington Wells was played by George Grossmith, another fortunate find. Grossmith was just thirty years old and with his distinctive, somewhat impish face, brimming with intelligence, he had first attracted Sullivan's notice at a private drawing-room entertainment when he had sung accompanying himself on the piano. This led to his taking part in a charity performance of *Trial by Jury* at the Haymarket Theatre as a juryman. Then on a further occasion he had played the main part of the judge at the Bijou Hall, Bayswater, a benefit performance for which Gilbert himself had conducted the rehearsals, and in 'training' Grossmith had evidently been impressed. In particular he could not have helped noticing Grossmith's agility and how clearly he enunciated his words. Thus it was that although Grossmith was a fairly experienced entertainer he had yet to make a professional appearance on the stage as an actor. In 1877 for a season he had joined Mrs Howard Paul's touring company, and so was well acquainted not only with her but also with Rutland Barrington.

'Under any circumstances, and at some sacrifice, do not fail to accept the part,' Mrs Paul wrote, when she learnt that Grossmith was under consideration. 'It will be a new and magnificent introduction for you, and be a very great service afterwards.'[23] When she heard that Grossmith had indeed accepted she threw a party with a display of fireworks on 5 November for him and Barrington in the back garden of her house in Bedford Park.

Grossmith has himself described the anxious time leading up to his accepting the part. During August he had received a letter from Sullivan addressed from the Beefsteak Club: 'Are you inclined to go on the stage for a time? There is a part in the new piece I am doing with Gilbert which I think you would play admirably. I can't find a good man for it.'[24]

Sullivan invited the young man to reply or even better, if he was interested, to present himself at No. 9 Albert Mansions. It was not very easy for Grossmith to make up his mind; he had accepted all kinds of engagements in the provinces in the coming months and any commitment to the opera would mean cancelling. There was no guarantee that the opera would be a success, and his father was very much against the idea: at least the provincial engagements were certainties; besides, he doubted if George had a good enough voice to appear in opera. This was not Sullivan's view, however. When

Grossmith appeared at Albert Mansions Sullivan struck the D, fourth line in treble clef, on the piano, and said, 'Sing it out as loud as you can.' Grossmith did so and Sullivan looked up with a humorous expression on his face – even his eye-glass seemed to smile – and he simply said, 'Beautiful!' Then Sullivan sang, 'My name is John Wellington Wells,' and invited Grossmith to repeat it. 'You can do that?' he asked. Grossmith replied: 'Yes, I think I can do that.' 'Very well,' said Sullivan. 'If you can do that you can do the rest.'

It was then time to visit Gilbert at No. 24 The Boltons.

Mr Gilbert was very kind and seemed pleased that I meditated accepting the engagement. He read me the opening speech of John Wellington Wells, with reference to the sale, 'Penny Curses', etc., with which, of course, I was much amused, and said he had not completed the second Act yet; but the part of Wells had developed into greater prominence than was at first anticipated. I saw that the part would suit me excellently, but I said to Mr Gilbert, 'For the part of a Magician I should have thought you required a fine man with a fine voice.' 'That,' replied Gilbert, 'is exactly what we don't want.'[25]

As far as Gilbert and Sullivan were concerned Grossmith was just what they wanted, but this was not a view shared by the directors of the company, one of whom even went so far as to send D'Oyly Carte a telegram. 'Whatever you do don't engage Grossmith.' Fortunately Carte had the good sense to ignore it, so Grossmith was engaged and remained with the company until 1889 as its star performer. On the opening night of *The Sorcerer* there was a great roar of applause as Grossmith danced about the stage as John Wellington Wells brandishing an almost exploding teapot and then, crouching down, made his exit imitating a steam railway engine. Gilbert had certainly made the right choice.

Nevertheless, there was also Cellier's *Dora's Dream* to be considered and so other members of the cast were trained opera singers: one of them, the baritone Richard Temple, the stage-name of Richard Cobb, had made his debut in Bellini's *La Sonnambula* at the Crystal Palace in 1869. Temple sang in both pieces, and as Sir Marmaduke Pointdextre in *The Sorcerer* set the seal on his future with the company with which he remained, singing in another eight Gilbert and Sullivan operas. Then there was the tenor George Bentham, a member of Her Majesty's Opera Company, who sang the part of Alexis; Giulia Warwick, of the Carl Rosa Company, as Constance, who also sang in *Dora's Dream*; Henriette Everard as Mrs Partlet; Alice May as Aline; and the chorus was chiefly made up of students from the Royal Academy of Music.

The Sorcerer ran until 22 May 1878, in all 175 performances. Yet it was in no way a smooth run. From the start D'Oyly Carte was under pressure from his co-directors, who, after all, had put up the money. These four gentlemen were dissatisfied unless the theatre was full every night, and when the takings were less than they thought acceptable they were all for cutting their losses and giving the cast a fortnight's notice. Suddenly, the house would be full again, then it was a different matter: another opera should be commissioned. Carte became frustrated: on 9 February a different curtain-raiser was put on, another Alfred Cellier piece with a libretto by James Albery, *The Spectre Knight*. During the following weeks *The Sorcerer* continued to play to diminishing houses. On 13 April Gilbert entered in his diary that Sullivan and he had taken the train to Portsmouth.

4

The Ruler of the Queen's Navee!

⚜ 1878–1880 ⚜

In 1878 Disraeli had been Prime Minister for four years. As leader of the Conservative Party he was anxious to promote what he saw as the twin ideals of patriotism and imperialism, in pursuit of which, two years earlier, he had purchased on behalf of the government the Khedive of Egypt's shares in the Suez Canal Company, a move which furthered British interests in the region; in addition, the canal itself was of vital importance in making communication and shipping easier, in particular reducing considerably the time it took to reach India and the Far East.

The year 1878 also saw the outbreak of further hostilities in Afghanistan when, after the murder of an English envoy, Lord Roberts mobilised his Anglo-Indian forces and marched to the frontier to begin a fierce campaign; in southern Africa the British tried unsuccessfully to impose terms on Cetewayo, the King of the Zulus, which led to the Zulu War in the following year. The movement and maintenance of troops to and from these far-away regions, and an ever-increasing trade, required a strong merchant fleet carefully protected by the Royal Navy. England's navy was thought of quite simply as Britannia ruling the waves.

Few in England therefore doubted for a moment that the British would soon subdue disruptive natives. It was true England was involved, with her chief rivals Germany and France, in what was termed 'the scramble for Africa', but she felt a stern sense of duty in taking up 'the white man's burden', and in bringing civilisation, law and religion to 'new-caught, sullen peoples, half devil and half child'.[1] To further British influence was seen as a crusade, and imperialistic ambition, however self-interested it might be in reality, aroused at home a feeling of pride as reports of British daring, individual heroism and the exploits of the 'empire-builders' appeared in the popular press, while on the throne, at the centre, at the heart of the Empire, ruled a Queen who would soon become the symbol of all these things.

It was in January 1878 that Gilbert first read to D'Oyly Carte the plot of his new opera, HMS *Pinafore*. Sullivan, who was in Paris, was sent a copy with a covering letter.

'I have very little doubt whatever but that you will be pleased with it,' Gilbert wrote. 'I should have liked to have talked it over with you, as there is a good deal of fun in it which I haven't set down on paper.'[2]

As he had done with *The Sorcerer*, Gilbert drew the plot of HMS *Pinafore* from his own published work, this time from the *Bab Ballads* – not only the one about Captain Reece, commander of the *Mantelpiece*, already described, but from several others besides, such as 'The Baby's Vengeance', in which the swapping of infants is the central theme, and 'The Bumboat Woman's Story', in which Poll Pineapple, now an old lady, reminisces about how a gunboat commander, Lieutenant Belaye of the *Hot Cross Bun*, seemed to encourage her affection and liked to call her 'Little Buttercup'. Poll tells how she disguised herself as a sailor and sailed off with the crew, but it transpired after a fortnight's cruise when the ship put into port that the Lieutenant returned from shore with a wife; it was then revealed that the whole crew was made up of girls in disguise, each one equally besotted with Lieutenant Belaye and now equally broken-hearted. It was obvious now why the crew had been so gentle, so polite to one another, and such bad sailors.

> We sailed that afternoon at the mystic hour of one, –
> Remarkably nice young men were the crew of the *Hot Cross Bun*.
> I'm sorry to say I've heard that sailors sometimes swear,
> But I never yet heard a Bun say anything wrong, I declare.
>
> When Jack Tars meet, they meet with a 'Messmate, ho! What cheer?'
> But here, on the *Hot Cross Bun*, it was 'How do you do, my dear?'
> When Jack Tars growl, I believe they growl with a big, big D–
> But the strongest oath of the Hot Cross Buns was a mild 'Dear me!'
>
> Yet, though they were all well bred, you could scarcely call them slick:
> Whenever a sea was on, they were all extremely sick;

And whenever the weather was calm, and the wind was light and fair.
They spent more time than a sailor should on his back back hair.[3]

Gilbert took details from here for his new opera, and more than the
'big, big D–'. Readers of 'General John', 'Joe Golightly', 'Little
Oliver' and 'Lieutenant-Colonel Flare' may well recognise themes
that also appear in HMS *Pinafore*. However, there was one theme
uppermost in Gilbert's mind, one for which oddly enough Disraeli
had inadvertently been responsible when he appointed W. H. Smith
First Lord of the Admiralty. It certainly seemed strange to elevate to
such a position not only a self-made man who did not come from the
same class socially as the vast majority of naval officers but also a man
who had never been to sea!

When some years later Gilbert retold the story of HMS *Pinafore*
specially for children he made much of this fact.

One of the most important personages in the Government of that day was
Sir Joseph Porter, First Lord of the Admiralty. You would naturally think
that a person who commanded the entire Navy would be the most
accomplished sailor who could be found, but that is not the way in which
such things are managed in England. Sir Joseph Porter knew nothing
whatever about ships. Now as England is a great maritime country it is very
important that all Englishmen should understand something about men-of-
war. So as soon as it was discovered that his ignorance of a ship was so
complete that he did not know one end of it from the other, some important
person said: 'Let us set this poor ignorant gentleman to command the
British Fleet, and by that means give him an opportunity of ascertaining
what a ship really is.' This was considered to be a most wise and sensible
suggestion, and so Sir Joseph Porter was at once appointed 'First Lord of the
Admiralty of Great Britain and Ireland.' I daresay you think I am joking, but
indeed I am quite serious. That is the way in which things are managed in
this great and happy country.[4]

Gilbert was, of course, writing after the tremendous success of the
opera, but while it was in the process of creation he was a little
cautious: 'Among other things a song for the First Lord – tracing his
career as an office-boy in a cotton-broker's office, clerk, traveller,
junior partner, and First Lord of Britain's Navy,' he had informed
Sullivan. 'I think a splendid song can be made of this. Of course, there
will be no personality in this – the fact that the First Lord in the opera
is a Radical of the most pronounced type will do away with any
suspicion that W. H. Smith is intended.'[5]

How could Gilbert have appeared so naïve? Perhaps he was not at all; perhaps he was trying to convince Sullivan that there was no cause for alarm, for he knew well enough Sullivan's intimacy with people in 'high places', and to pillory a member of the Cabinet might be thought to be going too far. In any event the song was set and the point was not lost on the public when the opera opened at the Opera Comique on the night of 25 May, and it came as no surprise that very soon the First Lord was being referred to as 'Pinafore Smith'.

The action of HMS *Pinafore; or The Lass that Loved a Sailor* takes place on the quarterdeck of the ship as it lies at anchor off Portsmouth. Act I opens at noon as the sailors make the ship spick and span, cleaning brasswork, splicing ropes and so on. Little Buttercup, the bumboat woman, enters carrying a large basket of wares to sell to the crew: anything from snuff and tobacco to succulent chops and peppermint drops. As she is described as 'the reddest beauty in all Spithead', it is clear that Buttercup is elderly, though, as she says, she has dissembled well.

Two sailors stand out from the rest of the crew: Dick Deadeye, whose ugliness is mocked by the rest, since 'you can't expect a chap with such a name as Dick Deadeye to be a popular character'. As he himself admits, 'From such a face and form as mine the noblest sentiments sound like the utterances of a depraved imagination.'[6] The other is Ralph Rackstraw, 'the smartest lad in all the fleet', whose sorrow is that he is love-sick for a lass above his station, Josephine, the Captain's daughter. Captain Corcoran comes on deck and it is obvious that in the manner of Captain Reece he likes to make his men feel as comfortable as possible.

When he is left alone with Little Butercup the Captain admits he is worried that Josephine is not in the least pleased that she is sought in marriage by Sir Joseph Porter, the First Lord of the Admiralty, who, it is expected, will arrive that very afternoon to claim her promised hand. When Josephine enters carrying a basket of small flowers she tells her father that she might be able to esteem, reverence, even venerate Sir Joseph, but she cannot love him because her heart is already given to a humble sailor on the ship.

'I blush for the weakness that allows me to cherish such a passion. I hate myself when I think of the depth I have stooped in permitting myself to think tenderly of one ignobly born, but I love him! I love him! I love him!'[7]

Josephine affirms, however, that she will never reveal her love to the sailor in question, who is, of course, Rackstraw. The Captain sees Sir Joseph Porter's barge approaching, 'manned by twelve trusty oarsmen and accompanied by the admiring crowd of sisters, cousins and aunts that attend him wherever he goes'. Josephine leaves the quarterdeck, and her father ascends the poop-deck as a barcarolle is sung off-stage.

> Over the bright blue sea
> Comes Sir Joseph Porter K.C.B,
> Wherever he may go
> Bang-bang the loud nine-pounders go!
> Shout o'er the bright blue sea
> For Sir Joseph Porter K.C.B.[8]

The sailors tiptoe on to the deck listening attentively to the song. Sir Joseph's female relations arrive and dance round the deck. Sir Joseph's entrance is certainly one of the finest Gilbert and Sullivan wrote:

SIR JOSEPH.	I am the monarch of the sea,
	The ruler of the Queen's Navee.
	Whose praise Great Britain loudly chants.
COUSIN HEBE.	And we are his sisters, and his cousins, and his aunts!
RELATIONS.	And we are his sisters, and his cousins, and his aunts! . . .
SIR JOSEPH.	But when the breezes blow,
	I generally go below,
	And seek the seclusion that a cabin grants!
COUSIN HEBE.	And so do his sisters, and his cousins, and his aunts!
ALL.	And so do his sisters, and his cousin, and his aunts!
	His sisters and his cousins,
	Whom he reckons up in dozens,
	And his aunts![9]

This might be the right place to mention that Cousin Hebe was the first part played by Jessie Bond, who soon became an essential member of the company, much loved by all who worked with her, and particularly by Gilbert and Sullivan themselves.

In the same way as the judge in *Trial by Jury* had outlined the strange progress he had made towards his present important position Sir Joseph Porter reveals how he had risen unctuously from obscurity.

When I was a lad I served my term
As office boy to an Attorney's firm.
I cleaned the windows and I swept the floor,
And I polished up the handle of the big front door.
    I polished up that handle so carefullee
    That now I am the Ruler of the Queen's Navee!

As office boy I made such a mark
That they gave me the post of a junior clerk.
I served the writs with a smile so bland.
And I copied all the letters in a big round hand –
    I copied all the letters in a hand so free,
    That now I am the Ruler of the Queen's Navee!

In serving writs I made such a name
That an articled clerk I soon became;
I wore clean collars and a brand new suit
For the pass examination at the Institute.
    And that pass examination did so well for me,
    That now I am the Ruler of the Queen's Navee!

Of legal knowledge I acquired such a grip
That they took me into the partnership.
And that junior partnership I ween
Was the only ship I had ever seen.
    But that kind of ship so suited me,
    That now I am the Ruler of the Queen's Navee!

I grew so rich that I was sent
By a pocket borough into Parliament.
I always voted at my party's call,
And I never thought of thinking for myself at all.
    I thought so little they rewarded me,
    By making me the Ruler of the Queen's Navee!

Now landsmen all, whoever you may be,
If you want to rise to the top of the tree,
If your soul isn't fettered to an office stool,
Be careful to be guided by this golden rule –
    Stick close to your desks and never go to sea,
    And you all may be Rulers of the Queen's Navee![10]

This is surely a brilliant lyric by any standard, but Gilbert seems here to excel even himself in the thought that the junior partnership in an attorney's office was the only ship the First Lord of the Admiralty had ever seen!

Sir Joseph insists that Captain Corcoran should treat his crew respectfully at all times. 'That you are their Captain is an accident of birth,' he says. 'I cannot permit these noble fellows to be patronised because an accident of birth has placed you above them and them below you.' The Captain must always give his orders with an 'if you please', and Ralph Rackstraw is handed a song the First Lord has specially composed for use by the whole Royal Navy: 'A British tar is a soaring soul,/ As free as a mountain bird.'[11]

When Sir Joseph has gone to his cabin Ralph and Josephine are alone on deck. Ralph addresses her with high-flown eloquence, which hints that he is no ordinary seaman, admitting how he is 'Driven hither by objective influences – thither by subjective emotions – wafted one moment into blazing day, by mocking hope – plunged the next into the Cimmerian darkness of tangible despair.' He decides it is the time to declare himself:

Even though Jove's armoury were launched at the head of the audacious mortal whose lips, unhallowed by relationship, dared to breathe that precious word, yet I would breathe it once, and then perchance be silent evermore. Josephine, in one breath I will concentrate all the hopes, the doubts, the anxious fears of six weary months. Josephine, I am a British sailor, and I love you.[12]

In the duet which follows Josephine appears to rebuff Ralph while she reveals the truth about her feelings, but only in an aside.

JOSEPHINE. Refrain audacious tar,
             Your suit from pressing;
             Remember what you are,
             And whom addressing!
             [*Aside*]
             I'd laugh my rank to scorn
             In union holy,
             Were he more highly born
             Or I were lowly!

RALPH.   Proud lady, have your way,
             Unfeeling beauty!

You speak and I obey,
It is my duty!
I am the lowliest tar
That sails the water,
And you, proud maiden, are
My Captain's daughter!
[*Aside*]
My heart with anguish torn
Bows down before her;
She laughs my love to scorn,
Yet I adore her![13]

Ralph, thinking he is completely spurned, decides there is nothing left but to blow his brains out, much to the delight of Dick Deadeye. The Boatswain hands Ralph a loaded pistol, the sailors stop their ears. Just when all seems inevitable Josephine rushes on to the deck: 'Ah! Stay your hand! I love you.' Dick Deadeye remains cynical and issues a stern reproach:

Our Captain, ere the day is gone,
Will be extremely down upon
The wicked men who art employ
To make his Josephine less coy
In many different ways.[14]

Nobody heeds Deadeye's further warning given to Ralph when he hears that the two lovers plan to go ashore that night to get married:

Forbear, nor carry out the scheme you've planned
She is a lady – you a foremost hand!
Remember, she's your gallant captain's daughter,
And you the meanest slave that crawls the water![15]

The first act ends with great joy as the sailors give three cheers for the 'sailor's bride/Who casts all thought of rank aside,/Who gives up home and fortune too/For the honest love of a sailor true,' and sing the song Sir Joseph had composed for them.

That same night by moonlight Captain Corcoran is on the poop-deck singing as he accompanies himself on the mandoline. Little Buttercup is seated below on the quarterdeck gazing sentimentally at him, having remained on board long after she would normally have gone ashore. The Captain is in a melancholy mood, everything is now at sixes and sevens, the crew is rebellious and his daughter 'to a tar is partial'. Worse still, Sir Joseph is furious and has threatened a court martial. Buttercup gives her sympathy and reveals clearly how strong her feelings are for him, but the Captain insists he and she can never be more than friends.

'I understand!' says Buttercup. 'You hold aloof from me because you are rich and lofty – and I, poor and lowly. But take care! The poor bumboat woman has gipsy blood in her veins, and she can read destinies.'[16]

Things are never what they seem. Buttercup has a secret to reveal, and the Captain will 'learn the truth with sorrow'. However, the secret will not come out just yet. Sir Joseph must be placated, and the Captain assures him that it is only the high position he holds that makes Josephine shrink from showing her affection – his exalted rank dazzles her. Sir Joseph is satisfied for the moment. Josephine herself enters from her cabin to confess she has misgivings about the momentous step she is about to take, leaving her father's luxurious home, hung with ancestral armour and old brasses, for a dark and dingy room in some back street with snuffly children crying, which would be all her simple sailor, lowly born, would be able to offer:

> Where organs yell, and clacking housewives fume,
>   And clothes are hanging all day a-drying.
> With one cracked looking-glass to see your face in,
>   And dinner served up in a pudding basin![17]

Yet she is in love, and it is a question between love and reason. Sir Joseph, still thinking that Josephine is in awe of his rank, assures her that 'the high and the lowly may be truly happy together, provided that they truly love one another.' This is just what Josephine wishes to hear, and with Sir Joseph thinking the 'humble captain's child' is now his and Captain Corcoran excited that his only daughter will soon be the bride of a Cabinet Minister, 'the prospect is Elysian', as a happy trio is sung with the merry bells 'on board-ship' rhyming with 'his Lordship,' since 'Love can level ranks'.[18]

The Captain is once again left alone, but the happy moment is wrecked by the entrance of Dick Deadeye, who reveals the truth that Josephine 'this very night with Rackstraw will be flying'. The Captain just has time to don his large boat cloak and crouch beside the ship's wheel as the sailors tiptoe on deck with Ralph, and Josephine

enters from her cabin carrying a bundle of necessaries accompanied
by Little Buttercup. A sudden noise makes them all freeze. It is only
the cat, Dick Deadeye assures them, but it is a cat of a different sort,
the cat-o'-nine-tails, which the Captain brandishes as he confronts
them demanding an explanation. Ralph obliges:

> I humble, poor, and lowly born,
>   The meanest of the port division –
>   The butt of epauletted scorn –
> The mark of quarter-deck derision –
>   Have dared to raise my wormy eyes
> Above the dust to which you mould me
>   In manhood's glorious pride to rise,
> I am an Englishman – behold me!

ALL.   He is an Englishman!
BOATSWAIN. He is an Englishman!!
>   For he himself has said it,
>   And it's greatly to his credit,
> That he is an Englishman!

ALL.   That he is an Englishman!
BOATSWAIN. For he might have been a Roosian,
>   A French, or Turk, or Proosian,
>   Or perhaps Ital-ian!

ALL.   Or perhaps Ital-ian!
BOATSWAIN. But in spite of all temptations.
>   To belong to other nations,
>   He remains an Englishman![19]

Surely this will be sufficient to assuage the Captain's anger? Not in
the least.

> In uttering a reprobation
>   To any British Tar,
> I try to speak with moderation,
>   But you have gone too far.
> I'm very sorry to disparage
>   A humble foremast lad,
> But to seek your captain's child in marriage
>   Why, damme, it's too bad![20]

All are horrified as the Captain swears the 'big, big D–', none more so
than Sir Joseph and his female relations who have appeared on the

poop-deck. Sir Joseph will hear of no defence and the Captain is sent to his cabin in disgrace, swiftly followed by Josephine.

Sir Joseph is prepared to hear a true account of what happened from Ralph, but he is profoundly shocked when he learns that 'love burns as brightly in the foksle as it does on the quarter-deck, and Josephine is the fairest bud that ever bloosomed upon the tree of a poor fellow's wildest hopes.' At which point Josephine rushes in and flings herself into Ralph's arms. This is too much for Sir Joseph who orders Ralph to be loaded with chains and thrown into the dungeon.

Seeing Ralph's sorry plight, Buttercup decides this is the moment to reveal her secret. When she had been young and charming she had practised baby-farming and had nursed two babies, one was of 'low condition' while the other was 'upper-crust, a regular patrician', but Little Buttercup has to admit the awful truth:

> Oh, bitter is my cup!
>   However could I do it?
> I mixed these children up,
>   And not a creature knew it! . . .
>
> In time each little waif
>   Forsook his foster mother,
> The well-born babe was Ralph –
>   Your Captain was the other!!![21]

So it turns out that Ralph is the Captain and the Captain a common sailor. The two appear in their changed uniforms, a 'very singular occurrence', and Sir Joseph commands Ralph, now the Captain, to let Corcoran 'stand forward'.

RALPH.   Corcoran. Three paces to the front – march!
CAPTAIN.   If what?
RALPH.   If what? I don't think I understand you.
CAPTAIN.   If you please.
SIR JOSEPH.   Perfectly right. If you please.
RALPH.   Oh. If you please. [*Captain stands forward.*]
SIR JOSEPH.   [*To Captain*]. You are an extremely fine fellow.
CAPTAIN.   Yes, your honour.
SIR JOSEPH.   So it seems that you were Ralph and Ralph was you.
CAPTAIN.   So it seems, your honour.

SIR JOSEPH. Well I need hardly tell you that after this change in your
            condition, a marriage with your daughter will be out of the
            question.
CAPTAIN.   Don't say that, your honour – love levels all ranks.
SIR JOSEPH. It does to a considerable extent, but it does not level them as
            much as that.[22]

Sir Joseph hands Josephine to Ralph; the Captain turns to Buttercup,
and Sir Joseph himself, thinking his lot is sad and sorry, finds a
willing hand in his cousin Hebe who promises never to desert him and
to soothe and comfort his declining days. The opera ends with
reprises and the final thought that it's greatly to anyone's credit that
he is an Englishman! Rule Britannia!

When on 13 April 1878 Lord Charles Beresford entertained Gilbert
and Sullivan to lunch on board HMS *Thunderer* at Portsmouth he was
unlikely to have known, more than in a vague way, what they were up
to. He showed them round his ship and then instructed a boatman
and four sailors to take them on board various other ships in the
harbour: *Invincible*, *St Vincent*, and Nelson's flagship, *Victory*. On
the last two Gilbert made copious notes and sketches of the quarter-
decks before catching the 4.40 train back to London. The visit was
important, because he was determined to recreate an authentic
replica of a British man-of-war for the stage, exact in every detail,
even to the smallest ring, bolt, thole-pin and halyard.

It had been a difficult time for both men: Sullivan out in Nice had
found composing arduous, and he had been in acute pain with kidney
trouble for much of the while. 'I would compose a few bars and then
be almost insensible with pain,' he recalled. 'When the paroxysm was
past, I would write a little more, until the pain overwhelmed me
again.'[23] It was remarkable, as Sullivan himself admitted, that what
was considered such merry and spontaneous music should have been
written under such distressing conditions.

Gilbert also had been suffering from migraine and gout. He had
begun to assemble the lyrics for HMS *Pinafore* at the beginning of the
New Year, but he did not write out the dialogue until 3 May. From
that time onward he was supplying Sullivan with alterations to the
lyrics and revising and rehearsing at the same time. He was used to
such a situation, for in January he had been revising and rehearsing
his play *The Ne'er Do well* for the Olympic Theatre. Marion Terry,
the third of the famous Terry sisters, was in the cast and in order to

give her special coaching, and partly for his health, he had taken her and his wife to Brighton for a few days in the middle of February. The play opened on the 25th but was soon taken off. Nothing daunted, Gilbert rewrote the third act, changed the title back to the original, *The Vagabond*, and the following month it ran for a short while 'magnificently'.

A few days after he and Sullivan had visited Portsmouth, Gilbert toyed with the thought of covering the Afghan War for *The Times*. The idea was hardly practicable and instead he took Marion and Kitty to Paris, then to Antwerp and Brussels. The field of Waterloo brought on a migraine. More exercise was needed: on his return he had an 'indoor' tennis court set out in a tent in the garden.

However, another task had occupied him after visiting Portsmouth: the building or, at least, supervising the building of a model of the set on which he could plan the action of the opera. Every move, every situation and grouping, every entrance and exit had to be clear in his mind before he began to rehearse with the actors. It is known that he used differently coloured and variously sized wooden blocks to represent characters and chorus. HMS *Pinafore* had an important innovation in the way the chorus was involved in the action, particularly the male chorus of sailors which, though in most ways a caricature crew, must seem to be manning the ship in a realistic way at all times; here Gilbert's knowledge of the sea and ships was invaluable, and the cast was so well drilled that it seems the professional seamen in his audience were satisfied with the result.

Gilbert too was satisfied: 'Piece went extremely well. I went in and out three or four times during evening,'[24] he recorded on the opening night. In his usual way he had paced about the streets rather than sit through the whole performance, something denied to Sullivan who was conducting the orchestra. At the final curtain there were enthusiastic curtain calls for them both.

When he left the theatre Gilbert made his way to the Beefsteak Club to dine with friends, and on the following morning, a Sunday, he took a hansom round to Sullivan's house and they scoured the newspapers together for reviews. On the whole the critics were kind, though the general impression was that Gilbert's part in the work had been more understandable than Sullivan's. The next morning *The Times* was wondering what Sullivan was doing involving himself in such a venture anyway.

'While recording this decided success of Mr Sullivan's new work we cannot suppress a word of regret that the composer on whom before all others the chance of a national school of music depends should confine himself, or be confined by circumstances, to a class of production which, however attractive, is hardly worthy of the efforts of an accomplished and serious artist.'[25]

Another critic wrote of the first night:

Seldom, indeed, have we been in the company of a more joyous audience, more confidently anticipating an evening's amusement than that which filled the Opera Comique in every corner. The expectation was fulfilled completely. Those who believe in the power of Mr Gilbert to tickle the fancy with quaint suggestions and unexpected forms of humour were more than satisfied, and those who appreciated Mr Arthur Sullivan's inexhaustible gift of melody were equally gratified. The result, therefore, was 'a hit, a palpable hit' – a success in fact, there could be no mistaking, and which, great as it was on Saturday, will be even more decided when the work has been played a few nights.[26]

There was only one dismissive voice: the *Daily Telegraph* which described the piece as 'a frothy production destined soon to subside into nothingness'.[27]

After a few weeks it seemed as though the *Daily Telegraph* might have been right. The audiences began to dwindle and the subsequent loss of revenue began to worry the directors. In fact, the small audiences were not really because the opera was considered bad, but more because May that year was hotter than usual and people did not wish to spend their evenings cooped up in a stuffy theatre. Surely the heatwave would not last, but June was just as hot. Soon the cast was on a fortnight's notice and working for a cut of a third in its wage; the orchestra was scaled down and cheaper musicians employed. On returning from a short holiday in Switzerland Sullivan was annoyed to discover the fact. He informed Carte that unless better instrumentalists were engaged he would withdraw his music. 'You know perfectly well that what I say I mean,' he wrote. 'Kindly advise the Directors of this.'[28]

The *Pinafore* seemed to be listing badly, then quite suddenly she righted herself, or rather Sullivan righted her. It happened that Sullivan had been engaged to conduct a series of Promenade Concerts at Covent Garden. One evening he included in the programme a selection of tunes from HMS *Pinafore* arranged by Hamilton Clarke. The effect was immediate, the audience was enthusiastic to the point of wanting to see the opera for themselves; soon the Opera Comique was packed every night, and by the end of August it was realised even by the directors that they had a success on their hands.

The opera was not only a success in England, but in America also, where, according to Jessie Bond, enthusiasm was even greater. It was performed at the Boston Museum in November 1878, a 'decent and delightful' experience reported the *Boston Advertiser*.[29] Soon it was being staged in differing versions in New York where there was beginning what has been described as 'a *Pinafore* epidemic'. At its height the 'epidemic' was so contagious that nine productions were running concurrently, for the copyright laws did not extend to scores published abroad and there was nothing to prevent any theatre in any place mounting a 'pirated' version without any consideration towards the author or composer. However, it is true that Sullivan had been approached by a theatre in Philadelphia with the offer to conduct *Pinafore* for a fortnight, but he declined. Clearly something had to be done, and D'Oyly Carte, furious at the news, made plans to mount a production in America with his own company.

In the last week of June he set off across the Atlantic in the steamship *Gallia*. Before his departure he had made arrangements for the running of the company, and most members had been satisfied with his appointment by power of attorney of Michael Gunn to manage the theatre in his absence and act as his substitute. It is certain also that he had agreed with Gilbert and Sullivan that the three of them, together with a small group of leading singers, would cross the Atlantic in the autumn.

It was while Carte was in America that the Opera Comique became the scene of a bizarre naval battle, or at least the crew of the *Pinafore* were involved in a brawl. The Comedy Opera Company's lease of the theatre was due to expire on the last day of July, but at a time when the opera was still running to packed houses. For long bored and dissatisfied at the attitude of his fellow directors Carte had decided in view of the opera's undoubted success to take out a new lease in the three names of Carte, Sullivan and Gilbert and pay off Chappell and the others, who had each put up £500. This proposed arrangement soon reached the ears of the disaffected directors who on the night of 31 July took it upon themselves to disrupt the opera and with vans and furniture removers attempted to take away the scenery claiming it belonged to them! As Jessie Bond remembered:

The performance was nearly over. Miss Everard, as 'Buttercup,' was singing at the time, and she pluckily tried to continue her part, in spite of the noise going on behind the scenes, and heard all over the house. There was no panic, though the startled audience suspected fire, and a few people left the theatre. Alfred Cellier had to stop the orchestra, Frank Thornton ran round to a box and spoke to the people, and George Grossmith advanced to the footlights and explained the exact situation. For us young women at the back of the stage it was most unpleasant, as a battle royal was taking place between the burly workmen and the crew of the *Pinafore*. However, the jolly Jack Tars expelled the intruders – it was quite a glorious naval victory.[30]

Gilbert informed Sullivan about all this by letter. The poor fellow was on a short Swiss–Italian holiday convalescing from an operation to crush the kidney stone that had caused him so much pain. The episode had not been quite as mild or amusing as Jessie Bond described, for in the broil Richard Barker, who held the licence for the theatre, had been quite seriously injured. In fact the matter did not end until some three years later after a long-drawn-out battle of a different sort in the law courts.

Gilbert and Sullivan landed in New York on Guy Fawkes Day having crossed the Atlantic in the Cunard Line's *Bothnia*. Also on board had been Alfred Cellier who would be the company's regular conductor, alhough Sullivan himself intended to conduct the first nights. Carte followed a few days later, again travelling in the *Gallia*, and bringing with him several members of the company. The plan was that HMS *Pinafore* would open at the Fifth Avenue Theatre in the first week of December, but also that some of the authors' other work should receive an airing, and Sullivan had journeyed to Boston to conduct his *The Prodigal Son* performed by the Handel and Haydn Society. Gilbert's opera *Princess Toto*, for which, it will be remembered, Frederick Clay had composed the music, opened at the Standard Theatre on 13 December. However, the major project for both men was the preparation of their new piece, the title of which was still a closely guarded secret, though Gilbert had already decided on *The Pirates of Penzance*.

There has been much discussion, chiefly by Americans who naturally were the more interested, as to how much of this new opera was written and composed after the pair had arrived in New York. Certainly much of the music was, and there is a plaque advertising the fact at No. 45 East Twentieth Street, though it implies that Sullivan composed the whole piece there. 'We took with us the half-completed opera. I had only composed the second act, without any orchestration, in England. Soon after my arrival in America I wrote the first act, and scored the whole opera.'[31] Sullivan says 'Soon after my arrival', so Gilbert had completed the libretto, but it had most likely been written back to front as the main theme of the *Pirates* was a rehash of his unpublished operetta 'Our Island Home'. On 7 August he had informed Sullivan that he had 'broken the neck of Act II'.[32] 'I see my way clearly to the end. I think it comes out very well.' He then went on to describe in some detail how he had made great use of the 'Tarantara' business in the second act.

The Police always sing 'Tarantara' when they desire to work their courage to the sticking-point. They are naturally timid, but through the agency of this talisman they are enabled to acquit themselves well when concealed. In Act II, when the robbers approach, their courage begins to fail them, but recourse to 'Tarantara' (pianissimo) has the desired effect. I mention this that you may bear it in mind in setting the General's 'Tarantara' song. I mean that it may be treated as an important feature and not as a mere incidental effect. I need not say that this is a mere suggestion. If you don't like it, it won't be done.[33]

We know, of course, that it was done, and with great effect, but in a slightly different way from how Gilbert had suggested.

The Pirates of Penzance; or The Slave of Duty is set on the Cornish coast. Act I opens with a group of pirates making merry and drinking sherry in celebration of Frederic, one of their band, who has just completed his apprenticeship. The fact that sherry, a rather genteel drink, is being imbibed instead of the expected rum is significant, but the truth about the identity of these pirates only comes out at the end. There is nothing hidden about Frederic, however, because Ruth, 'a kind of piratical maid-of-all-work', announces that she had been the young man's nurse since he was a 'little lad', but in binding him as apprentice to a seafaring career had committed a gross error because of her deafness.

I was a stupid nurserymaid, on breakers always steering,
And I did not catch the word aright, through being hard of hearing;
Mistaking my instructions, which within my brain did gyrate,
I took and bound this promising boy apprentice to a pirate.

A sad mistake it was to make and doom him to a vile lot,
I bound him to a pirate – you – instead of to a pilot.[34]

Frederic is despondent and faces a serious dilemma: as a pirate he owes allegiance to the rest, but as a conscientious member of society he feels it his duty to bring his friends to book. But it is more desperate than that: he feels bound to exterminate them, not that they have ever been very successful at their trade; they are far too tender-hearted. As Frederic says: 'The last three ships we took proved to be manned entirely by orphans, and so we had to let them go. One would think that Great Britain's mercantile navy was recruited solely from her orphan asylums – which we know is not the case.'[35] The extermination would only become unnecessary if the whole band would accompany Frederic back to civilisation. The Pirate King replies that he does not think much of his profession, 'but contrasted with respectability, it is comparatively honest'.[36]

Ruth begs to be allowed to accompany him. Since she has been the only woman Frederic has set eyes on since the age of eight she has managed to persuade him that she is comely if not beautiful. However, the arrival on the scene of a chorus of young girls, the daughters of Major-General Stanley, soon opens Frederic's eyes and he chides Ruth with: 'O false one, you have deceived me!'[37] After his renunciation of her she goes off in despair while Frederic hides in a cave.

The girls being separated from their father for a while and thinking the place deserted decide to paddle and are removing their shoes and stockings for the purpose when Frederic emerges from the cave. Feigning to be quite horrified at the presence of 'A man!' each hops about on one foot while Frederic apologises for his strange appearance, but manages to convince them that he is about to give up his wild profession, and this would be made so much easier if he could be carried off in marriage.

> Oh, is there not one maiden breast
>   Which does not feel the moral beauty
> Of making worldly interest
>   Subordinate to sense of duty?
> Who would not give up willingly
>   All matrimonial ambition,
> To rescue such a one as I
>   From his unfortunate position?[38]

At first it seems there is not, but one of the girls, Mabel, responds to the plea and offers herself, but the question then arises, as her sisters ask, that had Frederic not been a 'thing of beauty, would she not be swayed by quite as keen a sense of duty'.[39] The other girls decide to stay a little distance away; although they chatter about the weather, their ears are straining to hear the lovers' conversation. Suddenly the pirate band arrives and see a chance too good to be missed.

> Here's a first rate opportunity
> To get married with impunity,
> And indulge in the felicity
> Of unbounded domesticity.
> You shall quickly be parsonified,
> Conjugally matrimonified,
> By a doctor of divinity,
> Who resides in this vicinity.[40]

The 'opportunity' is soon thwarted by the entrance of Major-General Stanley, who introduces himself in one of the best-known patter-songs: 'I am the very model of a modern Major-General',[41] in which Gilbert matches Byron in his handling of the triple rhyme, using a few familiar to readers of *Don Juan* like 'gunnery' rhyming with 'nunnery'. All the girls are the Major-General's daughters, and when the pirates are deceived into thinking that this fine upstanding military figure is in reality only a poor orphan boy they have not the heart to pursue their plan. Gilbert makes great play on the words 'orphan' and 'often', a matter rather tedious to a modern ear, but the first Act ends dramatically enough with the girls and the General going up the rocks while the pirates indulge in a wild dance of delight. The General produces a Union Jack, and the Pirate King unfurls a black flag with skull and cross-bones, while Ruth makes a final plea with Frederick not to leave her, but he casts her aside.

Act 2 is set in a ruined Gothic chapel. The moon is shining brightly and the Major-General has risen from his bed and is surrounded by his daughters. It seems he could not sleep for the shame of having lied to the pirates about his background, and has come to the chapel to humble himself before the tombs of his ancestors, to implore their pardon for having brought dishonour on the family escutcheon. Here is another lie, if anything worse than the first, since the Major-General, as Frederic is quick to remind him, had only bought Tremorden Castle a year ago. 'The stucco in your baronial hall is scarcely dry.'[42]

'Frederic, in this chapel are ancestors: you cannot deny that. With the estate, I bought the chapel and its contents. I don't know whose ancestors they were, but I know whose ancestors they are, and I shudder to think that their descendant by purchase (if I may so describe myself) should have brought disgrace upon what, I have no doubt, was an unstained escutcheon.'[43]

Frederic assures him that in spite of this undoubted truth he had done the right thing in protecting his daughters from the pirates. Frederic too has arranged to bring the scoundrels to book at eleven o'clock, having assembled a force of policemen under the command of their sergeant for the purpose. The policemen enter nervously, but keep up their courage by beating their chests and much 'tarantara-ing', while the girls do their best to encourage them. When Frederic is eventually left alone he is immediately accosted by the Pirate King and Ruth who each hold a pistol to his ear and present him with 'a most ingenious paradox'. They inform him that because he was born on 29 February, during a leap year, he is in fact 'only five and a little bit over', and so has not served his twenty-one years' pirate appren-ticeship at all: that will not come to an end until 1940! Realising that he is still a pirate, Frederic knows where his duty lies and tells the King the truth about the Major-General; the King orders the castle to be attacked that very night and the deceiver to be put to death.

Frederic informs a distressed Mabel that he will not be free to claim her for another fifty-three years! The policemen return after failing to find the pirates, and Mabel explains that as dearly as she had loved Frederic before, his heroic sacrifice to his sense of duty has endeared him to her tenfold. 'He has done his duty. I will do mine,'[44] she says, and urges the policemen to go and do theirs. It is then that the Sergeant reflects on the nature of constabulary duty, a policeman's lot, which, he reflects, if one consideration is taken with another, 'is not a happy one'.[45] The opera soon reaches its climax as Major-General Stanley enters, watched by both the policemen and pirates in hiding; the policemen intent on catching the pirates, and the pirates now determined to vary piracy 'with a little burglaree', wait to capture the General. The daughters, all in white peignoirs and night-caps and carrying lighted candles, join their father, who is immedi-ately seized by Frederic and the pirates to face what seems his unhappy death.

'Is he to die, unshriven – unannealed?'[46] asks Mabel wildly, echoing the Ghost in *Hamlet*. The girls plead for mercy. Is there anyone to wield a weapon in his cause? The policeman leap in: a struggle ensues and the pirates get the better of them, and stand over their prostrate quarry with drawn swords. However, no pirate band will take its stand at the Central Criminal Court, and their proud triumph will not be long-lived. For a moment the Pirate King fears the policemen might claim to be orphans, but he knew that game well enough. No. There was a much stronger claim on their allegiance and the Sergeant charges them to yield 'in Queen Victoria's name!' The King yields with little hesitation because with all their faults the pirates love their Queen. The police holding the pirates by the collar take out handkerchiefs and weep as they lead the supposed felons away, and the Major-General orders them to be placed at the bar, when Ruth enters to reveal that the pirates are really 'all noblemen, who have gone wrong'. The Major-General's attitude changes instantly:

> No Englishman unmoved that statement hears,
> Because with all their faults, we love our House of Peers.
>
> I pray you pardon me, ex-Pirate King,
> Peers will be peers, and youth will have its fling.
> Resume your ranks, and legislative duties,
> And take my daughters, all of whom are beauties.[47]

The Pirates of Penzance opened grandly at the Fifth Avenue Theatre, New York, on 31 December 1879, but ironically it was not its first performance. In order to establish the opera's copyright in England, D'Oyly Carte had arranged for it to be played at a special matinee performance a day earlier at the Royal Bijou Theatre, Paignton. Why Paignton? Quite simply because one of Carte's companies was performing HMS *Pinafore* at Torquay, a fact which explains why the pirates of Paignton seemed unfamiliar with both words and music and wore naval uniforms decked out with a few coloured handkerchiefs. It hardly mattered: there were only about fifty people in the audience!

5

I'm an Aesthetic Sham

1880–1882

By the latter part of 1880 Gilbert was hard at work on a new opera. On 1 November he informed Sullivan he had written two-thirds of it, although he felt dissatisfied. Once again he had drawn upon one of his Bab Ballads; this time 'The Rival Curates', but he was having very grave doubts whether even a sympathetic audience would accept a satire on the clergy. Certainly Dr Daly in *The Sorcerer* had been accepted; nevertheless he mistrusted the clerical element.

'I feel hampered by the restrictions which the nature of the subject places upon my freedom of action,' he wrote.[1] It was probably better to play safe and revert to an earlier idea of rivalry between two aesthetic fanatics worshipped by a chorus of female aesthetes instead of a couple of clergymen worshipped by a chorus of female devotees. He would be able to get much more fun from the aesthetes, making them painters or poets, and he could keep his idea of bringing in a chorus of Hussars in dress uniform who would all become aesthetes in order to attract the female variety, and forsake their profession for the purpose, carry lilies in their hands, wear long hair, and stand in stained-glass attitudes.

'I entertained this idea at first, as you may remember, but abandoned it because I foresaw great difficulty in getting the chorus to dress and make up aesthetically. But if you can get Du Maurier to design the costumes, I don't know that the difficulty will be insuperable.'[2]

With such feelings of uncertainty were sown the seeds of *Patience; or Bunthorne's Bride!*, a new and original Aesthetic Opera in Two Acts. When the libretto finally reached him Sullivan was delighted, and produced such happy music that Gilbert himself always maintained that the opera's immense popularity was 'mainly referable to the delightful music'.[3]

The theme and manner of *Patience* were topical, and Du Maurier had much to do with that; for he had been lampooning the pretensions of aestheticism for some years in the pages of *Punch* and in February 1880 had begun a series of caricatures, one of which he termed 'Nincompoopiana'. The central character attacked was Oscar Wilde, who had recently taken up residence in London. Wilde's extravagant clothes, worn, it should be noted in fairness to him, usually in the evening, of 'a velvet coat edged with braid, knee-breeches, black silk stockings, a soft loose shirt and a wide turn-down collar and a large flowing green tie ',[4] had achieved their purpose and become a talking point. For Wilde proclaimed 'reformation of dress was of far more importance than a reformation of religion'.[5] However, Wilde was not by any means the originator of the so-called Aesthetic Movement: in fact, he was rather late on the scene, and, if anything, a product of it. The movement, if it may be called a 'movement' at all, had its origins a few years earlier and is chiefly associated with Whistler and Swinburne, who, through their friendship with Rossetti and William Morris and their families, were imbued with all the images and decorative ideals of Pre-Raphaelitism. Aestheticism had also been given a certain philosophical respectability through the writings of the Oxford don, Walter Pater. 'Art for Art's sake' was the ideal that aroused that enthusiasm for art and beauty which had the rich and the more enlightened members of the middle class crowding into Arthur Liberty's recently opened store in Regent Street to buy Japanese fans, Oriental jars, screens and vases. By 1880, then, the word 'aesthetic' had become a general term for a fashionable trend, some might say, for good taste, much in the way 'psychedelic' in the 1960s might have been used to describe the extravagant colours in fabric and clothing to be bought in Carnaby Street, or excitable modes of speech and behaviour displayed by those likely to have been unaware of the mescaline-induced visions of Aldous Huxley, whose *Doors of Perception* and *Heaven and Hell* had helped to start it all off. In 1879 Du Maurier had drawn attention to one of the 'Refinements of Modern Speech' in a cartoon showing a drawing-room in 'Passionate Brompton' where a 'Fair Aesthete', a girl dressed in a long flowing gown and looking as though she has stepped out of a Burne-Jones stained-glass window, is asking a dull-looking philistine of a man in a dinner jacket to whom just been introduced: 'Are you intense?'

'If folly grow romantic, I must paint it,' Alexander Pope wrote, a spur to the satirist, and this was very much Gilbert's attitude. He had both Swinburne and Wilde and all their imitators in mind when he created the character of Reginald Bunthorne, but he also seems to have been aware of Robert Buchanan's forceful attack on the 'Fleshly School of Poetry' which had appeared in 1871 in the *Contemporary Review*.

Patience has remained one of Gilbert and Sullivan's most popular operas because it satirises a constant conflict, that between the artist and the philistine; the artist and what W.A. Darlington in discussing the opera calls 'the plain man'.

Aestheticism has gone, but all sorts of other -isms have followed in its wake, and each of them has followed the same course. An artist or group of artists reacting against the conventions of the time enunciates a new principle. Lesser artists follow, and a 'school' is formed. Lesser artists still imitate the work of the school, carry its principle to exaggerated extremes, and are received with acclamation by half-baked hangers-on. And the plain man, listening to these hangers-on with distaste, dismisses the whole movement as nonsense. Gilbert in *Patience* hit off the plain man's attitude so exactly that his opera is still topical. You can still find his Rapturous Maidens in the artistic quarters of any large town – differently dressed, perhaps, and using a different jargon, but easy to recognise, and still pouring out admiration of the 'Precious nonsense' uttered by the Bunthornes and Grosvenors of the day.[6]

The opera's first act takes place outside Castle Bunthorne, an ancient edifice with a drawbridge over a moat. Young ladies, some twenty of them, led by Angela, Ella and Saphir, are grouped about the place, dressed in aesthetic draperies and playing various musical instruments, the lutes and mandolines of Pre-Raphaelite angels. They are in the last stages of despair because all twenty of them are passionately, not to say intensely, in love with the scion of the castle, Reginald Bunthorne, a 'fleshly poet'. As Angela expresses it: 'the very hopelessness of our love is a bond that binds us to one another.' Lady Jane enters to tell them their love is hopeless indeed because Reginald is himself in love with Patience, the village milkmaid, though Patience boasts that she has never loved. Lady Jane is another of Gilbert's middle-aged pining women: she too is in love with Bunthorne:

'O, Reginald, if you but knew what a wealth of golden love is waiting for you, stored up in this rugged old bosom of mine, the milkmaid's triumph would be short-lived.'[7] It is through the mouth of Lady Jane that Gilbert makes most of his sarcastic attack on aestheticism. When Patience is chided by Angela that if she has never loved anyone – except a great-aunt – she can never have known true happiness, she replies that the truly happy always sem to have so much on their minds, adding that the truly happy never seem quite well; Lady Jane explains:

'There is a transcendentality of delirium – an acute accentuation of supreme ecstasy – which the earthly might easily mistake for indigestion. But it is not indigestion – it is aesthetic transfiguration.'[8]

Patience announces the good news that the 35th Dragoon Guards have halted in the village, all fleshly men, of full habit. A year ago the girls were all engaged to them, but now they will have nothing to do with them. The Dragoon officers, led by Colonel Calverley, Major Murgatroyd and Lieutenant, the Duke of Dunstable, expecting to be the centre of attention, are soon disillusioned when the girls ignore them because Bunthorne is in the throes of poetic composition, or at least he appears to be. Besides, as Lady Jane points out, the Guards' uniform of red and yellow is so unfashionable. Primary colours! Oh, South Kensington! The Lieutenant assures her that they did not design their own uniforms, but he does not see how they might be altered. Lady Jane has a quick reply. 'Still, there is a cobwebby grey velvet, with a tender bloom like cold gravy, which, made Florentine fourteenth-century, trimmed with Venetian leather and Spanish altar lace, and surmounted with something Japanese – it matters not what – would at least be Early English'[9]

When Bunthorne finds himself alone he confesses to the audience that he is really an aesthetic sham, his 'mediaevalism's affection/ Born of a morbid love of admiration'.[10] However, he can see that pretence has its advantages, and he might as well cash in while the going is good. 'Though the Philistines may jostle, you will rank as an apostle in the high aesthetic band,/If you walk down Piccadilly with a poppy or a lily in your mediaeval hand.'[11]

When Patience returns he declares his love for her but, in spite of confessing that he really loathes poetry and offering to cut his long hair, is rejected. When Bunthorne has departed disconsolately, Patience, now in a state of anxiety, is comforted by Angela, who persuades her that love is essentially an unselfish matter. Patience realises that she should not reject anything unselfish, but the problem is that she has not loved anyone except her great-aunt, because as a child of four she had formed an affection for a little boy she used to play with. Nevertheless, realising now that it is her duty to love somebody she is determined to fall in love as soon as possible. Just at that moment Archibald Grosvenor wanders in deeply engrossed in a book. He is an Idyllic poet, an Apostle of Simplicity, the appointed trustee of beauty, and it is his duty to see that the conditions of his trust are faithfully discharged. He also happens to be, one is not surprised to discover, Patience's little boy friend!

Grosvenor and Patience vow to live and die together, but suddenly Patience realises that as he is absolute perfection there could be nothing unselfish on her part in loving him; they will have to part, but then as Patience remembers she herself is 'plain, homely and unattractive',[12] it would be true unselfishness for him to love her. With this resolution they depart.

Bunthorne enters, crowned with roses and hung about with garlands and looking very miserable. He is led by Angela and Saphir, each holding a rose-garland by which he is bound, and accompanied by a procession of maidens. They dance classically, and play on cymbals, double pipes and other archaic instruments. The Dragoons arrive on the scene and are astonished at this strange spectacle. Bunthorne is miserable at Patience's rejection of him and with the aid of his solicitor has resolved to put himself up for auction. For a moment the Lieutenant seems to persuade the girls to choose the soldiers after all, but Bunthorne is able to show what a great advantage he might be to any girl who wins him:

> Such a judge of blue-and-white and other kinds of pottery –
> From early Oriental down to modern terra-cotta-ry –
> Put in half a guinea – you may draw him in a lottery –
>   Such an opportunity may not occur again.[13]

Immediately the girls crowd round to buy tickets, with Lady Jane more eager than most. Suddenly Patience returns and falls to her knees before Bunthorne and pleads to be forgiven. As it would be an unselfish act to love him against her will, she is pleased to do so. Bunthorne is delighted; the pair embrace and go off together. This leaves the girls to the Dragoons and all seems resolved. Patience and Bunthorne return as Grosvenor appears. The girls take one look at him and crowd round him adoringly and so the act ends with

Bunthorne in a fury as he recognises he has a rival!

The second act is set in a wooded glade. Lady Jane accompanies herself on the cello as she tells of the sadness of losing her beauty: 'Reduced with rouge, lip-salve, and pearly grey,/To "make up" for lost time, as best she may.'[14] However, she feels her situation is not hopeless; the girls are engrossed in Grosvenor and it is only a matter of time before Reginald Bunthorne will tire of Patience and come running for her.

Grosvenor is still surrounded by the girls, now playing their instruments. They coax him to recite some of his poetry, which turns out to be much more like Gilbert's own ballad style, and very different from Bunthorne's. The rhyming couplets recounting the exploits of those irksome children, Gentle Jane and Teasing Tom, are the happy forerunners of, and probably the models for, Belloc's *Cautionary Tales*.

> Teasing Tom was a very bad boy.
> A great big squirt was his favourite toy;
> He put live shrimps in his father's boots,
> And sewed up the sleeves of his Sunday suits;
> He punched his little sisters' heads,
> And cayenne-peppered their four-post beds,
> He plastered their hair with cobbler's wax,
> And dropped hot halfpennies down their backs.
> The consequence was he was lost totally,
> He married a girl in the corps de bally![15]

Angela is impressed by this: 'how grandly, how relentlessly the damning catalogue of crime strode on, till Retribution like a poised hawk, came swooping down upon the Wrong-doer!'[16] It was indeed terrible! Grosvenor is a true poet! But he goes on to tell them the tale of the Magnet and the Churn, the silver churn which no magnet whose power is only over iron could ever attract. So Grosvenor can only love the overseer of such a churn, his milkmaid.

Patience appears and persuades him that it is her duty to love Bunthorne, but she is not happy, in fact miserable beyond description. Yet she is happy that Grosvenor still loves her. When he has gone Bunthorne arrives followed by Jane; they had seen Patience and Grosvenor together and Bunthorne has a plan to humiliate his rival and goes off discussing this with Jane. The Dragoon officers appear dressed as aesthetes, this being the only way to win the girls' attention.

'We are doing this at some personal inconvenience with a view to expressing the extremity of our devotion to you,'[17] the Colonel explains.

This is the funniest scene in the opera if it is not overplayed, which is often a temptation. Although, as the Colonel continues, they have not quite mastered the angular attitudes of the Inner Brotherhood, and the Major wonders what the Brotherhood usually recommends for cramp, the girls see their efforts as 'not quite too all-but', and 'jolly utter!'

The two poets come together and Bunthorne threatens to place a curse on his rival unless he alters his appearance by cutting his hair and having a back parting. In appearance and costume he must become absolutely commonplace. Once he realises Bunthorne is serious Grosvenor yields, in fact he is quite relieved and dances off. Bunthorne is a changed man; he has committed his last act of ill-nature, and when Patience appears he is dancing about the stage in a mood she has never seen him in before. He has modelled himself on Grosvenor, as he tells her:

'Henceforth I am mildly cheerful. My conversation will blend amusement with instruction. I shall still be aesthetic; but my aestheticism will be of the most pastoral kind.'[18]

Patience realises that this frees her from her duty, since she can no longer love him unselfishly. 'Love to be pure, must be absolutely unselfish, and there can be nothing unselfish in loving so perfect a being as you have now become!'

Bunthorne sees that he is trapped. 'But stop a bit,' he says. 'I don't want to change – I'll relapse – I'll be as I was – interrupted.'[19]

It is too late. Grosvenor enters, followed by all the young ladies, who are followed by a chorus of Dragoons. He has had his hair cut, and is dressed in an ordinary suit of dittos and a pot hat. They all dance cheerfully round the stage in marked contrast to their former languor. Grosvenor is no longer an aesthete and neither is anyone else, except Bunthorne and, as it appears in a moment, Lady Jane. Patience, now assured that Archibald will always be a commonplace young man, feels it safe to give herself to him. Jane is still there for Bunthorne, she has never left him, she says, and she never will; but there is a flourish as the Colonel, Duke and Major enter. The Duke has at length determined to select a bride! However, he will not deprive his fellow officers of those girls who are truly lovely.

'In common fairness,' he says, 'I think I ought to choose the only one among you who has the misfortune to be distinctly plain. Jane!'[20] Jane immediately releases herself from Bunthorne's arms and Bunthorne is 'Crushed again!'

> In that case unprecedented
> Single I must live and die –
> I shall have to be contented
> With a tulip or lily!

He takes a lily from his buttonhole and gazes affectionately at it. So, although each is free to wed the other, 'Nobody be Bunthorne's Bride!'[21]

When *Patience* opened at the Opera Comique on St George's Day 1881 it was an instant success and received eight encores. The audience was delighted by Gilbert's mocking of the aesthetes, and his libretto was seen as cultural, but 'with the absence of anything approaching to coarseness or vulgarity'.[22] In particular, all the topical allusions in which the piece abounded were greatly appreciated, although one critic feared some had been missed. This was probably so, but hardly true in the main. The Grosvenor Gallery in New Bond Street founded by Sir Coutts Lindsay four years earlier, and where the first exhibition had shown paintings by Burne-Jones and Whistler, not only gave its name to one of the chief characters, but also provided what are, perhaps, the opera's most often quoted lines: 'A greenery-yallery, Grosvenor Gallery, Foot-in-the-grave young man!'[23]

Then there were the references to fashionable shops: Howell and James, of Regent Street, and Sewell and Cross, both well-known drapers; and the furriers Swears and Wells. In dressing the cast to his own designs Gilbert took particular care to be authentic and purchased the necessary materials from Liberty's; for example the rich black Japanese material for Lady Jane's costume was meant to suggest a painting by Whistler, and the dragoons' uniforms were specially made by a military tailor. In his plotting of the action he had recreated the grouping of other topical paintings, and the opera opened with the twenty love-sick maidens in the position of the girls in Burne-Jones's *The Triumph of Love*. The procession of Bunthorne garlanded and crowned with flowers was meant to represent Leighton's *Triumph of Cimabue*, and in the second act the actors sang a trio, using grouping and gestures to suggest *The Seasons*, another well-known painting by Burne-Jones.

Likewise the costumes and make-up of the leading characters were meant to suggest either paintings or personalities. Patience herself was dressed, as Gilbert admitted, in the milkmaid's costume borrowed from Luke Filde's 'Where are you going to, my pretty maid'. George Grossmith, who played the part of Bunthorne, sported a combination of Whistler's white streak in his hair, Walter Crane's velvet coat and Oscar Wilde's knee-breeches. It is likely the cast did not know the paintings or the models so well as Gilbert, and the rehearsals, Jessie Bond remembered, were hectic and Gilbert was well into them before he had finally settled on the opera's title, or Sullivan had completed the orchestral score. In fact, Sullivan did not begin it until ten days before the opening night![24] It was hardly surprising that this should be so, for he had had much on his mind and many other commitments. At the full dress rehearsal on 21 April he was distressed that everyone sang flat and he had a heated discussion with Gilbert about things generally. Later that evening at the Argus he lost £400 gambling.

On the night of the first performance, which seemed a great success from the rostrum, he felt so tired afterwards that he refused all invitations to supper, but he called in at the Fielding Club for a lemon and soda where he chatted for a while to friends. Then he got down to the real business of the day; he made a return visit to the Argus and won back £300 of the sum lost forty-eight hours earlier. Of two things he might have been certain: that Gilbert would already be thinking about the next opera, and D'Oyly Carte scheming how to cram more people into the theatre.

The result of D'Oyly Carte's scheming was the opening of the Savoy Theatre in October that same year, 1881. The site chosen was situated between the Victoria Embankment and the Strand, near to the Savoy Chapel and on the site of John of Gaunt's old Savoy Palace. D'Oyly Carte was also aware that close by on the Savoy Manor there had at one time been a theatre. 'I have used the ancient name as an appropriate title for the present one. The theatre is large and commodious, but a little smaller than the Gaiety, and will seat 1,292 persons,'[25] he wrote in the prospectus he issued to the public. The architect, C. J. Phipps, soon drew up the plans and the work only took a short time to complete. The building was a combination of red brick and Portland stone; inside it was spacious and decorated in the

Renaissance style uncluttered by 'cherubim, muses, angels, and mythological deities'.[26] The back walls of the boxes were in two tones of Venetian red and the curtains there were of yellowish silk, brocaded with a pattern of decorative flowers in broken colour. The stalls were covered with blue plush of an inky hue, and the balcony seats were stamped velvet of the same tint. Carte had a right to feel proud. Instead of the painted act-drop the company had been used to, the Savoy stage had a creamy satin curtain, which draped from the centre. It was described by Carte as 'quilted, having a fringe at the bottom and a valence of embroidery of the character of Spanish work'.[27]

Yet there was even more than all this, for the Savoy was the first theatre to be lit thoroughly by electricity. The Embankment outside had been lit by electric street lamps since 1878 and Hollingshead had employed some battery-operated electric arc lamps to illuminate the outside of the Gaiety as early as ten years before that. This fact did not deter D'Oyly Carte. He announced:

This is the first time that it has been attempted to light any public building by electricity. What is being done is an experiment and may succeed or fail. It is not possible to guarantee absolutely against any breakdown of the electric light. To provide for such a contingency, gas is laid on throughout the building, and the 'pilot' light on the central sun-burner will always be kept alight, so that in case of accidents the theatre can be flooded with gas-light in a few seconds.[28]

The innovation was a success, however, and 'the old, hot, yellow, evil-smelling and air-exhausting gaslamps were discarded for ever'.[29]

Another of D'Oyly Carte's Savoy improvements in service was his 'No fees' policy; everything was included in the price of the ticket – programmes, cloak-room – the staff were paid an adequate wage and tipping of any sort was forbidden. Anyone found to have accepted a tip would be dismissed immediately. Not only that, but the audience was expected to behave in an orderly manner, and D'Oyly Carte introduced the queue, something he had seen working to good effect in American theatres.

Once the Savoy was ready, the production of *Patience*, which was still showing to packed houses at the Opera Comique, was transferred, but with repainted scenery, something necessary owing to the extra brightness of the electric stage lighting. So it was that on 10 October *Patience* became the first Savoy Opera, a term which in time came to be applied to all Gilbert and Sullivan's comic operas, even those that had not been launched there, though, of course, all were revived at that theatre at a later time.

Patience also made certain of another consideration: it made its authors, and Cartre himself, very rich. Sullivan was able to spend much of 1881 abroad. In June he and Fred Clay sailed via Copenhagen to St Petersburg with the Duke of Edinburgh and received a royal reception at every port they called at. At Kiel the party was greeted by Prince Wilhelm and Prince Heinrich of Prussia. The future Kaiser bowed politely to Sullivan and sang 'He polished up the handle of the big front door!'

On returning to London Sullivan moved into No. 1 Queen's Mansions on Victoria Street; this was to be his home for the rest of his life. However, he did not stay at home that autumn, preferring to set off for a three-month holiday in Egypt.

The Gilberts were also enjoying the benefits of success, and their plans were even more elaborate, deciding to have a large house built for themselves with the very latest modern amenties, central heating, bathrooms on each floor and a telephone! This was in Harrington Gardens, Kensington, but the building work would not be completed for many months and they did not take up residence there until the October of 1883, by which time another opera had been performed.

Gilbert and his wife had a great passion for the sea and during the summer of 1881 they spent many happy weeks sailing round the south coast in their yacht. At the time Gilbert might be said to be suffering from fairies on the brain. Not that that was anything particularly unusual, since they had never been far from the honeycomb of his imagination and had appeared in 'The Fairy Curate', one of the Bab Ballads, in 1870. But in 1881 they came fluttering on to his stage; firstly in his three-act farce *Foggerty's Fairy* which opened at the Criterion on 15 December and, more importantly, in the new libretto he was preparing for Sullivan, 'Periola', though its name was changed at the last moment to *Iolanthe*.

Foggerty's Fairy was adapted from one of Gilbert's earlier short stories. The theme bears some resemblance to what has become known as Gilbert's lozenge plot, the idea that irritated Sullivan so much that he refused to have anything to do with it, where the characters by swallowing a magic lozenge could either change instantly into whoever they were claiming to be or become more truly themselves. In the play the fairy Rebecca supplies Frederick

Foggerty with a small phial and a box of prepared pills.

'When you wish to eliminate a factor from your social equation, all you have to do is to express your wish and swallow the draught. When you wish to see me, all you have to do is to express your wish and swallow a pill.'[30]

It all seemed so simple, but the effects were catastrophic, for if Foggerty were to obliterate an act and its consequences, it was impossible to know what incidents may not have taken their place. As the fairy warned him: 'You are pretty nearly sure to find yourself in an entirely altered state of circumstances.'[31]

The plot is packed with typically Gilbertian situations: Jennie Talbot is about to marry Foggerty, a penniless young apothecary, because he fits her special requirement; she has already called off her engagement to another young surgeon without practice, Walkinshaw, because he failed to meet it. As her father explains: 'Jennie has somehow got a ridiculous idea into her head, that she could never love any man who had ever loved before, and she is weak enough to believe that she has found this monstrosity in Foggerty.'[32] But Foggerty has already a fiancée, Miss Delia Spiff, described in the *dramatis personae* as a 'matter-of-fact old Lady'; she happens to be Jennie's aunt. At her entrance at the end of the first act she brandishes a large green umbrella and her autocratic 'That young man belongs to me' heralds the dramatic arrival of Katisha in *The Mikado*.

Here is yet another of Gilbert's thwarted older women, not middle-aged this time, but old and very eccentric-looking.

'He admired me. I can't imagine what he saw in me to admire, but he saw something. I attracted him; he grew attentive. I fascinated him; he grew sentimental. I was coy; he proposed to me. I accepted him; he grew indifferent. I sang to him; he wearied of me. I danced before him; he fled.'[33]

Understandably Foggerty wastes no time in fumbling for the fairy's phial and Miss Spiff is 'Spiffed out' for ever, but as the fairy says as she opens the next act, 'Poor fellow, he little thinks how materially his acquaintance with Miss Spiff has affected his subsequent adventures! Now that he has obliterated her and all the complicated consequences that came of his having known her, he won't know whether he's on his head or his heels. I'm really rather sorry for him. However, I mustn't allow sentiment to interfere with duty.'[34]

Soon the situation becomes incomprehensible to Foggerty as

Gilbert indeed 'stands him on his head'. He is apparently, and quite unknown to himself, passionately loved by a Miss Malvina de Vere, a girl he has never seen before; thinking it is still his wedding day to Jennie, he is amazed to discover that she is about to marry Walkinshaw. The confusion becomes even more bizarre. Jennie's father attempts to have him declared insane, but Foggerty agrees to marry Malvina rather than pay the damages in her breach of promise suit against him. Inevitably the fairy brings the confusion to a happy ending: Foggerty does marry Jennie whom he has loved since the age of nine, Malvina marries Walkinshaw, and even the minor characters pair off, all laughing heartily. Gilbert's stage-direction for the ending reads: 'The scene opens at the back during this. Fairies enter, laughing heartily, and waving wands. Rebecca ascends on stool at back, also laughing. Red fire. Curtain.'[35]

It must be emphasised that there was nothing unique or odd about Gilbert's delight in fairies, but it is not always appreciated that *Iolanthe* had an immediate predessor in *Foggerty's Fairy*. Iolanthe itself took its title from a play of the same name by W. G. Wills, in which Ellen Terry and Henry Irving took the leading parts, and which had been performed at the Lyceum Theatre in the previous year. Wills had adapted *King Rene's Daughter* by the Danish poet Henrik Hertz, a lyrical drama derived from Hans Andersen, on which Tchaikovsky later based his opera *Yolanta*. In Hertz's play and Tchaikovsky's opera Iolanthe is blind, but there is nothing of this in Gilbert except the name.

Of course, Shakespeare had pre-empted all this fairy business in *A Midsummer Night's Dream* and *The Tempest*, and, to a lesser extent, in the Queen Mab speech in *Romeo and Juliet*. Sullivan, it will be remembered, had composed incidental music for *The Tempest*, and the Pre-Raphaelite painters and their followers had depicted many scenes from those particular plays. Millais, for instance, had exhibited his *Ferdinand Lured by Ariel* at the Royal Academy as early as 1850. The Tate Gallery has one of the strangest paintings of this sort in Richard Dadd's weird *The Fairy Feller's Master Stroke*, painted over a period of nine years, but the Victorian predilection for this aspect of the supernatural would seem to have taken impetus from the spiritualism and table-tapping that had begun to intrigue people at about this time. All some kind of a reaction, no doubt, against an ever-dwindling religious faith and a consequent increase of rationalism. As the author of a recent book on Victorian painting pointed out: 'Fairy painting was close to the centre of the Victorian subconscious.'[36]

After his work with Sullivan was over, and indeed after Sullivan had died, Gilbert returned to the fays with *The Fairy Dilemma*, performed at the Garrick Theatre in 1904, and five years later his last opera for which Edward German set the music was *Fallen Fairies*, based on his earlier play, *The Wicked World*.

Gilbert worked away at the libretto of *Iolanthe*, or 'Periola', as it was then called, during the winter. On 16 February 1882 he informed Sullivan out in Egypt that although he was hard at work on Act 2, he was having 'infinite difficulty with it'. It comes as a surprise that his plot-book reveals that his original idea was to have the fairies all falling in love with barristers of the Northern Circuit, and that the piece was to have been another courtroom drama. However, the plot soon developed; superfluous characters like the Attorney General, which Rutland Barrington was earmarked to play, and the Admiral of the Fleet, disappeared. The Lord Chancellor was already included, and Gilbert scrawled across the page 'They must be Peers.' When the lovers, Phyllis and Corydon, and the Arcadian, open-air idylls of Watteau came into his mind, he was home and dry at last.

Sullivan already had some of the work with him, but he lazed over it. *Patience* was still playing to packed houses, and there seemed no hurry. Then in the middle of May came sudden sadness, Clementina Sullivan, now aged seventy, was stricken with a 'nearly unmanageable' illness and on 27 May she died. The house in Fulham where she had lived with his brother's widow, Charlotte, and where he had all the time supported them, was in semi-darkness with the blinds all down when he arrived a little after nine in the morning. It was too late. 'I rushed upstairs,' he recorded in his diary, 'and was alone in the room – alone, that is, with my Mother's lifeless body – her soul had gone to God.'[37] How he regretted having gone back home earlier that same morning; he had returned to town at 3.30 a.m. to get a few hours' rest. Now his closest friend had gone. Only three weeks before his mother had come with Charlotte and the children to visit him on his fortieth birthday. He would feel dreadfully lonely; very few days had passed without the two exchanging letters. There was only one obvious course open now; he must really hurl himself into the composition of the new opera.

6

The Peer and the Peri

1882–1883

The last performance of *Patience* took place on 22 November 1882, a Wednesday. *Iolanthe* was scheduled to open on the following Saturday night, but Gilbert had been rehearsing the cast for many weeks, two casts, in fact, because it had been decided to open in London and New York on the same day in order to defeat the pirates who had again made a killing out of *Patience*. This new plan of Carte's seemed to be foolproof, and a full cast with Alfred Cellier as conductor had sailed to New York ready to open simultaneously, which it did, allowing for the five hours' difference in time!

Cellier had received a message from Sullivan advising him of the change of name from 'Periola' to *Iolanthe*, and he had had to compose his own overture because Sullivan had not completed his before Cellier's departure. When at the final dress rehearsal at the Savoy Sullivan announced the alteration of name to the cast there was consternation. Surely they would get the names muddled at such short notice, although in some ways it might be easier. Instead of singing: 'Come Periola,' 'Iolanthe' had a haunting quality about it. Seeing the company's anxiety Sullivan quipped:

'Never mind so long as you sing the music. Use any name that happens to occur to you! Nobody in the audience will be any the wiser, except Mr Gilbert – and he won't be there.'[1]

What did the audience that cheered the composer so rousingly as he mounted the podium see on that first night of *Iolanthe*? After the overture, which Sullivan three days earlier had sat up all night to complete, the curtain rose to reveal an Arcadian landscape with a river running round the back of the stage, crossed by a rustic bridge; and fairies tripping round the stage singing as they danced. The fairies bemoan their lot; things have never been quite the same since Iolanthe, the most popular of their group, had been banished by the Fairy Queen to live at the bottom of a stream because she had married a mortal. Iolanthe had kept the rest going, writing their songs and arranging dances. 'We sing her songs and we trip her measures, but we do not enjoy ourselves.'[2]

Under the terms of fairy law Iolanthe deserved to die, but the Queen had such a love for her that she had commuted the sentence to penal servitude for life. It was Iolanthe's own choice to spend her punishment at the bottom of a stream.

All this happened twenty-five years ago. The fairies beg the Queen to pardon Iolanthe who is summoned from the stream. Her weeds fall from her as she rises, and she appears clothed as a fairy. The Queen places a diamond coronet on her head, and embraces her, as do all the others. When asked why she had chosen such an unpleasant spot for her punishment, Iolanthe explains that it was to be near her son, Strephon, an Arcadian shepherd, aged twenty-four, who loves Phyllis, a Ward in Chancery. Strephon is only half a mortal, as his mother explains:'He's a fairy down to the waist – but his legs are mortal'[3]

Strephon himself enters singing and dancing and playing on a flageolet. He shows no surprise whatsoever at seeing his mother, wishes her 'Good morrow' and announces that he is to be married that day. There is one snag, however: the Lord Chancellor has not given his permission, neither is Phyllis aware of his fairyhood, but Strephon is happy 'to brave the upshot'. The Queen, admiring his mettle and seeing that his fairy brain should seek some intellectual sphere of action, offers him a seat in Parliament, since she has a borough or two at her disposal. Strephon doubts his suitability for the favour:

'You see down to the waist, I'm a Tory of the most determined description, but my legs are a couple of confounded Radicals, and, on the division, they'd be sure to take me into the wrong lobby. You see, they're two to one, which is a strong working majority.'[4]

The Queen has an admirable solution: he shall be returned as a Liberal-Unionist, and his legs should be in her peculiar care. The fairies and Queen trip off after assuring Strephon that they will always come to his aid if he is in any doubt or danger. Iolanthe takes an affectionate farewell of her son and joins the others.

Phyllis now arrives; like Strephon she is singing and dancing and playing the flageolet. She is concerned because she knows it will mean penal servitude for life for a Ward of Court to marry without the Lord Chancellor's consent. As she will only come of age in two years she wonders if Strephon is prepared to wait. Certainly not, and for a very good reason; not only is Phyllis far too beautiful for any man in his senses to wait, but half the members of the House of Lords are sighing at her feet:

'Why did five-and-twenty Liberal Peers come down to shoot over your grass-plot last autumn? It couldn't have been the sparrows, Why did five-and-twenty Conservative Peers come down to fish your pond? Don't tell me it was the gold-fish! No, no, delays are dangerous, and if we are to marry, the sooner the better.'[5] Resolved to carry their arrangement through the lovers depart declaring that none shall ever part them.

A procession of peers fully robed and wearing coronets marches in to 'Loudly let the trumpet bray,' with sounding brasses, and much Tarantara, Tzing and Boom! This unique procession must be a constant example of nobility to which the lower middle classes, tradesmen and the masses should bow down to:

> We are peers of highest station,
> Paragons of legislation
> Pillars of the British Nation!
> Tarantara! Tzing! Boom![6]

The peers are followed by the Lord Chancellor himself in his wig and black and gold gown. In a state of some anxiety he tells them of the problems he has with his susceptible nature in fulfilling the law with regard to the young Wards in Chancery,

> All very agreeable girls – and none
> Are over the age of twenty-one.
> For I'm not so old, and not so plain;
> And I'm quite prepared to marry again,
> But there'd be the deuce to pay in the Lords
> If I fell in love with one of my Wards!
> Which rather tries my temper, for
> I'm such a susceptible Chancellor![7]

Lord Tolloller announces that the business of the day is for the Lord Chancellor to award Phyllis's hand in marriage to the most deserving, but the Lord Chancellor has to admit that he is 'singularly attracted' himself, so much so that his regard for her is rapidly undermining his constitution.

'Three months ago I was a stout man. I need to say no more. If I could reconcile it with my duty, I should unhesitatingly award her to myself, but I can conscientiously say that I know no man who is so well fitted to render her expectionally happy.'[8]

Nevertheless he must continue to wrestle with his own conscience over the matter.

The feelings of a Lord Chancellor in love with a Ward of Court are not to be envied. What is his position? Can he give his own consent to his own marriage with his own Ward? Can he marry his own Ward without his own consent? And if he marries his own Ward without his own consent, can he commit himself for contempt of his own Court? And if he commit himself for contempt of his own Court, can he appear by counsel before himself, to move for arrest of his own judgment? Ah, my Lords, it is indeed painful to have to sit upon a woolsack which is stuffed with such thorns as these![9]

Phyllis's announcement when she arrives accompanied by Lord Mountararat puts all in a quandary, for even after the peer's praises of her beauty and virtue, she does not wish for any of the nobly born, but only her shepherd, Strephon. It is not that she is not moved by the protestations of her blue-blooded admirers. Had not Lord Tolloller been convincing as he pleaded.

> Spare us the bitter pain
> Of stern denials,
> Nor with lowborn disdain
> Augment our trials.
> Hearts just as pure and fair
> May beat in Belgrave Square
> As in the lowly air
> Of Seven Dials![10]

No, Phyllis's heart may be riven with grief, but her heart is given!

When Strephon enters to claim his darling's hand, the peers are horrified beneath a 'blow worse than stab of dagger'; they make an attempt to laugh the matter off and execute a dignified and stately exit. The Lord Chancellor separates Phyllis from Strephon and orders her off so that he can upbraid the audacious shepherd for having disobeyed the order of the court. Strephon gains the upper hand by insisting that he goes by Nature's Act of Parliament and not by any Court of Chancery.

'When chorused Nature bids me take my love, shall I reply, "Nay, but a certain Chancellor forbids it?" Sir, your are England's Lord High Chancellor, but are you Chancellor of the birds and trees, King of the winds and Prince of thunderclouds?'[11]

The Lord Chancellor agrees it is a nice point, one he has never met before, but where is the evidence that Nature has interested herself in the matter? Strephon insists that Nature had told him to take his love. It is not evidence to say what somebody else has said and this does not satisfy the Lord Chancellor:

'Now an affidavit from a thunderstorm, or a few words on oath from a heavy shower, would meet with all the attention they deserve.'[12]

Strephon is surprised that anyone could apply the prosaic rules of evidence to a case which bubbles over with such poetic emotion, and when the Lord Chancellor has departed he feels despondent enough to break down. Iolanthe comes to comfort him and, on hearing that it was the Lord Chancellor who has caused his misery, utters an enigmatic 'Oh, if he did but know!'[13]

While Iolanthe and Strephon are talking the peers arrive with Phyllis at the back of the stage. They advance unseen on tiptoe. They overhear only a garbled version of what the two are saying, but when they reveal their presence and Strephon explains that Iolanthe is his mother they refuse to believe it, and understandably so, because Iolanthe being immortal has kept the youthful features of a girl of seventeen, while her son is twenty-five! It is all too much for Phyllis who, thinking she has been deceived, renounces her love for Strephon and offers herself to the most worthy of the peers. Strephon calls upon the Queen of the Fairies who enters with all her train, all Iolanthe's sisters and therefore Strephon's aunts. The Queen explains that Strephon is telling the truth about his relationship to Iolanthe, but the Lord Chancellor and the peers are not convinced and react mockingly:

> I wouldn't say a word that could be reckoned as injurious,
> But to find a mother younger than her son is very curious,
> And that's a kind of mother that is usually spurious.[14]

Their attitude makes the Queen furious.

> Bearded by these puny mortals!
> I will launch from fairy portals

> All the most terrific thunders
> In my armoury of wonders![15]

She admonishes the Lord Chancellor by revealing her true identity.

QUEEN.

> Oh! Chancellor unweary
> It's highly necessary
>   Your tongue to teach
>   Respectful speech –
> Your attitude to vary!
>
> Your badinage so airy,
> Your manner arbitrary,
>   Are out of place
>   When face to face
> With an influential Fairy.

ALL THE PEERS [*Aside*].

> We never knew
> We were talking to
> An influential Fairy!

LORD CHANCELLOR.

> A plague on this vagary
> I'm in a nice quandary
>   Of hasty tone
>   With Dames unknown;
> I ought to be more chary
> It seems that she's a fairy
> From Andersen's library,
>   And I took her for
>   The proprietor
> Of a Ladies' Seminary!

PEERS.

> We took her for
> The proprietor
> Of a Ladies' Seminary![16]

The Queen informs the peers that Strephon is to cast his crooks, pipes and ribbons away, forsake his flocks and herds and go into Parliament. Backed by the Queen's supreme authority he'll command a large majority. Into Parliament he shall go, but there is some doubt as to which party he would support:

> In the Parliamentary hive,
> Liberal or Conservative –
> Whig or Tory – I don't know –
> But into Parliament you shall go![17]

There is even worse to come as the Queen continues to intone the peers' sentence with a list of Strephon's extraordinary powers:

> Every bill and every measure
> That may gratify his pleasure,
> Though your fury it arouses,
> Shall be passed by both your Houses!
> You shall sit, if he sees reason,
> Through the grouse and salmon season:
> He shall end the cherished rights
> You enjoy on Friday nights:
> He shall prick that annual blister
> Marriage with deceased wife's sister:
> Titles shall ennoble, then,
> All the common Councilmen:
>> Peers shall team in Christendom
>>> And a Duke's exalted station
>> Be attainable by Com-
>>> Petitive Examination![18]

Such a suggestion horrifies the peers who promise vengeance on Strephon, 'the kind of lout they do not care a fig about'.[19] The fairies threaten them with their wands and the peers kneel begging for mercy. Phyllis implores Strephon to relent, but he casts her aside, and she falls fainting into the arms of Lord Mountararat and Lord Tolloller. So the first act comes to an end.

The curtain rises for the second act to reveal a very well-known scene: the Palace Yard, Westminster, on a moonlit night. Westminster Hall to the left and the Clock Tower up right centre. Private Willis, 1st Battalion Grenadier Guards, is on sentry duty, and his solitary vigil provokes reflection upon how Nature curiously contrives that every boy and girl 'That's born into the world alive/Is either a little Liberal or else a little Conservative!' Suddenly the Palace Yard is full of fairies who tell how Strephon is making both the Lords and Commons shake in their shoes with his legislation. The peers come from Westminster Hall with much the same information.

That very night sees the second reading of Strephon's Bill to throw the peerage open to competitive examination!

Seeing the peers' obvious distress the fairies' hearts are moved and they begin to find the men attractive; as Celia says: 'for self-contained dignity, combined with airy condescension, give me a British Representative Peer.'[20] The Queen reminds them of the dire penalty for anyone even contemplating marrying a mortal. Yet the Queen herself, confronted by the manly, even godlike form of Private Willis, has to keep her passionate feelings in check.

'If I yielded to a natural impulse, I should fall down and worship that man. But I mortify this inclination. I wrestle with it and it lies beneath my feet! That is how I treat my regard for that man.'[21]

When the fairies have gone Phyllis comes into the Yard wondering why being engaged to two noblemen at once makes her so miserable. One thing is certain; she absolutely hates Strephon: 'No girl could care for a man who goes about with a mother considerably younger than himself!'[22]

Lord Mountararat and Lord Tolloller cannot decide which of them is the more likely to bring Phyllis lasting happiness. They are far too close friends to fight over her, and Phyllis manages to persuade them she is not worth spoiling their friendship for. The Lord Chancellor is in a wretched state suffering from unrequited, hopeless love which plagues his nights with either insomnia or phantasmagoric dreams. These two states he describes with all their restlessness, and in the case of the dreams, inconsequential imagery.

> For you dream you are crossing the Channel, and tossing about in a
>   steamer from Harwich –
> Which is something between a large bathing machine and a very small
>   second class carriage.[23]

The two Lords persuade him to make one last effort to approach himself in his official capacity as Lord Chancellor 'respectfully and with a proper show of deference',[24] since faint heart never won fair lady.

Strephon is in very low spirits; he does not enjoy being a Member of Parliament, especially when he leads both parties. He cannot forget Phyllis, who conveniently enters at that moment. He confesses to her that he is half a fairy; Phyllis, somewhat dazed by this information, decides that she would rather have half a mortal she did love than half a dozen she didn't, and the two decide they will not wait for each other any longer. Iolanthe comes to welcome her new daughter-in-law, and she reveals to the lovers that the Lord Chancellor is her husband and Strephon's father, but he must never know:

'He believes me to have died childless, and, dearly as I love him, I am bound, under penalty of death, not to undeceive him. But see – he comes! Quick, my veil!'[25]

Strephon and Phyllis leave the scene on tiptoe as the Lord Chancellor enters excited that he has at last resolved the legal difficulties of his situation.

Victory! Victory! Success has crowned my efforts, and I may consider myself engaged to Phyllis! At first I wouldn't hear of it – it was out of the question. But I took heart, I pointed out to myself that I was no stranger to myself; that, in point of fact, I have been personally acquainted with myself for some years. This had its effect, I admitted that I had watched my personal advancement with considerable interest, and I had handsomely added that I yielded to no one in admiration for my private and professional virtues. This was a great point gained. I then endeavoured to work upon my feelings. Conceive my joy when I distinctly perceived a tear glistening in my own eye! Eventually, after a severe struggle with myself, I reluctantly – most reluctantly – consented.[26]

Iolanthe comes forward, still veiled, and pleads for Strephon, but the Lord Chancellor tells her that he is engaged to Phyllis herself. Iolanthe removes her veil and is recognised immediately. The Fairy Queen and the fairies enter and Iolanthe kneels before the Queen. Once again Iolanthe has broken a vow; she must bow her head to destiny and die.

Strephon and the peers arrive and the Queen raises her spear. The fairy Leila reveals the awful truth that if Iolanthe deserves death so do they all since they are now all fairy 'duchesses, marchionesses, countesses, viscountesses and baronesses'.[27]

The Queen is put on the spot. 'You have all incurred death; but I can't slaughter the whole company!' She unrolls a scroll on which the law is clearly set out: 'Every fairy must die who marries a mortal!'[28]

The Lord Chancellor has the answer: 'Allow me, as an old equity draughtsman, to make a suggestion. The subtleties of the legal mind are equal to the emergency. The thing is really quite simple – the insertion of a single word will do it. Let it stand that every fairy shall die who doesn't marry a mortal, and there you are, out of your difficulty at once!'[29]

The Queen pencils in the alteration and turns to Private Willis and explains that she must marry at once to save her own life. How would Willis like to be a fairy guardsman?

'Well, ma'am, I don't think much of the British soldier who wouldn't ill-convenience himself to save a female in distress.'[30]

What a brave fellow! Willis becomes a fairy from that moment and wings spring from his shoulders. What of the peers, now that all must be recruited from persons of intelligence, Lord Mountararat wonders. There will not be much use for the likes of Lord Tolloller and him if they remain where they are. That is good, and as wings spring from the shoulders of all the peers, the Queen leads everyone, lover by lover, up into the air to fairyland:

> Up in the sky,
> Ever so high,
> Pleasures come in endless series;
> We will arrange
> Happy exchange –
> House of Peers for House of Peris![31]

Gilbert had written the part of Iolanthe specially for Jessie Bond, a part which would require little dancing about because she was suffering from a weak ankle. 'You will not have to dance, and hardly to move,' he had said, 'and as you are always laughing, I have written a song to show that you can be serious when you like.'[32] Gilbert was referring to the song, 'He loves', in which Iolanthe pleads Strephon's cause with the Lord Chancellor, played, as might have been expected, by George Grossmith. Gilbert, no doubt, had had all the company in mind in one way or another. Rutland Barrington and Durward Lely took the parts of Lord Mountararat and Lord Tolloller, Richard Temple was Strephon, and the bass, Charles Manners, had been promoted from the chorus to take the small but important part of Private Willis. The contralto, Alice Barnett, who had played Lady Jane in *Patience*, was suitably hefty and Brünhilde-like to be the Fairy Queen, and the petite Leonora Braham, Phyllis.

The first performance was rapturously received, and although the second act seemed to Sullivan to have dragged, Gilbert and he were called and heartily cheered. Sullivan felt very low afterwards and went straight home, for unknown to anyone at the theatre he had received earlier in the day some shattering news: his broker, E.A. Hall, had informed him that he was ruined and had lost the £7,000

Sullivan had entrusted to him. For Sullivan the loss was a bitter setback, but it in no way meant ruin for him; besides he had just conducted the first performance of a winner.

The critics were on the whole in favour. They liked Grossmith's performance in particular. Nevertheless, there was a feeling of *déjà-vu* about it all. It was, as the critic of *The Echo* noted, 'the same set of puppets as Mr Gilbert has dressed over and over before'.[33] Another critic wondered, 'Where is this topsy-turvydom, this musical and dramatic turning of ideas wrong side out, to end?'[34] The answer, of course, was 'Never.' Gilbert knew of no other way. In one sense there is but one character in all Gilbert's work and that is Gilbert himself. G.K. Chesterton said much the same thing about Bernard Shaw, that his characters only existed for the argument, that 'all Shaw's plays are prefaces.'[35] It might be said that all Gilbert's characters exist only for the joke. But the 'joke' always has a sting in it. Gilbert's wit was staccato and often harsh and the joke was aimed like a dart at a society for whose smug values he felt a loathing. 'He was not happy in his own age and atmosphere. It did not provide him with any positive philosophy for which to fight, but that was not his fault. He did fight for what he conceived to be common sense, and he found plenty of things that wanted fighting.'[36]

Gilbert's characters, if indeed 'character' is the correct word to use, have their origins in folklore, they exist in a world apart from time. One can never imagine them in any other circumstances than those in which we find them, and this is odd because they appear to inhabit and belong to the real world. Sometimes, as in the case of the Lord Chancellor or Sir Joseph Porter, they hold respectable offices with which all are familiar, and yet Gilbert's Chancellor has far more in common with Puck or Father Christmas than he has with anyone who ever sat on the woolsack, however sharp the thorns. At the end of *Iolanthe* Gilbert sends everyone off to fairyland, but that is where he had already sent John Wellington Wells, Little Buttercup, the pirates and the poets, and, with the exception of Jack Point in *The Yeoman of the Guard*, where he would send everyone else!

This is why the audiences who flocked into the Savoy were able to feel so safe in their laughter; although Gilbert might seem to be portraying the real world in exactness of scene and costume he was really parading before them a fantasy, but it was a fantasy about which, however absurd a course the action might take, there was an underlying common sense. In all Gilbert's work there is also the feeling of wrongs being righted, of falsehood exposed and of love triumphant. If it is true that fairy-tales are about the uncommon things as seen by the common people, then Gilbert was producing fairy-tales, but it was his unique achievement that he inhabited his fairyland with characters from the real world. That Sullivan was able to match Gilbert in this with his music, 'giving wings to his words, and sending them soaring to the sky',[37] explains the remarkable popularity of Gilbert and Sullivan to this day. Somehow the operas never seem stale or old-fashioned; they have the eternal youthfulness of fairy-tales, and this is true of *Iolanthe* especially.

Once the opera was running smoothly, and after several songs had been omitted, Sullivan invited Gladstone to attend a performance as his guest: 'Nothing, I thought, could have been happier than the manner in which the comic strain of the piece was blended with its harmonious sight and sound, so good in taste and so admirable in execution from beginning to end,'[38] Gladstone wrote. He would have relished the portrayal of the House of Lords as a House of Numskulls. There was a strong feeling at the time in the Liberal Party that the peers, nearly all of whom were Tories, by holding up legislation were obstructing progress. Thus there was deep irony when Gilbert wrote:

> And while the House of Peers withholds
>   Its legislative hand,
> And noble statesmen do not itch
> To interfere with matters which
>   They do not understand.[39]

Yet it was not only the Upper House which Gilbert lampooned, and Strephon's going into Parliament was, of course, a joke at the Commons' expense, with the insinuation that when the House divides the members have to leave their brains outside, 'And vote just as their leaders tell 'em to.'[40]

The critic of *Theatre* spoke of Gilbert's 'scathing satire upon the hereditary moiety of our Legislature',[41] but most people, like Gladstone, accepted Gilbert's point and laughed heartily. However, when Gladstone was thinking of awarding honours, it was Sullivan who would be offered a knighthood in May 1884, while Gilbert had to wait for his until 1907. Gilbert was hurt, but perhaps he understood that he was regarded as an oddity, dangerous even. No one knew what he might do next. If you dared to honour such a man, you might very well find yourself pilloried in his next opera!

Gilbert had included a joke at the expense of Captain Byre Massey Shaw, the Chief of the Metropolitan Fire Brigade. Not that Shaw would have minded; he was a close friend to Sullivan and appears among his guests at Queen's Mansions; but he was taken completely by surprise and there was great hilarity when Alice Barnett in breast-plate and winged helmet as the Fairy Queen came to the front of the stage and sang of her sudden surge of passion for Private Willis with:

> On fire that glows
>   With heat intense,
> I turn the hose
>   Of common sense,
> And out it goes,
>   At small expense.

> We must maintain
>   Our Fairy law;
> That in the main
>   On which to draw –
> In that we gain
>   A Captain Shaw!

> [*Aside*] Oh, Captain Shaw,
> Type of true love kept under!
> Could thy Brigade
> With cold cascade
> Quench my great love? – I wonder.[42]

Obviously this will have had its greatest impact on the opening night when Shaw was present; today the reference is obscure and needs a footnote, but Sullivan's setting of the song was magnificent and there is no indication that Gilbert ever considered leaving it out, as he did with one of Strephon's songs in Act 2. This was thought to be in bad taste and unsuitable to be included in a comic work; the song was about delinquency and its theme was that crime was largely the result of poverty and deprivation. Gilbert had boys like the Artful Dodger and Charlie Bates in *Oliver Twist* in mind when he had Strephon pricking the consciousness of the rich and powerful as he threatened to introduce 'some rather urgent measures':

Take a watchful thief
　Through the City sneaking,
Pocket handkerchief
　Ever, ever seeking;
What is he but I
　Robbed of all my chances –
Picking pockets by
　Force of circumstances?
　　I might be as bad –
　　　As unlucky, rather –
　　If I'd only had
　　　Fagin for a father![43]

One cannot help wishing that Gilbert had had the courage to leave this in, for he certainly thought it true, but such sentiments were held to 'jar upon the ear and taste alike when brought to bear upon us through the medium of a song sung by a half-fairy in a professedly comic opera'.[44] The *Theatre* critic objected that Gilbert's pathos had an underlying note of anger, 'a passion altogether out of place in a "fairy opera"',[45] and the author's politics were thought to be bitterly aggressive too. For the moment Gilbert was quite satisfied; those illuminaries who had occupied the boxes, stalls and circles on the opening night had heard loudly and clearly what he had to say.

7

Castle Adamant

⊷❦ 1883–1884 ❦⊶

Gilbert was among those invited to celebrate Sullivan's forty-first birthday; the dinner was given a day late on 14 May 1883, Whit-sunday, and the Prince of Wales was the chief guest; other guests included the Duke of Edinburgh, the Marquess of Hartington, the Earl of Kenmare, Baron Ferdinand de Rothschild, Millais, the artist, and F. C. Burnand. It was not merely a birthday party since Sullivan was also celebrating his acceptance of a knighthood, the honour he was due to receive from the Queen at Windsor a week later, together with his friends George Grove and George Macfarren. To entertain his birthday guests he had arranged a musical progamme in which Madame Albani and Paolo Tosti took part, but there was a greater treat in store; Sullivan had installed a telephone connecting his flat with the Savoy Theatre, so that it was possible to listen to a live selection of songs from *Iolanthe*, especially performed by the cast which had agreed to go into the theatre on a Sunday evening. The Prince was delighted and, as he presented Sullivan with an enamel match-box, said it had been the most successful party Sullivan had given.

The opera was still running to packed houses, and the words and tunes had become very popular; Chappell reported that he had sent out 10,000 copies of the vocal and piano scores in one night. To meet this great demand he had paid his staff to work through until the orders had been dispatched. There seemed no sign of the audiences dwindling, and in fact *Iolanthe* ran for almost 400 performances, but Gilbert had already prepared his next libretto, part of which he had read to Sullivan and D'Oyly Carte back in February. This was *Princess Ida*, a reworking of Gilbert's earlier dramatisation of Tennyson's 'The Princess' performed, it may be remembered, somewhat unsuccessfully at the Olympic Theatre in 1870.

Gilbert's irony in *Princess Ida* was aimed at women's emancipation and women's education in particular, a subject highly topical at the time, as was the lesser theme of Darwinian man. Following the successful example of Queen's College, London, the first university college for women, Emily Davies had founded Girton College at Hitchin in 1869. It subsequently moved to Cambridge and with Newnham College, founded the year before, became the first women's colleges at the two ancient universities. Oxford almost ten years later founded Lady Margaret Hall and Somerville College, and St Hugh's would soon follow in 1886. To begin with, girls at these colleges were not admitted as full members of either university, but they were allowed to attend lectures and take the degree examinations. It was not long before women's names were appearing high up in the class lists. It is unlikely that Gilbert himself really thought such establishments 'the maddest folly going', as he makes one character say in the opera, but he was a fairly typical man of his time who would probably have agreed with Dr Johnson that a man is in general better pleased when he has a good dinner upon his table than when his wife talks Greek.

Princess Ida; or Castle Adamant broke new ground for it had three acts instead of two, and all the dialogue was written in blank verse rather than prose. Advertised as a 'Respectful Operatic Perversion of Tennyson's "Princess", it opened at the Savoy on the evening of Saturday, 5 Janury 1884, and was Gilbert and Sullivan's sixth full-grown operetta.

There had been the usual rush to have the piece ready, and Sullivan still had two songs to set four days before the opening. He had carried the libretto about with him for months during the early summer of 1883 when he had travelled out to Carlsbad to take the waters. Once again his health was very low and his kidneys were playing him up. However, he was not alone, for Frederic Clay was there with his sister. Clay was hoping to complete the cantata on Byron's 'Sardanapalus' he was preparing for the forthcoming Leeds Festival in the autumn, something in which he failed, much to Sullivan's embarrassment, although the festival proved to be a great personal success for Sullivan himself, and he conducted Beethoven's *Grand Mass in D*, better known as the *Missa Solemnis*, for the first time.

It was hardly surprising that with such a 'stupendous performance', as Sullivan described the event in his diary, the setting of

Gilbert's lyrics should be felt in comparison as 'penal servitude'. By the middle of December the scoring of the opera was 'heavy work'.

The first full dress rehearsal was on 2 January and went on until the early hours of the following morning. The final rehearsal lasted from 6.30 p.m. on the 4th to 2.30 a.m. on the morning of the first performance. Sullivan was thoroughly exhausted and, on the verge of collapse, staggered to his room at the theatre to inject himself with morphine. The chances of his being fit enough for the opening seemed slight and Carte had special programmes printed with François Cellier's name as conductor. Sullivan was determined to overcome his pain and see *Princess Ida* launched. His diary records:

At 7 p.m. had another strong hypodermic injection to ease the pain and a strong cup of black coffee to keep me awake. Managed to get up and dressed, and drove to the theatre more dead than alive – went into the orchestra at 8.10. Tremendous house – usual reception.

Very fine first performance – not a hitch. Brilliant success. After the performance very faint and could not stand.[1]

Carte, Cellier and Sullivan's secretary, Walter Smythe, took the stricken conductor home and put him to bed in dreadful pain. It was officially put about that Sullivan was suffering from a 'muscular affection of the neck'!

The general feeling on the opening night was that Gilbert had once again given abundant proof that he was the monarch of the Realm of Topsy-Turvydom; but that his incongruities were more elaborately worked up than usual and therefore less funny. In fact, *Princess Ida* is exceedingly funny, and Sullivan certainly showed no sign of ill-health in his score, which was one of his best.

The opening scene is the Pavilion attached to King Hildebrand's Palace. Soldiers and courtiers, encouraged by Florian, are discovered looking out through opera-glasses and telescopes in anticipation of the imminent arrival of King Gama and his fascinating daughter, Princess Ida, who is betrothed to Hildebrand's son, Hilarion. There are some forebodings expressed that Gama might not keep his promise, but he would surely not make a deadly foe of Hildebrand. Hilarion enters and relates how he and Ida had been plighted as babies; Ida had been a twelvemonth old, and Hilarion had been two, and 'Husband twice as old as wife/Argues ill for married life', but Ida is now twenty-one; but it soon becomes clear that she is not with her father and

That Princess Ida has forsworn the world,
And, with a band of women, shut herself
Within a lonely country house, and there
Devotes herself to stern philos'phies![2]

King Gama's entrance is preceded by that of his three sons, Arac, Guron and Scynthius, all warriors dressed in heavy armour, but not very intelligent, to say the least. Yet they are bold and fierce and strong and burning for a war. Gama arrives; he is a deformed, waspish little man, 'a twisted monster – all awry', and he reveals something of himself immediately in words which Gilbert playfully told the cast in rehearsal referred to himself. 'I thought it my duty to live up to my reputation,'[3] he quipped to Grossmith.

If you give me your attention, I will tell you what I am;
I'm a genuine philanthropist – all other kinds are sham.
Each little fault of temper and each social defect
In my erring fellow creatures, I endeavour to correct.
To all their little weaknesses I open people's eyes;
And little plans to snub the self-sufficient I devise;
I love my fellow creatures – I do all the good I can –
Yet everybody says I'm such a disagreeable man!
      And I can't think why!

To compliments inflated I've a withering reply;
And vanity I always do my best to mortify;
A charitable action I can skilfully dissect;
And interested motives I'm delighted to detect:
I know everybody's income and what everybody earns;
And I carefully compare it with the income-tax returns;
But to benefit humanity however much I plan.
Yet everybody says I'm such a disagreeable man!
      And I can't think why!

I'm sure I'm no ascetic; I'm as pleasant as can be;
You'll always find me ready with a crushing repartee,
I've an irritating chuckle, I've a celebrated sneer,
I've an entertaining snigger, I've a fascinating leer,
To everybody's prejudices I know a thing or two;
I can tell a woman's age in half a minute – and I do.
But although I try to make myself as pleasant as I can,

> Yet everybody says I'm such a disagreeable, man!
> And I can't think why![4]

Gama treats Hildebrand's demand that Ida be brought with disdain. Ida, he says, has 'beauty, virtue, wit, grace, humour, wisdom, charity, and pluck and it would hardly be fair on Hildebrand to parade such qualities before him. Ida is at Castle Adamant, one of Gama's country houses, where she rules a women's university, 'With full a hundred girls, who learn of her'. No men are allowed in the place, nor anything created by a man. 'She'll scarcely suffer Dr Watt's hymns.' All the animals are female, and in the mornings the girls rise at 'cockcrow', the crowing done by 'an accomplished hen'!

Hildebrand orders Gama and his sons to be kept hostage until Ida comes to her senses, and if by any chance Hilarion should disappear they will be hanged. Hilarion has every intention of disappearing and with his friends Cyril and Florian seeking out Castle Adamant and overpowering the inhabitant with love. Gama and his sons, now in heavy leg-irons, are led off to prison.

> For a month to dwell
> In a dungeon cell;
> > Growing thin and wizen
> > In a solitary prison,
> Is a poor look-out
> For a soldier stout,
> > Who is longing for the rattle
> > Of a complicated battle –
> For the rum-tum-tum
> Of the military drum,
> > And the guns that go boom! boom![5]

Such conditions will prevail until Hilarion's bride has at length complied with the just conditions of Hildebrand's requisitions.

Act 2 is set in the gardens of Castle Adamant. A river runs across the back of the stage crossed by a rustic bridge. The castle is seen in the distance. Girl graduates are discovered seated at the feet of Lady Psyche, the Professor of Humanities; they are told which classical authors they should read, Anacreon, Ovid, Aristophanes and Juvenal, but if they have any sense they should obtain bowdlerised versions. One of the graduates, Sacharissa, asks the more pertinent question: 'What is this thing known as Man?' Lady Psyche answers

that man is many unpleasant things, but above all 'Man is Nature's
sole mistake!' The girls agree to remember this and continue to
search for wisdom's pure delight.

Lady Blanche, the Professor of Abstract Science, comes in with
Princess Ida's list of punishments. First, Sacharissa is expelled for
bringing a set of chessmen into the castle. Sacharissa bursts into tears
and pleads that she meant no harm, 'they're only men of wood.'
'They're men with whom you give each other mate,/And that's
enough'[6] is the stern reply. Chloe will lose three terms for drawing a
sketch of a perambulator in her drawing-book, a double
perambulator, shameless girl!

The Princess herself appears to give her inaugural address for the
young ladies who have only just joined the university. She offers a
prayer to the Goddess Minerva that she might endow the girls'
unillumined eyes with sight, and then proceeds to address her 'fair
neophytes' on the processes that have led to a hundred maidens
swearing to place their feet upon Man's neck. Lady Blanche is
prepared to give her lecture on Abstract Philosophy, the three points,
the Is, the Might Be and the Must, which she illustrates thus:

> Madame, I take three possibilities,
> And strike a balance, then, between the three:
> And thus: The Princess Ida is our head,
> The Lady Psyche Might Be – Lady Blanche,
> Neglected Blanche, inevitably Must.[7]

The 'Must' is the point, as Lady Blanche insists once the Princess and
the maidens have departed. She was born to rule, and one day she will
rule again, but she must bide her time.

Hilarion, Cyril and Florian climb over the wall, after braving
prickly cacti, stinging nettles, bulldogs and broken bottles on a wall.
They creep cautiously among the trees and rocks at the back of the
stage. Florian wonders what girls can learn worth knowing in such a
place and is prepared to lay a crown that he could teach the inmates of
the college as much in half-an-hour outside it, but Hilarion and Cyril
are more speculative, although the chief principle of the place is to
repudiate the tyrant known as Man and to do without him, if they can.
They soon come across some academic robes worn by the lady
undergraduates when they matriculate, and they decide to try them
on, and they are prancing about showing off to each other as they
pretend to be girls when Princess Ida comes on the scene reading. She

does not see them until they bow and then, correcting themselves, curtsy before her as they beg, three well-born maids of liberal estate, to become students at the university. The Princess assures them that they may be noblewomen, but the only nobility that stands for anything is nobility of brain. There are a hundred maids within the walls, 'All good, all learned, and all beautiful'. The three promise with little difficulty that they are more than willing to love their fellow students and that they will never marry a man. If a hundred lovely maidens wait within to welcome them with smiles and open arms, then they are quite happy to renounce the world, since the world is but a broken toy and its pains alone are true.

When the Princess has left Lady Psyche enters and looks at the three with amazement. Florian immediately recognises her as his sister. There is only one way out of their dilemma, which is to let Psyche into their secret. After reminiscing on their common childhood, for both Hilarion and Cyril used to play with Psyche, she tells them that they have risked death to enter the place since all have promised to renounce mankind, and the reason, Lady Psyche explains, is simple: 'We are all taught, and being taught, believe/That Man, sprung from an Ape, is Ape at heart.'[8] She continues to expound to them the moral tale of 'The Ape and the Lady'.

> A Lady Fair, of lineage high,
> Was loved by an Ape, in the days gone by –
> The Maid was radiant as the sun,
> The Ape was a most unsightly one –
> So it would not do –
> His scheme fell through,
> For the Maid when his love took formal shape,
> Expressed such terror
> At his monstrous error,
> That he stammered an apology and made his 'scape,
> The picture of a disconcerted ape.
>
> With a view to rise in the social scale,
> He shaved his bristles, and he docked his tail,
> He grew moutachios, and he took his tub,
> And he paid a guinea to a toilet club –
> But it would not do,
> The scheme fell through –

For the Maid was beauty's fairest Queen,
　　With golden tresses,
　　Like a real princess's,
While the Ape, despite his razor keen,
Was the apiest Ape that ever was seen!

He bought white ties, and he bought white suits,
He crammed his feet into tight bright boots –
And to start in life on a brand-new plan,
He christened himself Darwinian Man!
　　But it would not do,
　　The scheme fell through –
For the Maiden fair, whom the monkey craved,
　　Was a radiant Being,
　　With a brain far-seeing –
While Darwinian Man, though well-behaved,
At best is only a monkey shaved![9]

While Lady Psyche is telling this sad story Melissa, Lady Blanche's daughter, enters unobserved and looks on in amazement. She comes forward and is struck by the attractiveness of these, the first men she has ever set eyes on. She promises to keep the secret. Lady Psyche admits that her faith in Ida's views is somewhat shaken too. They all dance with joy that the truth has at last been found. Men, far from being hideous, idiotic and deformed, are in fact, 'quite as beautiful as women are'. Lady Psyche and the three men depart and Melissa is confronted by her mother, who has already realised the three new students are men disguised. Melissa attempts to persuade her otherwise, but is eventually forced to admit the truth. However, she placates her mother with the thought that if Princess Ida should marry Hilarion, then Lady Blanche would automatically become the principal, and the mighty Must, the inevitable Shall, would find her destiny fulfilled.

　　Left alone, Melissa sees Florian entering on tiptoe; she tells him the three are recognised as being men, but that for reasons of her own Lady Blanche is likely to keep the secret. The luncheon bell sounds and Hilarion arrives with the Princess, Cyril with Pysche, and Lady Blanche and the other ladies. The new students, the Daughters of the Plough, bring in the luncheon. The conversation gets round to the subject of King Hildebrand's court, and Prince Hilarion in particular. The Princess is surprised to find that the three seem to have known Hilarion rather well, and, as Cyril is getting increasingly tipsy over luncheon, he becomes more and more indiscreet, and ends up singing an old kissing-song of the kind Hilarion used to sing to the blushing Mistress Lalage, the hostess of the Pigeon. Ida is horrified, and Hilarion, who has been with difficulty restrained by Florian during Cyril's singing, breaks from him and strikes Cyril on the breast. Cyril's 'Hilarion, are you mad?' reveals their true identity as Ida runs towards the bridge away from these 'Man-monsters'. She loses her footing and tumbles into the stream. Hilarion springs in after her to save her.

Although all who witnessed the rescue are impressed by Hilarion's swift action, the Princess soon recovers her autocratic pose:

> I know not mercy, men in women's clothes!
>   The man whose sacrilegious eyes
> Invade our strict seclusion dies.
> Arrest these coarse intruding spies![10]

The three men beg Ida for mercy, but to no avail, and they are marched off. Melissa hurries in to inform the Princess that an armed band of men is at the gates. They must be defied, but it is too late: the gate yields and the soldiers rush in. Arac, Guron and Scynthius are with them, though they are still handcuffed. Hildebrand arrives and shows he will have none of the Princess's defiance. He is a peppery kind of king who is indisposed for parleying, especially when it comes to 'fit the wit of a bit of chit'.[11] If Ida will pocket her pride and let Hilarion claim her as his bride, he says, he will let bygones go by, but if not he will raze the castle to the ground. Ida's three brothers support this view, since their lives are held in the balance. Ida reassures them that Hildebrand's threats are all bluster and that vengeance lurks behind! Hildebrand gives Ida until tomorow afternoon: 'Release Hilarion, then, and be his bride,/Or you'll incur the guilt of fratricide.'[12]

The Princess is still adamant and although she sees Hilarion is fair and strong and tall she will die before she will become his wife.

> Though I am a girl,
> Defiance thus I hurl,
>   Our banners all
>   On outer wall
> We fearlessly unfurl.[13]

She stands surrounded by her followers who all kneel before her. The King and his soldiers stand on built rocks at the back and side of the stage. The curtain falls at the end of the second act.

The Outer Walls and Courtyard of Castle Adamant is the setting for Act 3. Melissa, Sacharissa and the other girls are armed with battle-axes crying death to the invader and speaking of their martial thunder, but such valour is a sham: their true feelings naturally are those of fright, not that there is anything strictly feminine about that! A flourish sounds and Princess Ida enters fully armed for the fray attended by Blanche and Psyche: 'We have to meet stern bearded warriors in fight today,' she says. 'Wear naught but what is necessary to/Preserve your dignity before their eyes/And give your limbs full play.'[14] The task to hand is clear:

> Women of Adamant, we have to show
> That Woman, educated to the task,
> Can meet Man, face to face, on his own ground.
> And beat him there.[15]

Sacharissa, who is acting as surgeon, is alarmed at the prospect of cutting off the live arms and legs of the wounded. 'You have often cut them off in theory!' the Princess insists. Sacharissa can face theory but not practice, so Ida says she will do the job herself – not the only job she must do, for it soon becomes clear that many girls are feeling too unwell to fight, so the Princess resolves to meet the men alone. Her rock has turned to sand, her oak to a bruised reed, and her sword is but a lath:

> Ah, coward steel
> That fear can unanneal!
> False fire indeed,
> To fail me in my need![16]

She sinks down on a seat, and Chloe, one of the girl graduates, accompanied by all the ladies, comes in to announce that King Gama and his three sons have come to fight on her behalf. It is an infamous situation when one has to resort to the help of men, but in an emergency, 'even one's brothers may be turned to use'.[17] King Gama has been released from captivity merely to bring words from Hildebrand: Hildebrand is loth to war with women and is prepared to settle the issue in a fight between Hilarion, Florian and Cyril, and the Princess's three brothers. For Ida this is 'Insult on insult's head', but

Gama explains that he cannot stand up against Hildebrand any longer because Hildebrand had made his captivity so pleasant that he no longer has anything to grumble about.

> He finds out what particular meats I love,
> And gives me them. The very choicest wines,
> The costliest robes – the richest rooms are mine:
> He suffers none to thwart my simplest plan,
> And gives strict orders none should contradict me!
> He's made my life a curse![18]

Life is extremely flat for Gama with nothing whatever to grumble at! He bursts into tears, and falls sobbing on his seat. The Princess knows how much her father has had to suffer and decides to yield. The gates are opened immediately, the girls mount the battlements as the soldiers surge forward. Hilarion, Florian and Cyril are brought in; they are still bound and wearing women's clothes. Hilarion is taunted by Gama to the extent that had he not been Princess Ida's father Hilarion would have wrung his shrivelled neck. The three are led off to prepare for the fight, while Arac, Guron and Scynthius decide to take off their heavy Hungarian armour for the conflict; beneath their armour they are wearing close-fitting shape suits.

When the three knights return a desperate fight takes place in which Arac and his brothers are eventually overcome. Princess Ida arrives with Hildebrand and Gama, and she formally yields; she orders the girls to bind up her brothers' wounds, but to be careful to look the other way. There is now no alternative but for the Princess to resign as principal and hand over to Lady Blanche.

> So ends my cherished scheme! Oh, I had hoped
> To band all women with my maiden throng,
> And make them all abjure tyrannic Man![19]

Had she been successful, Ida continues, her name would have been exalted and posterity would bow in gratitude. Hildebrand reminds her that had she succeeded there would have been no posterity to do the bowing. Ida had never thought of that; she turns to Lady Blanche for an answer. Lady Blanche admits that there is no answer that Abstract Philosophy could provide.

Love between the sexes is the answer; Cyril claims Psyche, and Florian Melissa. Ida admits that her views had been mistaken as she takes Hilarion for her husband:

I have been wrong – I see my error now.
Take me, Hilarion – We will walk the world
Yoked in all exercise of noble end!
And so through those dark gates across the wild
That no man knows! Indeed, I love thee – Come![20]

The truest happiness is found after all in a right balance between man and woman, for

> It were profanity
> For poor humanity
> To treat as vanity
>   The sway of Love.
> In no locality
> Or principality
> Is our mortality
>   Its sway above.[21]

It will have been noticed that Gilbert concluded the Princess's last speech with a quotation; the words are Tennyson's, and in his poem are spoken by Hilarion, but Tennyson had a little more to say. 'My hopes and thine are one/Accomplish thou my manhood and thyself;/Lay thy sweet hands in mine and trust to me.'[22] It is clear in giving the speech to Ida that Gilbert did not need Tennyson's words, fine as they were.

The part of the Princess was sung on the opening night by Leonora Braham, but she had not been the first choice in spite of her successes in *Patience* and *Iolanthe*. It had been decided, because of the taxing demands of the part, to bring in a well-known American soprano, Lillian Russell; however, Miss Russell soon displeased Gilbert by missing a rehearsal, something unforgivable in his eyes, and she was instantly dismissed. 'I won't speak to her and she shan't play in any piece of mine,' he said. The result was a court case in which the company was sued for breach of contract, a matter eventually settled out of court.

Gilbert was happy enough at the opera's reception, though the critic of *The World* had written of a 'desperately dull performance'. He was soon in for a very great shock, for it became evident that Sullivan was losing interest. Gilbert had been making all the running; he took pride of place in the partnership. Indeed, it is true that Gilbert did see himself, and quite rightly, as the instigator of each opera; the ideas were his, the humour, and the intelligence of the plots; yet he was always ready to praise Sullivan, and frequently took his advice. He also knew perfectly well how much their successes owed to the music, and that Sullivan's contribution had increased the humour and raised the pieces to a unique level. It was a considerable blow, therefore, when he discovered that Sullivan had confided in D'Oyly Carte behind his back.

The problem was that *Princes Ida* was not proving to be another *Iolanthe* at the box-office; the takings were already dropping away after it had been running for a month; it looked as though a successor to it might be called for very soon – far too soon for a composer who had begun to find Gilbert's words a tedious chore to set. By March D'Oyly Carte was worried. He wrote to both men requesting that in accordance with the contract drawn up between the three of them only twelve months earlier, in which it was agreed that a new opera could be called for at six months' notice, they must prepare, or at least begin to think about preparing, a successor to *Princess Ida* for the autumn. In fact, with his usual energy, Gilbert was already busily at work on a new libretto. Sullivan's reply to Carte from Brussels was to the point.

'I ought to tell you at once that it is impossible for me to do another piece of the character of those already written by Gilbert and myself,'[23] he wrote. On receiving this information Gilbert's reaction was swift.

'I learnt from Carte yesterday, to my unbounded surprise, that you do not intend to write any more operas of the class with which you and I have been so long identified,'[24] he complained. He was very bewildered at the news, he insisted that he had invariably subordinated his own view to those of his collaborator. Of course, Sullivan had thought the exact opposite was the case.

'I will be quite frank,' he wrote from Paris. 'With *Princess Ida* I have come to the end of my tether – the end of my capability in that class of piece.'[25]

He went on to say that his tunes were in danger of becoming mere repetitions of his former pieces, and his concerted movements were getting to possess a strong family likeness. This was certainly true, but the audiences were not worried about that. Then came something which hurt Gilbert's feelings very much.

I have looked upon the words as being of such importance that I have been continually keeping down the music in order that not one should be lost. And this my suppression is most difficult, most fatiguing, and I may say most disheartening, for the music is never allowed to arise and speak for itself.

I want a chance for the music to act in its own proper sphere – to intensify the emotional element not only of the actual words but of the situation. I should set a story of human interest and probability, where the humorous words would come in a humorous (not serious) situation, and where, if the situation were a tender or a dramatic one the words would be of a similar character. There would then be a feeling of reality about it which would give fresh interest in writing, and fresh vitality to our joint work.[26]

The letter went on to hope that there would be no break in the chain of their joint workmanship.

In his response Gilbert assumed that the letter had been written hurriedly. Surely Sullivan had not intended to gall and wound him. 'Your reflections on the character of the libretti with which I have supplied you have caused me considerable pain,'[27] he wrote. He hardly understood how Sullivan could request that humorous words should come in a humorous situation and tender and dramatic situations should be treated tenderly and dramatically. Was Sullivan trying to teach him the ABC of his profession?

'It is inconceivable that any sane author should ever write otherwise than as you propose I should write in the future,'[28] he insisted.

However, the matter of human interest and probability was really the central issue. Sullivan was tired of topsy-turvydom, the wizardry and improbable fancifulness that seemed to be the pivot of Gilbert's imagination. Neither was he too surprised when on his return to London Gilbert showed him his new libretto, and it turned out to be a reworking of the old lozenge plot! Nevertheless, he had made his point and he would now make his stand; under no circumstances would he have anything to do with such an unreal and artificial piece. There was a long argument with no concession on either side; it seemed to be a complete deadlock, although Sullivan recorded in his diary that the atmosphere had been quite friendly throughout the meeting.

Gilbert, for his part, thought that Sullivan's attitude was arbitrary and capricious, and he affected not to grasp its meaning. Perhaps Sullivan would like to collaborate with someone else for a change, he was always receiving other writers' offerings. Gilbert made the offer, but Sullivan would not entertain it for a moment, he did not see why just because an idea seemed to fail in his judgement to afford sufficient musical suggestion the partnership should necessarily come to a standstill. Gilbert remained adamant; he would not consent to change his mind, he would not construct another plot for the new opera. Sullivan wrote in hurt terms:

'The tone of your letter convinces me that your decision is final and therefore further discussion is useless. I regret it very much.'[29]

Gilbert regretted it too. He needed time to reflect, to consider the full implications of the situation. Perhaps the partnership was indeed over; after all they had achieved much together, perhaps that was enough, and it had been chiefly a working partnership, one that had not enjoyed the very close ties of loyalty and friendship such as might have been expected. A few days after he had received Sullivan's final letter Gilbert was pacing up and down the long study Ernest George had designed for him on the first floor at No. 39 Harrington Gardens, a room whose deep bay with its leaded window overlooked the gardens, but which was, unusually for the time, double-glazed to keep out the clopping trundle of the London streets round about, and so to closet undisturbed the active mind of the occupant within. That day, however, the mind was overwhelmed by a mood as dark as the Spanish leather frieze around the room itself, a mind nursing a grudge that seemed to have no limit to its destructive power, when the completely unexpected happened, an incident to heal everything, though it might seem to have threatened to end Gilbert's life for ever. Suddenly a very large Japanese sword, that had only recently been hung on the wall as a decoration, became dislodged and pitched to the floor with a terrifying clatter.

Part II

Alone
Bereft

8

The Mikado

ᴖ᳁1884–1885 ᳁ᴖ

Gilbert made much of the Japanese sword incident when he came to retell the story of *The Mikado* especially for children after the opera had been successfully performed. The sword had come as a sign, and brought to the forefront of his mind what must have been lurking there already, for at the time the inhabitants of Kensington, and Knightsbridge in particular, were bemused by the exotic sight of Japanese men and women walking about the streets dressed in their traditional clothes. In November *Punch* had included a cartoon of the House of Commons supposedly from a design by a Japanese artist; some members are holding fans, and the speaker seems to be the Mikado himself.

The reason for all this was the Japanese exhibition now in preparation: a whole village was being created at Humphrey's Hall, Albert Gate, Hyde Park, near the top of Sloane Street, with rows of Japanese houses, temples and gardens, and cherry blossom and chrysanthemums galore. Most interesting, perhaps, were the Japanese craftstmen going about their normal daily work.

If Whistler and Burne-Jones had fostered a passion for Oriental fabrics and pottery, their enthusiasm was nothing compared with the rage which was about to overtake London in January 1885 when parents and children, paying a shilling and sixpence to get in, could watch grand entertainments on free seats and seem to experience the everyday life of the Land of the Rising Sun.

Why on earth had Gilbert not seen the significance of all this before? The answer is, he already had, but the idea just needed to be brought out. One thing was certain: the sword had sliced away the lozenge plot, at least for the time being, but it had suggested the broad idea of a new opera set in Japan, or, perhaps more accurately, at the exhibition. Gilbert worked away with speed and enthusiasm. He later described how he set out the scheme in no time, the characters rose before him as he sketched the little figures in his plot-book, and wrote short notes about them. This was all very exciting; he must let Sullivan know immediately.

The news was received at Queen's Mansions with considerable relief. Gilbert had written of picturesque scenery and costumes, such things were his own concern of course, but he had also mentioned the chance of unusual music. It would be wise to go out to Albert Gate and perhaps gain some ideas. Sullivan had spent much time in Egypt listening to Arab music, but he had little or no experience of Japan. Nevertheless, he would not quibble with Gilbert now; he was pleased that this new idea showed that Gilbert wished to continue the collaboration which had been such an advantage to them both.

'If I understand you to propose you will construct a plot without the supernatural or improbable elements, and on the lines you describe,' he wrote on 8 May 1884, 'I gladly undertake to set it without further discussing the matter, or asking what the subject is to be.'[1] It was asking rather too much of Gilbert to produce a plot without 'improbable elements', and it would hardly have been Gilbertian if he had, even were it possible. It was also asking too much of them both after all the time wasted wrangling to have the new opera written and rehearsed for the autumn. D'Oyly Carte was ready with a solution: the company would revive *Trial by Jury* and *The Sorcerer* as a double-bill when *Princess Ida* closed.

During the summer of 1884 Gilbert completed his libretto, spending time between Harrington Gardens and the house Kitty and he had taken in the country, Breakspeare, at Harefield, near Uxbridge. The place was fully furnished, the garden had an outsize tennis court, and the Gilberts paid £800 a year for a seven-year lease. There they entertained many friends at weekends, and it provided a peaceful haven from the more rigorous life in London. Sullivan also spent the latter part of the summer in Hertfordshire at Stagenhoe Park, a rented house, near Hitchin. On 11 October both men were in London for the first performance of the revived operas, which Sullivan conducted. The joyous reception of *Trial by Jury* came as no surprise, but now that the audience knew what to expect from Gilbert *The Sorcerer* was received with far more enjoyment than it had been in 1877. Grossmith, Barrington and Temple played their orginal parts, and Barrington also took the part of the learned judge in *Trial by Jury*. This, the first of many revivals over the coming years, was a great and pleasing surprise to all involved, and news came that the two operas had been given a similar reception in America. There was no doubting D'Oyly Carte's sagacity, and the operas ran for 150 performances, long enough for *The Mikado* to be ready for its opening on 14 March the following year.

Sullivan's hope that Gilbert would produce a libretto free from all improbability was hardly fulfilled in *The Mikado; or the Town of Titipu*; the plot was as far-fetched as ever. Gilbert had toyed with the idea of setting the first scene of the opera in a street in Nagasaki, possibly the market-place, even a junk-lined wharf. In fact, Act I is set in the Palace Courtyard of Ko-Ko, the Lord High Executioner of Titipu. Japanese nobles are discovered standing and sitting in attitudes suggested by native drawings. They are, as they quickly tell the audience, gentlemen of Japan such as may be seen on many a vase and jar, or screen or fan. If their actions appear to be like marionettes it is only that court etiquette demands it so. Nanki-Poo comes on the scene in great excitement. He carries a native guitar on his back and a bundle of ballads in his hand. He is looking for Yum-Yum, Ko-Ko's ward, with whom he has been in love for a year, ever since as a member of the Titipu town band he had taken the cap round for contributions. He had been shocked to learn that Yum-Yum was betrothed to her guardian, but now it seems Ko-Ko has been condemned to death for flirting. Was this really true? Pish-Tush, a noble lord, confirms that the great Mikado of Japan has indeed issued a decree that anyone who flirted, leered or winked should be forthwith beheaded. However, the people had managed to evade the penalty by appointing Ko-Ko as Lord High Executioner. Ko-Ko was only a cheap tailor and a convict in the county jail awaiting execution himself. There was logic in the appointment for it was argued that 'Who's next to be decapited/Cannot cut off another's head/Until he's cut his own off.'[2]

Pooh-Bah, who has become Lord High Everything Else now that all other nobles have resigned their offices, explains to Nanki-Poo the intricacies of the ruler's reasoning:

'Our logical Mikado, seeing no moral difference between the dignified judge, who condemns a criminal to die, and the industrious mechanic who carries out the sentence, has rolled the two offices into one, and every judge is now his own executioner.'[3]

He goes on to explain his own position, as holder of a wide range of appointments: First Lord of the Treasury, Lord Chief Justice, Commander-in-Chief, Lord High Admiral, Master of the Buckhounds, Groom of the Back Stairs, Archbiship of Titipu, and Lord Mayor, both acting and elect. He naturally draws a salary from each: 'It revolts me, but I do it!'[4] Yet he is admirably suited for all these tasks, being 'a particularly haughty and exclusive person', and a descendant of pre-Adamite ancestors. 'I can trace my ancestry back to a protoplasmal primordial atomic globule. Consequently my family pride is something inconceivable. I can't help it. I was born sneering. But I struggle hard to overcome this defect. I mortify my pride continually.'[5] He is always ready to retail state secrets for a very low figure and he is prepared to receive Nanki-Poo's 'insult', a sum of money to provide information about Yum-Yum. In short, there is no point in hoping for her hand because that very afternoon she is to be married to her guardian, Ko-Ko, the Lord High Executioner. Has Nanki-Poo then travelled for almost a month on a fruitless errand? It would seem so.

The Lord High Executioner enters bearing his sword of office and preceded by a chorus of nobles, whose ceremony and adulation make the unprepossessing figure of Ko-Ko appear absurd. He describes his sudden release from jail, liberated on bail on his own recognisances and elevated to a height that few can scale. If he is ever called upon to act professionally he has a little list of likely candidates who never would be missed. He discusses the arrangements for his imminent marriage with Pooh-Bah, who in each of his offices offers advice:

'I don't say that all these distinguished people couldn't be squared; but it is right to tell you that they wouldn't be sufficiently degraded in their own estimation unless they were insulted with a very consider-able bribe.'[6] Ko-Ko is prepared to give the matter a careful consid-eration and the two leave in deep discussion, just as his bride and her sisters approach.

A procession of girls trips in in characteristic Japanese fashion:

> Schoolgirls we, eighteen and under,
> From scholastic trammels free,
> And we wonder – how we wonder! –
> What on earth the world can be![7]

These are Yum-Yum's school friends who herald her entrance with her sisters, Peep-Bo and Pitti-Sing, also Ko-Ko's wards: three little maids from school, for whom life is a joke that's just begun.

> Three little maids who, all unwary,
> Come from a ladies' seminary,
> Freed from its genious tutelary.
> Three little maids from school![8]

Ko-Ko returns with Pooh-Bah and attempts to embrace his bride. There is a short altercation on the etiquette of kissing in public, but Yum-Yum acquiesces: 'I've no objection if it's usual.'[9] She is nevertheless very pleased to get the moment over. Suddenly the girls recognise Nanki-Poo and dash across to him, the musician who used to play on the Marine Parade. Ko-Ko asks to be introduced, and Nanki-Poo confesses to loving Yum-Yum. Surely he must deserve her guardian's anger?

'Anger! Not a bit, my boy. Why, I love her myself/ Charming little girl, isn't she? Pretty eyes, nice hair. Taking little thing, altogether. Very glad to hear my opinion backed by a competent authority. Thank you very much. Good-bye.'[10]

The girls then make fun of Pooh-Bah, but apologise for failing in etiquette towards a man of rank so high. Pooh-Bah is understanding:

> I think you ought to recollect
> You cannot show too much respect
> Towards the highly titled few;
> But nobody does, and why should you?[11]

When Nanki-Pooh and Yum-Yum at last find themselves alone two important truths are revealed: Yum-Yum has no wish whatsoever to marry Ko-Ko, and Nanki-Poo confesses to being the son of the Mikado, disguised in order to escape the advances of an elderly woman of the court, Katisha:

She misconstrued my customary affability into expressions of affection, and claimed me in marriage, under my father's law. My father, the Lucius Junius Brutus of his race, ordered me to marry her within a week, or perish ignominiously on the scaffold. That night I fled his Court, and, assuming the disguise of a Second Trombone, I joined the band in which you found me when I had the happiness of seeing you?[12]

If only things were different! If there were no law against flirting, and Yum-Yum were not already plighted, how much they would love one another; how seriously they would flirt and kiss, as indeed they do!

Ko-Ko has seen Yum-Yum depart: 'To think how entirely my future happiness is wrapped up in that little parcel!'[13] He is wondering about the step he is about to take when Pish-Tush brings in a letter from the Mikado. The Mikado is struck by the fact that no executions have taken place in Titipu for a year, and decrees that unless somebody is beheaded within one month the post of Lord High Executioner shall be abolished, and the city reduced to the rank of a village! Such a reduction would mean irretrievable ruin: someone will have to be executed at once – in fact, Ko-Ko will have to execute himself, if he cannot find a substitute. Perhaps Pooh-Bah would consent to add the title of Lord High Substitute to his many honours. Such an appointment would realise his fondest dreams, but he must set bounds to his insatiable ambition. Nobody in the town cares very much.

> To sit in solemn silence in a dull, dark dock,
> In a pestilential prison, with a life-long lock.
> Awaiting the sensation of a short, sharp shock,
> From a cheap and chippy chopper on a big black block![14]

Ko-Ko is left alone to face death within a month for the sake of the town, but Nanki-Poo enters carrying a rope ready to hang himself out of love-sick despair. Here is an ideal substitute! KooKo agrees that Nanki-Poo and Yum-Yum shall marry immediately, but the marriage will only last for a month, then Nanki-Poo will be executed! Ko-Ko's sense of loss will be unpleasant for a month, but not as unpleasant as Nanki-Poo's at the end of it. Nanki-Poo promises not to prejudice Yum-Yum against her guardian; she has been educated to be Ko-Ko's wife and taught to regard him as a wise and good man. 'Trust me,' Nanki-Poo insists, 'she shall never learn the truth from me.'[15]

Ko-Ko is pleased to have found a 'volunteer', even if it does mean surrendering Yum-Yum. At the announcement of the news everyone is happy; 'with joyous shout and ringing clear' they wish Nanki-Poo a long life – till the dreadful 'then'. A dance of joy begins, but is melodramatically interrupted by the arrival of Katisha, come to claim her 'perjured lover, Nanki-Poo!'[16] Nanki-Poo tries to escape his fate, but Katisha prevents him with 'No!'/You shall not go,/These arms shall thus enfold you!'

> Oh fool, that fleest
> My hallowed joys!

Oh blind, that seest
No equipoise![17]

She pleads with Nanki-Poo to unbind his heart and give her her rightful place; then she turns upon Yum-Yum to assure her that her pink cheek, bright eye, rose lip and smooth tongue have met their doom. Pitti-Sing intervenes to say that Katisha's connubial views are of no concern to anyone present and Nanki-Poo is going to marry Yum-Yum, so Katisha had better succumb and join in the general expressions of glee since there are lots of fish in the sea, and many who's wed for a penny!

Katisha seems to accept her fate that she must live alone, that all has perished save love which never dies. She attempts to unmask Nanki-Poo and reveal his true identity as the son of the Mikado, but her attempts at revelation are drowned by the chorus interrupting with Japanese words.

KATISHA. In vain you interrupt with this tornado!
He is the son of your –
ALL. O ni! bikkuri shakkuri to![18]

Katisha, realising she has failed, calls for her wrongs with vengeance to be crowned, while everyone else refuses to heed their dismal sound, for joy reigns everwhere around. Katisha rushes furiously up-stage, clearing the crowd away right and left, and finishes on the steps at the back of the stage, a fine finale to Act 1.

The setting for Act 2 is Ko-Ko's garden. Yum-Yum, surrounded by the other girls, is being prepared for her wedding; her hair is being brushed and her face and lips heavily painted, as she judges the effect in a mirror. The effect is certainly favourable in her own estimation:

'Yes, I am indeed beautiful! Sometimes I sit and wonder in my artless Japanese way, why it is I am so much more attractive than anybody else in the whole world. Can this be vanity? No! Nature is lovely and rejoices in her loveliness. I am a child of Nature and take after my mother.'[19]

As a child of Nature she is certainly in perfect harmony with the sun and moon, and everything seems to smile upon her. Today she is to be married to the man she loves and she must surely be the 'very happiest girl in Japan'. Her happiness, as her sisters hastily remind her, is great in all but perfection since she will be a widow in a month!

Nanki-Poo is alarmed to find his bride in tears, but he has a solution. The divisions of time are purely arbitrary. 'We'll call each second a minute – each minute an hour – each hour a day – each day a year. At that rate we've about thirty years of married happiness before us.'[20]

Feeling very much happier at the thought, Yum-Yum, Pitti-Sing, Nanki-Poo and Go-To, a character brought in specially for the purpose, sing the merry madrigal 'Brightly Dawns our Wedding Day.'

Ko-Ko arrives on the scene and suffers agony as he witnesses Yum-Yum and Nanki-Poo's love for each other; he begs them to go about their petting gently to make his torture more simple. He has some alarming news for Yum-Yum: if Nanki-Poo is to be beheaded, she, as his wife, according to the Mikado's law, must be buried alive. Here's a state of things! The laws of common sense ought not to be ignored, and so the wedding better not take place, at least not that wedding. Yum-Yum better marry Ko-Ko after all. At this suggestion Nanki-Poo says he will perform the Happy Despatch and hang himself. Ko-Ko cannot allow that, as Nanki-Poo is to be beheaded. While this chaotic situation is debated Pooh-Bah announces that the Mikado is coming to Titipu to see whether his orders have been carried out. With this information Ko-Ko is put on the spot; he had thought his duties were purely nominal, in fact he admits to being quite incapable of killing anybody or anything, but does he really have to?

Why should I kill you,' he says to Nanki-Poo, 'when making an affidavit that you've been executed will do just as well?'[21]

Pooh-Bah in all his Offices of State is prepared for a consideration to endorse the fiction, and, as Archbishop of Titipu, he agrees to solemnise the marriage between Yum-Yum and Nanki-Poo immediately!

The Mikado's procession marches in. It is led by troops of the Imperial Guard, and the Emperor is accompanied by Katisha, his daughter-in-law elect, 'as tough as a bone,/With a will of her own', to whom all should bow. The Mikado explains that his sublime object is to let each punishment fit the crime committed, 'to make each evil liver/A harmless river/Of harmless merriment'. He proceeds to give some examples of this humane endeavour to illustrate how far he is a true philanthropist.

> All prosy dull society sinners,
> Who chatter and bleat and bore,
> Are sent to hear sermons

From mystical Germans
Who preach from ten till four.
The amateur tenor, whose vocal villainies
All desire to shirk,
Shall during off-hours,
Exhibit his powers
To Madame Tussaud's waxwork.

The lady who dyes a chemical yellow,
Or stains her grey hair puce,
Or pinches her figger,
Is blacked like a nigger
With permanent walnut juice.
The idiot who, in railways carriages,
Scribbles on window-panes,
We only suffer
To ride on a buffer
In Parliamentary trains.

My object all sublime
I shall achieve in time –
To let the punishment fit the crime –
The punishment fit the crime;
And make each prisoner pent
Unwillingly represent
A source of innocent merriment!
Of innocent merriment.[22]

It turns out that the matter of executions is not the Emperor's chief concern, although Ko-Ko, Pitti-Sing and Pooh-Bah give a most lurid description of the supposed demise of Nanki-Poo, 'as the sabre true/ Cut cleanly through/His cervical vertebrae!' Far more to the point is the whereabouts of Nanki-Poo, since the Mikado is still unaware of the name on the certificate. The heir apparent is said to be masquerading in the town, disguised as a Second Trombone. Ko-Ko has to think quickly. Nanki-Poo has gone abroad. Where to? What is his address? Naturally, he is living in Knightsbridge!

Katisha is staring in horror at the certificate. The name of the felon executed that morning is Nanki-Poo, the heir to the throne of Japan! The Mikado is immediately comforting to the apologetic Lord

High Executioner. How could it possibly have been his fault?

'If a man of exalted rank chooses to disguise himself as a Second Trombone, he must take the consequences ... I've no doubt he thoroughly deserved what he got.'[23]

There had been no way of telling who the gentleman really was; his name was not written on his forehead. It might have been on his pocket-handkerchief, but Japanese don't use pocket-handkerchiefs. However, there is a set punishment for 'compassing the death of the Heir Apparent', but the Emperor has forgotten what it is for the moment, something lingering, anyway, humorous but lingering, with boiling oil or melted lead in it. Seeing Ko-Ko, Pooh-Bah and Pitti-Sing are grovelling on their knees the Mikado agrees to alter the law after luncheon. 'I'm really very sorry for you all, but it's an unjust world, and virtue is triumphant only in theatrical performances.'[24]

The Mikado and Katisha retire for luncheon, and Ko-Ko, Pooh-Bah and Pitti-Sing decide that Nanki-Poo must be hastily brought back to life. Just at that moment Yum-Yum and he appear on their way to their honeymoon. The arrival of Katisha has complicated everything:

'Katisha claims me in marriage, but I can't marry her because I am married already – consequently she will insist on my excecution, and if I'm executed, my wife will have to be buried alive.'[25]

There is only one way out of the dilemma: Katisha must be persuaded to marry Ko-Ko. When Katisha is married, existence for Nanki-Poo will be as welcome as the flowers that bloom in the spring. Ko-Ko, for his part, does not relish taking under his wing a most unattractive old thing with a caricature of a face.

Katisha herself is without hope, there is little left for a cheated maiden, she thinks, but death. She is all alone when Ko-Ko approaches her timidly and hurls himself at her knees in supplication. He begs for mercy. How can she give him mercy?

Had you mercy on him? See here, you! You have slain my love. He did not love me, but he would have loved me in time. I am an acquired taste – only the educated palate can appreciate me. I was educating his palate when he left me. Well, he is dead, and where shall I find another? It takes years to train a man to love me. Am I to go through the weary round again, and, at the same time, implore mercy for you who robbed me of my prey – I mean my pupil – just as his education was on the point of completion? Oh, where shall I find another?[26]

Ko-Ko offers himself: for years he has loved her with a white-hot passion that is slowly but surely consuming his very vitals! Katisha will have none of it, but Ko-Ko sets about wooing her with the tale of a little tomtit which drowned itself in a river. Surely it was blighted affection that caused it to do it. If Katisha remains callous and obdurate Ko-Ko will perish in the same way. During the sad story Katisha has been much affected, and at the end she is almost in tears, Had the bird really died for love, because of a cruel little hen? It had. Will Ko-Ko really do the same? He will. Katisha falls upon him saying she has been a silly little goose, and hopes that she won't be hated because she is 'just a little teeny weeny wee bit bloodthirsty. 'Hate you? Oh Katisha! is there not beauty even in bloodthirstiness?'[27] That is Katisha's idea exactly.

KATISHA. There is beauty in the bellow of the blast,
　　　　　There is grandeur in the growing of the gale,
　　　　　　There is eloquent outpouring
　　　　　　When the lion is a-roaring,
　　　　　And the tiger is a-lashing of its tail!
KO-KO.　　　Yes, I like to see a tiger
　　　　　　From the Congo or the Niger,
　　　　　And especially when lashing of its tail!
KATISHA. Volcanoes have a splendour that is grim,
　　　　　And earthquakes only terrify the dolts,
　　　　　　But to him who's scientific
　　　　　　There's nothing that's terrific
　　　　　In the falling of a flight of thunderbolts!
KO-KO.　　　Yes, in spite of all my meekness,
　　　　　　If I have a little weakness,
　　　　　It's a passion for a flight of thunderbolts!

So their tastes are one; there is no need to wait another moment to be married, unless, as Ko-Ko hopefully suggests, Katisha is not yet old enough to marry!

KO-KO.　　There is beauty in extreme old age –
　　　　　　Do you fancy you are elderly enough?
　　　　　　　Information I'm requesting
　　　　　　　On a subject interesting:
　　　　　Is a maiden all the better when she's tough?
KATISHA.　　　Throughout this wide dominion

> It's the general opinion
> That she'll last a good deal longer when she's tough.

KO-KO. Are you old enough to marry, do you think?
> Won't you wait until you're eighty in the shade?
> There's a fascination frantic
> In a ruin that's romantic;
> Do you think you are sufficiently decayed?

KATISHA. To the matter that you mention
> I have given some attention,
> And I think I am sufficiently decayed.

BOTH. If that is so,
> Sing derry down derry!
> It's evident, very,
> Our tastes are one!
> Away we'll go,
> And merrily marry,
> Nor tardily tarry
> Till day is done.[28]

The pair go off happily.

There is a flourish as the Mikado and his court enter. Pish-Tush is with them. They have had a capital lunch. The Mikado, seeming to have forgotten that he had agreed to alter the law, hopes that all the painful preparations have been made. Where is the unfortunate gentleman, and his two well-meaning and misguided accomplices?

Ko-Ko, Katisha, Pooh-Bah and Pitti-Sing enter and throw themselves at the Mikado's feet, and beg for mercy. Katisha explains that as her husband-that-was-to-have-been is dead, she has just married this 'miserable object'! However, the difficulty remains that Ko-Ko has slain the heir apparent. Not so! Nanki-Poo and Yum-Yum enter and kneel before the Emperor: the heir apparent is not slain, and here is his daughter-in-law elect. Katisha realises Ko-Ko has deceived her. An explanation is necessary: it is true that Ko-Ko had stated he had killed Nanki-Poo, but what exactly did that mean?

'When your Majesty says, "Let a thing be done," it's as good as done – practically it is done – because your Majesty's will is law. Your Majesty says, "Kill a gentleman," and a gentleman is told off to be killed. Consequently, that gentleman is as good as dead – practically, he is dead – and if he is dead – who not say so?'

His Majesty sees the point. 'Nothing,' he says, 'could possibly be more satisfactory!'²⁹ Nanki-Poo has gone and married Yum-Yum, an irreversible fact to which His Majesty and Katisha better succumb!

> The threatened cloud has passed away,
> And fairly shines the dawning day;
> What though the night may come too soon,
> There's yet a month of afternoon!
> > Then let the throng
> > Our joy advance,
> > With laughing song
> > And merry dance,
> With joyous shout and ringing cheer,
> Inaugurate our new career!³⁰

Although *The Mikado* was greeted with great enthusiasm on the opening night, it was not quite up to the Savoy mark. For one thing it was a disastrous evening for Grossmith; he felt thoroughly uncomfortable made up as Ko-Ko, and he suffered such stage fright that he fluffed some of his lines, and his nerves meant he did not always sing in tune. The audience was somewhat mystified, not to say alarmed, as the critic writing for *Punch* noted. 'It broke upon many of us there that George Grossmith's real humour had hitherto been less in his face and voice than in his legs.'³¹ Throughout Act I Grossmith' legs had been invisible, because his costume came down to his shoes. The audience knew something was wrong, but they did not know what it was exactly. Suddenly their favourite was not being funny. He did not even look funny. However, there was some improvement after the interval: 'Suddenly, in the Second Act, he gave a kick-up, and showed a pair of white stocking'd legs under the Japanese dress. It was an inspiration. Forthwith the house felt a strong sense of relief – it had got what it wanted, it had found out accidentally what it had really missed, and at the first glimpse of George Grossmith's legs there arose a shout of long pent-up laughter.'³²

Grossmith took the hint, he too had found out where the fault lay, and for the rest of the performance he kicked and twisted about till the audience shouted, applauded and encored, and actually joined in the action, unconsciously kicking up their own legs in their irrepressible delight.

Recalling his experience himself, Grossmith said it must have appeared to all that he was doing his best to spoil the evening:

'What with my own want of physical strength, prostration through the numerous and very long rehearsals, my anxiety to satisfy the author, and the long rows of critics rendered blasé by the modern custom of half-a-dozen matinees a week, I lost my voice, and the little there was of it, my confidence, and – what I maintain is most valuable to me – my own individuality.'[33]

In fact, Grossmith was quite prepared to plead guilty to being what one critic described as 'a lamentable spectacle'.

One may imagine what Gilbert's reaction might have been had he been there to see it; but his carefully thought-out plan and well-regulated drill momentarily abandoned, he was pacing about the London streets: 'What I suffered during those hours no man can tell,' he said. 'Agony and apprehension possessed me.'[34]

The rehearsals had been difficult and long. While the set was being installed at the Savoy the company had rehearsed at the Lyceum, and Sullivan had held musical rehearsals in Langham Hall. It had taken much effort to get Barrington to understand what was wanted of him; to begin with his interpretation had been no more like Gilbert's idea of Pooh-Bah than chalk is like cheese, and he had told him so. He had invited Barrington to his home to spend several hours working on the part. This had had the desired effect. He knew little Jessie Bond would be all right, he could always rely on her, her sense of timing, her fun. He had not been sure of Temple's opening song as the Mikado; at the dress rehearsal he had suggested leaving out 'My object all sublime', but Temple and the other singers had protested and overruled him.

The costumes had also been his concern. Some of the principals were dressed in genuine Japanese clothes, and Rosina Brandram's costume for Katisha was about two hundred years old; other fabrics he had bought at Liberty's. He had persuaded several Japanese from the exhibition to come to give advice about gesture and movement, especially the intricate fan movement. The words and music, except for the opening tune in the overture, were thoroughly English, the humour was English, the evils of English society he had continud to pursue and persecute; this was all intentional, but it was therefore important that the manner should be authentically Japanese. He had planned it all so carefully, and Hawes Craven, the stage designer, had risen to the occasion with two magnificent sets, yet until he returned to the theatre to the curtain calls and the thunderous applause Gilbert had been apprehensive, even afraid.

For Sullivan *The Mikado* showed every sign of a real success. It had been a most brilliant house, and it had given the piece a tremendous reception. The Duke and Duchess of Edinburgh were in the audience, so were Princess Louise and Prince Louis Alexander of Battenberg. From the rostrum Sullivan had certainly been aware of Grossmith's nervousness which had nearly upset the piece altogether, but Barrington's Pooh-Bah, Temple's Mikado and Lely's Nanki-Poo had been excellent, as had the women led by Leonora Braham as Yum-Yum; the 'Three Little Maids' had received three encores. There were a further three encores for 'The Flowers that Bloom in the Spring', and more had been called. Sullivan took seven, but, as he recorded in his diary, he might have taken twelve. The signs were right, *The Mikado* would run for 672 performances, much longer than anything else Gilbert and he wrote. Perhaps now he might be able to concentrate on some serious music, his main concern – a cantata, a symphony perhaps. It was a shock indeed to Sullivan when some years later his fellow composer, Ethel Smyth, told him that *The Mikado* was by far and away the best thing he had ever written!

9

The Witch's Curse

ᖍᖍ 1885–1887 ᖍᖍ

With another obvious success in his hands the fear of further piracy in the United States caused D'Oyly Carte much anxiety. He had already lost one copyright action in the American courts, on which occasion the judge had stated that 'no Englishman possesses any rights which a true-born American is bound to respect'.[1] If this were the prevailing opinion the rumours that the Americans had already sent musical copyists to London to take down *The Mikado* in performance were alarming.

In order to safeguard the situation the company had in 1884 allowed an arrangement of the orchestral score of *Princess Ida* to be published in Boston by one of Sullivan's former pupils, George Lowell Tracy, thus in effect giving him entire copyright for the United States. The opera had been performed, but it did not arouse sufficient interest to provoke a legal battle. With *The Mikado* the situation was different. Again Tracy was entrusted with a score, so that anybody attempting to play the opera would be infringing Tracy's rights, and Carte as his assignee would be able to stop them under the statute laws of the United States, or so it seemed.

Two other Americans, John Duff and John Stetson, had also visited England in an attempt to purchase rights to *The Mikado*, but Carte was unable to come to agreeable terms with either. However, it soon reached his ears that Duff was planning to open the opera at the Standard Theatre, New York, in September without authority. There was no time to lose, and it was important to pre-empt this with a fully rehearsed English cast, which could be shipped secretly across the Atlantic. It was fortunate also that Sullivan himself was leaving for America in the *Etruria* on 20 June 1885, so Carte decided to follow on the very next boat.

Sullivan's main reason for crossing the Atlantic was sad and personal; his sister-in-law, Charlotte, Frederick's widow, had died at the end of January in Los Angeles leaving six children between the ages of six and twenty-one, and this was the earliest opportunity he had had to visit. Charlotte had married Benjamin Hutchinson only two years before; she had recently borne him a child, and seemed to have settled happily. Sullivan had continued to send her a yearly allowance, but when she died he had advised against the family's coming back to England, although he was quite prepared to adopt Herbert Sullivan who had lived with his uncle since his mother had emigrated.

Sullivan joined Carte in New York, but he did not wish to be embroiled in any action against Duff: that was Carte's province, and Sullivan soon moved on to Chicago, where another production of *The Mikado* was being planned. There he was interviewed by a reporter from the *Chicago Tribune*, who observed after a cheery greeting, 'a typical Englishman between five-foot five and five-feet six in height, a picture of good nature and good health, and must have tipped the beam at 175 pounds. His beard was worn close-cut, and his hair was parted exactly in the middle.'[2] Sullivan complained of Sydney Rosenfeld's imminent production of *The Mikado*, a man who got 'all he knows about Japanese customs and everything else from a dollar score book'.[3] He was astounded to be told that HMS *Pinafore* was also opening that week. It hardly seemed possible that such a thing could be tolerated. He proceeded to refer to Rosenfeld in such rude terms that he asked the reporter not to publish them for fear of a libel suit against him.

The *Chicago Evening News* reported that it appeared Sir Arthur had come to America to teach people a thing or two, but implied that his attack had misfired. 'We know that Sir Arthur could handle a tuning-fork with considerable eclat, but we do not find him quoted as a legal authority in the revised statutes.'

Via Denver and Salt Lake City Sullivan travelled by rail to San Francisco and then to Los Angeles to spend several weeks with his nephews and nieces. During his time there he toured with them through the Yosemite Valley with its giant trees and waterfall. On 19 August Carte's authentic production of *The Mikado* opened at the Fifth Avenue Theatre, New York, where Stetson was manager, performed by a cast that had only disembarked the day before. The singers had been brought, one might almost say smuggled, across the Atlantic, since their cabins had been booked under false names and their true identity kept a closely guarded secret throughout the voyage. Carte, who had gone back to England to fetch them, travelled under the name of Henry Chapman!

Towards the end of September the company lost its case against Duff, but by that time it hardly mattered, as Duff's production was already running; if anything the publicity was good for the authentic version. On 24 September Sullivan himself took over from Alfred Cellier to conduct a special performance, for which the ticket prices were raised. New York society had been determined to show a right sense of propriety; a great many professional and social dignitaries were in the audience as a method of showing to the composer 'that the authorised *Mikado* is the only *Mikado* that possesses any attraction for the representative, right-thinking portion of the community'.[5]

A few days after this successful performance Sullivan travelled to Philadelphia to conduct another first night of *The Mikado* at McCaull's Opera House. This was a production Carte had sanctioned back in July, allowing McCaull sole rights for that city. It was about this time that Sullivan paid tribute to his great collaborator, who was busily working at a new libretto back in England.

'Have you noticed,' Sullivan said, 'what an extraordinary polish there is in his versification. There is never a weak syllable or halting foot. It is marvellous. He has a wonderful gift, too, of making rhythms, and it bothers me to death sometimes to make corresponding rhythms in music.'[6]

In one sense the spirit of Gilbert had haunted him during this American visit. With his usual gusto Gilbert had kept his partner in touch with the way his mind was working. There was a possibility of a libretto based on Mary Shelley's *Frankenstein*. Grossmith would make a good Frankenstein, and Barrington an equally good monster. Gilbert had written to ask what Sullivan thought. However, when Carte and Sullivan eventually received a draft of the new libretto there was no sign of Frankenstein, though the plot seemed dark and mysterious. But there seemed no real urgency in the autumn of 1885, because *The Mikado* was still playing to packed houses.

While Sullivan and Carte were in America Gilbert became suspicious. Were not the two of them building up some kind of resentment against him? It is true they were in many respects similar in character, and they had much in common; they came from similar backgrounds, and they enjoyed the high life, wining and dining, and took a more than usual number of the opportunities to cultivate the company of the aristocracy that success had made possible. They were probably both Freemasons, that would bind them together. What Gilbert knew of Sullivan's morals did not impress him either, the man was clearly a fornicator, and his gambling exploits were very well known. Gilbert nevertheless still felt he could trust Sullivan, a fellow artist, but he did not trust Carte, a mere commercial man, a broker.

'I confess I don't feel very keen about Carte,' Gilbert had been indiscreet enough to tell Sullivan. 'He owes every penny he posseses to us ... When we manage the theatre for him he succeeds splendidly. When he manages for himself, he fails. Moreover, when he succeeds, he shows a disposition to kick away the ladder by which he has risen.'[7]

Gilbert felt that Carte was unnecessarily extravagant: he mismanaged. For instance, he had been fool enough to send three touring companies into the provinces when one would have done. It had been the same with *The Pirates of Penzance* in America; he had sent out four companies when two would have been ample; this had resulted in the reduced profits he had moaned about. It had been his own fault entirely.

Furthermore, Gilbert had learnt from experience that Carte sided with Sullivan against him, and he would soon have the pain of knowing that Sullivan would side with Carte. It is important in this context to keep in mind, particularly because of the future misunderstandings that would eventually drive an irreversible wedge between Gilbert and the other two, that the members of the company sympathised with Gilbert throughout; not that they failed to see his obvious faults, but, as Jessie Bond realised, Gilbert was a man of far greater sensibility than Sullivan, who could be exceedingly churlish on occasion. Gilbert was a far greater man in every way, but he was stubborn when crossed; he liked to have his own way in matters which he thought were his prerogative. He was a perfectionist, and often over-tried the patience of his actors, though they continued to respect him; on the occasions when he was overruled he behaved childishly.

Sullivan was a shallower and less complicated character; he hated any kind of fuss, and he wished to be popular with all, something he managed to achieve. He certainly did not share Gilbert's view of

Carte, whom he regarded as a friend; he had had ample time to discuss the triple partnership with him, and it was natural in Gilbert's absence that they should be drawn closer together. They travelled back to England in October 1885 aboard the *Eros*, a German boat, only to discover Gilbert had taken his wife to Egypt.

Gilbert thought Carte had misled him even here. Had not he said Sullivan would not return until the middle of November? Had Gilbert known it was to be earlier, he would certainly not have gone to Cairo, at least not until later. He was anxious to know what Sullivan had thought of the plot he had sent. He also thought it possibly a good idea to revive HMS *Pinafore* while there were members of the original cast in the company.

'I think it is not unlikely that if we postpone its revival for another year, we may have lost Grossmith or Temple, or Barrington, or Bond – or all of them. They would remain to play it now, I think, knowing that it would be followed by another original piece.'[8]

On the other hand he thought it likely that if the cast knew they were in for a list of revivals they might try to look for work elsewhere. In fact, HMS *Pinafore* was not revived, although the plan would have suited Sullivan well enough. The foremost project in his mind was not meant for the Savoy at all, but for the forthcoming Leeds Festival in the October of 1886, where, besides the first performance of his own new piece, he had agreed to conduct Bach's Mass in B Minor. In the event he worked at both compositions, and completed his cantata *The Golden Legend*, based on a dramatic poem by Longfellow, which Joseph Bennet adapted for him, while he sketched out the score of Gilbert's new opera, the title of which was kept a secret, even from the performers. Besides compoing, Sullivan was conductor of the Philharmonic Society and Principal of the Royal College of Music, a busy man, but Mrs Ronalds, his American friend, remained loyal and willing, and he still found plenty of time to indulge himself!

The Mikado ran until 19 January 1887. This allowed only three days to prepare the theatre and perfect the production of its successor, now named *Ruddygore*, a more complicated piece to perform. It was barely ready on the opening night, and the general opinon was that it was something of a disaster. For one thing the title offended some in the audience. It was in poor taste, and although Gilbert had merely intended to suggest the 'blood and thunder' of melodrama, there was no getting away from the fact that 'ruddy' meant 'bloody' in most people's language, and thus Gilbert seemed to be swearing in public.

There are several stories relating to this, and all make the same point. When, for instance, someone asked Gilbert how was 'Bloodygore' going, he replied, 'It isn't "Bloodygore", it's *Ruddygore*.' 'Oh,' said the other, 'it's the same thing.' 'Is it?' Gilbert retorted. 'Then I suppose you'll take it that if I say "I admire your ruddy counte- nance," I mean "I like your bloody cheek!"'[9]

The *Observer* critic thought: 'There is something not at all pretty about the sound of *Ruddygore* which moreover threatens a grimmer mood of satire than that in which the author is here pleased to indulge.'[10]

George Grossmith tells another story of how Gilbert arrived at the theatre a few days after the opera's opening and announced: 'I propose altering the piece and calling it "Kensington Gore, or, Not So Good As The Mikado".'[11]

However, Gilbert took the point and changed the spelling to *Ruddigore*, with the result that the name is now often confused with Verdi's *Rigoletto*!

Ruddigore; or The Witch's Curse, described as 'An Entirely and Original Supernatural Opera in Two Acts', is set during the Napoleonic War, in 1810, at Rederring, in Cornwall, a small fishing village.

Act I takes place outside Rose Maybud's cottage situated to the left of the stage. A chorus of bridesmaids, led by Zorah and Ruth, range themselves in front of it. This is a daily ritual, but something of a fruitless one, for these are an endowed corps of professional brides- maids who are bound to be on duty every day between the hours of ten and four in the constant expectation that Rose Maybud, the fairest flower that blows, will get married. Old Hannah, Rose's aunt, comes from the cottage to announce that Rose is still 'heart-free, and looks coldly upon her many suitors'.[12] The suitors are 'many' indeed, and include every young man in the village, but not one has the courage to declare himself, so appalled are they by Rose's beauty and modesty.

If Rose won't marry, what about Hannah herself? Old Adam, the faithful servant of Robin Oakapple, is known to love her with all the frenzy of a boy of fourteen. It cannot be, Hannah explains; she is pledged to 'eternal maidenhood' because she was once let down by a youth who had wooed her under an assumed name.

'On the very day upon which our wedding was to have been

celebrated, I discovered that he was no other than Sir Roderic Murgatroyd, one of the bad Baronets of Ruddigore, and the uncle of the man who now bears that title.'[13]

Such a man could never have been a husband to an honest girl. Why not, Zorah asks. Why should one not marry a bad baronet of Ruddigore? It seems all baronets are bad, but this one was accursed! A curse had been on all the line since it was placed by a witch on Sir Rupert Murgatroyd, the first baronet. Hannah proceeds to tell the story of how Sir Rupert had spent much energy, and money, in persecuting witches:

> With fear he'd make them quake –
> He'd duck them in his lake –
> He'd break their bones
> With sticks and stones,
> And burn them at the stake.[14]

Sir Rupert showed no remorse at such action, no shame, no pity; in fact he looked upon it as a sport. One day he met his match. He was roasting a palsied hag on the village green when she yelled out a curse from the flames:

> Each Lord of Ruddigore,
>   Despite his best endeavour,
> Shall do one crime, or more,
>   Once every day, for ever!
> This doom he can't defy
> However he may try,
>   For should he stay
>   His hand, that day
> In torture he shall die.[15]

The prophecy had come true, because the ingenuity required to keep up the momentum of a crime each day was more than any could manage, and their feeling of guilt had become so overpowering that the moment they cried out 'I'll sin no more', they died in agony on the same day.

> And thus, with sinning cloyed,
> Has died each Murgatroyd,
>   And so shall fall,
>   Both one and all,
> Each coming Murgatroyd.[16]

On that ominous note the stage is left empty as Rose Maybud comes from the cottage, with a small basket on her arm. She tells her aunt she has a few gifts for deserving villagers, a peppermint rock for old gaffer Gadderby, a set of false teeth for pretty little Ruth Rowbottom, and a pound of snuff for the poor orphan girl, and things of that sort. Rose is an orphan herself, having been hung in a plated dish cover to the knocker of the workhouse door with nothing to call her own but a change of baby-linen and a book of etiquette. When her aunt wonders why so much goodness is not being used to make some young man happy, Rose produces her little book to explain what she thinks of the young men in the village, all of whom seem to break the rules, eating peas with a knife, combing their hair in public, and failing to enter a room correctly. Hannah suggests that Robin Oakapple is different, he combines the manners of a marquess with the morals of a Methodist. Surely, Rose could love him, but even if she could confess it to him Robin is too shy. It would certainly be almost impossible to declare love without breaking the strict rules of etiquette, particularly in the matter of hinting which is most unladylike, and she could not speak to him first, because the book says quite clearly: 'Don't speak until you are spoken to.'[17]

In spite of this when Hannah has returned into the house, Robin himself appears and fortunately he speaks first. Although they are both far too shy, there is an obvious attraction which they can only express by speaking about the cases of imaginary friends. 'I know a youth who loves a little maid', and so on. When Rose has departed Robin sits desponding, and is joined by Old Adam, who reveals that Robin Oakapple is an assumed name: Robin is really Sir Ruthven Murgatroyd, the rightful Baronet of Ruddigore, who had disappeared from the castle in order to evade the curse twenty years previously and was presumed dead; his younger brother, Despard, had therefore succeeded to the title and the curse. Adam also reveals that Robin's foster-brother, Richard Dauntless, a man-o'-war's man, has arrived in the village after ten years away at sea.

Richard makes a stirring entrance accompanied by the bridesmaids, and relates how his Revenue sloop, the *Tom-Tit*, had paralysed a French frigate off Cape Finistere, not with gun-fire, but by cheering. This had been the kindest thing to do because fighting with the Frenchman, a poor Mounseer, a miserable Parley-voo, would be like 'hittin' of a gal – It's a lubberly thing to do.'

So we up with our helm, and we scuds before the breeze
As we gives a compassionating cheer;
Froggee answers with a shout
As he sees us go about,
Which was grateful of the poor Mounseer,
D'ye see?
Which was grateful of the poor Mounseer!
And I'll wager in their joy they kissed each other's cheek
(Which is what them furriners do),
And they blessed their lucky stars
We were hardy British tars
Who had pity on a poor Parley-voo.
D'ye see?
Who had pity on a poor Parley-voo![18]

Robin and Richard greet each other. Richard's confidence, his 'bumptious self-assertiveness', is overbearing, but it is just what Robin lacks, and he would give his right arm for such 'modest assurance' where Rose is concerned, for he knows well enough if you wish to advance in the world you must be able to blow your own trumpet or you haven't a chance. It is suggested that Richard might persuade Rose for him. He is quite prepared to take on the task, but when Robin departs and Richard sees Rose he is smitten by her himself: she's a tight little craft and fit to marry Lord Nelson: 'By the Flag of Old England, I can't look at her unmoved.' The inevitable happens and Richard and Rose fall in love, though only after Rose has consulted her book and found that it is bad etiquette to keep anyone in unnecessary suspense. The pair exchange a first kiss and declare everlasting love, just as Robin and the bridesmaids arrive to 'Hail the Bridegroom and the Bride', thinking that Richard will have successfully pressed Robin's suit. Richard comes clean upon the matter, but when Rose realises the truth she begins to have doubts, as Richard's prospects do not seem as good as Robin's. What can a lowly mariner offer in comparison with a man who has 'fat oxen, and many sheep and swine, a considerable dairy farm and much corn and oil?' Besides sailors are but worldly men, and little prone to lead serious and thoughtful lives! It may also be that he drinks strong waters such as might bemuse a man and make him 'even as wild as beasts of the desert'. Faced with this choice Rose decides to love Robin immediately, while assuring Richard that should she change her mind again,

1 *W. S. Gilbert, 1883*

2 *Arthur Sullivan, Leipzig, 1860*

3 *Lucy 'Kitty' Gilbert, 1866*

4 *Richard D'Oyly Carte*

5 *Helen D'Oyly Carte*

6 *George Grossmith as Ko-Ko in* The Mikado

12 *Richard Temple as the Pirate King in* The Pirates of Penzance

13 *Ilka von Palmay as Julia Jellicoe in* The Grand Duke

14 *The Savoy Theatre, c 1881*

15 *Programme for the first performance of* Iolanthe, *1883*

16 *Grim's Dyke which became the Gilberts' last home in 1890*

17 *Nancy McIntosh as Princess Zara in* Utopia Limited

18 *W. S. Gilbert in the uniform of the Deputy Lieutenant of the County of Middlesex*

19 *Arthur Sullivan, c 1890*

she won't forget him, and with that she runs off with Robin to prepare for the wedding!

The mood of the opera changes suddenly as the wildly dressed figure of Mad Margaret enters, though, as the stage-direction says, she is in picturesque tatters, and is an obvious caricature of theatrical madness. Like Ophelia in *Hamlet*, whose mad scene Gilbert seems to have had in mind, Margaret is a rejected lover, having been rejected by the evil Sir Despard Murgatroyd. She has become completely deranged and cannot fix her mind on anything, and she keeps breaking into frenzied chuckles.

> Cheerily carols the lark
> Over the cot.
> Merrily whistles the clerk
> Scratching a blot.
> But the lark
> And the clerk,
> I remark
> Comfort me not![19]

Daft Madge! Crazy Meg! Mad Margaret! Poor Peg! Yes, she is very mad, and the reason is a mystery, she says; she has committed no crime, she is only in love – lonely! Her lover would gather for his posies only roses, only roses! She bursts into tears just as Rose herself enters/ She wishes to comfort Margaret and offers her an apple. Is Rose mad as well, Meg asks. Rose does not think so. Then she does not love Sir Despard Murgatroyd? All mad girls love him, Margaret says. 'I love him. I'm poor Mad Margaret!' Why has Margaret come to the cottage? To pinch Rose Maybud. Sir Despard is coming and with one Italian glance will make Rose Maybud his. Rose reveals that she is indeed Rose Maybud and she is pledged to another. There is therefore nothing for Meg to fear. The sound of voices is heard approaching, so Rose and Margaret tiptoe off together.

The bridesmaids herald the entry of a chorus of bucks and blades, all gentlemen, and men of station come from the city, whose charm and good looks quite disarm the girls and 'pillage their hearts'.

> The sons of the tillage
> Who dwell in this village
> Are people of lowly degree – degree.
> Though honest and active
> They're most unattractive

And awkward as awkward can be – can be.
They're clumsy clodhoppers
With axes and choppers.
And shepherds and ploughmen
And drovers and cowmen
And hedgers and reapers
And carters and keepers.
But never a lover for me![20]

The gentry are thus most welcome and the girls admit their entry has set their tender hearts a-beating.

Sir Despard Murgatroyd approaches. He is moody and sad and his youthful good looks have become haggard through crime. All the girls express their horror of Sir Despard and they fly from him terror-stricken, leaving him alone on the stage. What is a poor baronet to do in his situation, when a whole picture-gallery of ancestors step down from their frames and threaten him with an excruciating death if he hesitates to commit his daily crime? But he has worked out a system to get even with them:

'I get my crime over the first thing in the morning, and then, ha! ha! for the rest of the day I do good – I do good! Two days since, I stole a child and built an orphan asylum. Yesterday I robbed a bank and endowed a bishopric. Today I carry off Rose Maybud, and atone with a cathedral!'

His last two intentions are not carried out, because Richard Dauntless's heart is giving him trouble. He cannot forget Rose, which prompts him to reveal Robin's true identity to Sir Despard. 'Ruthven alive and going to marry Rose Maybud!'[21]

This shall not be: Ruthven must be unmasked, it is a matter of duty, painful though that duty be, in order to leave Sir Despard free to 'live a blameless life, and to die beloved and regretted by all who knew him.'

The bridesmaids and the bucks and blades come to the cottage, as do Robin, Richard and Old Adam, where they meet Rose attended by Zorah and Dame Hannah. Rose and Robin embrace on this beautiful spring day; all is budding and blossoming on this their wedding day in May, though their love will be everlasting and 'Life is lovely all the year.'

Suddenly the dancing of the gavotte is interrupted by the grim-faced Sir Despard:

> Hold, bride and bridegroom, ere you wed each other,
> I claim young Robin as my elder brother!
> His rightful title I have long enjoyed:
> I claim him as Sir Ruthven Murgatroyd![22]

Robin is unable to deny it, neither can Richard deny he is the betrayer, but it was his conscience, he explains, that made him do it. Rose turns away from Robin and offers herself to Sir Despard, but he is now virtuous and must keep his vow to Margaret, who is kneeling at his feet:

MARGARET.   Oh joy! with newly kindled rapture warmed
            I kneel before you!
SIR DESPARD. I once disliked you: now that I've reformed,
            How I adore you![23]

There is only one person left for Rose: Richard, whom she had bereft of love. So she shall now be his! Robin has the witch's curse on his head, the effects of evil are already building up inside him, his face becoming contorted, and he falls senseless to the ground.

The setting for Act 2 is the picture-gallery in Ruddigore Castle. The walls are covered with full-length portraits of the baronets of Ruddigore from the time of James I – the first being that of Sir Rupert Murgatroyd, alluded to in the legend; the last, that of the most recently deceased baronet, Sir Roderic.

Robin and Old Adam enter melodramatically. They are greatly changed in appearance, Robin wearing the haggard aspect of a guilty roué; Adam, that of the wicked steward to such a man! Robin is quite unfit for a life of villainy, and he relies on Adam to think up suitable crimes for him to commit. When it is known Richard and Rose are arriving at the castle to obtain permission to marry, Adam suggests poisoning their beer. Robin will have none of it, he may be a bad Bart, but not as bad a Bart as that! Perhaps he will tie Richard up to a post with a good stout rope and make hideous faces at him. When Richard and Rose enter with the chorus of bridesmaids, Robin tries out his ferocity:

'Know ye not that I have those within my call who, at my lightest bidding, would immure ye in an uncomfortable dungeon?'[24]

Richard had come prepared for this sort of thing and foils Robin by producing a Union Jack, a flag that none dare defy. All instantly kneel. Rose decides to plead with Robin:

'Sir Ruthven, have pity. In my book of etiquette the case of a maiden about to be wedded to one who unexpectedly turns out to be a baronet with a curse on his head, is not considered.'[25]

As there had been a time when he loved Rose madly, there was surely nothing selfish in his love, and Robin can prove that by now giving his consent to her marrying Richard, his dearest friend. Robin yields and all go to seek out the parson for the wedding.

Robin is left alone and wonders if his ghostly ancestors will be satisfied with his first week of crime. He addresses the pictures and begs them to look kindly upon his efforts. All darkens for a moment, and when there is light again the portraits, the painted emblems of a race, all accurst in days of yore, are seen to have become animated and the figures step from their frames and march round the kneeling Robin and show their obvious disapproval.

> Baronet of Ruddigore,
>   Last of our accursed line,
> Down upon the oaken floor –
>   Down upon those knees of thine.
>   Coward, poltroon, shaker, squeamer,
>   Blockhead, sluggard, dullard, dreamer,
>   Shirker, shuffler, crawler, creeper,
>   Sniffler, snuffler, wailer, weeper,
>   Earthworm, maggot, tadpole, weevil!
>   Set upon thy course of evil
>   Lest the King of Spectre-Land
>   Set on thee his grisly hand![26]

The spectre of Sir Roderic descends from his frame. He has a sterner, more relentless brow than the rest, but he assures Robin that he and his fellow ghosts are really a much jollier crew than might be supposed, and he gives the details of the spectres' holiday, the ghosts' high noon, which takes place 'When the night wind howls in the chimney cowls, and the bat in the moonlight flies' among the tombstones and lasts through the night until the cockcrow brings their merry-making to an end. The atmosphere of such revelling is grim indeed, 'As the sob of the breeze sweeps over the trees and the mists lie low on the fen', and the ghosts and their ladye-toasts exchange kisses, perhaps, on their lantern chaps, and wish each other a grisly, grim 'good-night!'

Sir Roderic subjects Robin to an interrogation about his crimes, and he is appalled at the lukewarmness of it all; feeble efforts like making a false income tax return, and forging a will, which happened to be his own, forging one of Adam's cheques, and disinheriting his unbegotten son. Only the shooting of a fox passes muster. No, something really dastardly must be accomplished, such as carrying off a lady. Robin is horrified at the suggestion.

'Certainly not, on any account. I've the greatest respect for ladies, and I would not do anything of the kind for worlds. No, no. I'm not that kind of baronet, I assure you!'[27]

If that is his attitude, then the agonies must commence. The ghosts make passes across him and Robin writhes in agony, but they ask Robin's pardon for doing so, and return back to their frames. Adam is quickly sent off to the nearest village to abduct the first lady he sees, and Robin is left to scour through *The Times* for suitable daily crimes to commit; 'a Baronet's rank is exceedingly nice,/But the title's uncommonly dear at the price!'[28]

When Robin has gone Sir Despard and Margaret arrive, dressed in sober black, in strong contrast to their former costumes. It is clear a reformation has taken place: Sir Despard has given up all his wild proceedings, and Margaret's taste for a wandering life is waning. They are now running a national school and have been married a week. However, Margaret fears she might relapse into madness again, a fear for which she has a possible remedy, as she tells her husband:

'If I could hit upon some word for you to use whenever I am about to relapse – some word that teems with hidden meaning – like "Basingstoke" – it might recall me to my saner self. For after all, I am only Mad Margaret! Daft Meg! Poor Peg! He! he! he!'[29]

'Basingstoke' is needed at once, for Robin enters, and the two try to persuade him to forsake his profligate ways. Furthermore, Sir Despard explains that as Robin had been the rightful heir to the baronetcy for the ten years he had held the title, Robin was guilty of all Sir Despard's crimes, including jilting Margaret. Robin then decides that he will defy his ancestors, he will refuse to obey their behests, and court death instead, so as to atone in some degree for all the infamy he has now inherited.

> My eyes are fully open to my awful situation –
> I shall go at once to Roderic and make him an oration.
> I shall tell him I've recovered my forgotten moral senses,
> And I don't care two-pence halfpenny for any consequences.

Now I do not want to perish by the sword or by the dagger,
But a martyr may indulge a little pardonable swagger,
And a word or two of compliment my vanity would flatter,
But I've got to die to-morrow, so it really doesn't matter![30]

Margaret and Sir Despard depart just as Adam arrives, having abducted Dame Hannah; it has been a hard task, for she had fought like a tiger-cat. Robin is full of apologies: this was not what he had intended at all. Dame Hannah berates Robin for his lack of chivalry. She, Stephen Trusty's daughter, is prepared to fight; she takes a formidable dagger from one of the armed figures in the gallery and throws her own much smaller dagger to Robin. Robin is so frightened by her fierce glare that he calls out to Sir Roderic for help, but as Sir Roderic descends from his frame and sees Hannah there is immediate recognition. She is his 'Little Nannikin!' and he is her 'Roddy-doddy'! The two were once lovers and engaged to be married. How could Robin have been so callous in his choice? He is told to leave them alone.

SIR RODERIC. This is a strange meeting after so many years!

HANNAH. Very. I thought you were dead.

SIR RODERIC. I am. I died ten years ago.

HANNAH. And are you pretty comfortable?

SIR RODERIC. Pretty well – that is – yes, pretty well.

HANNAH. You don't deserve to be, for I loved you all the while, dear, and it made me dreadfully unhappy to hear of all your goings on, you bad, bad boy![31]

Soon Hannah is weeping on Roderic's bossom; she is once again the little flower sheltering beneath her 'old oak tree'.

Suddenly Robin rushes in full of excitement, and everyone else from Rederring follows. An idea has just occurred to him, which might provide the perfect solution to all their problems: since a baronet of Ruddigore can only die through refusing to commit his daily crime, refusing to commit a daily crime is tantamount to suicide, but suicide is itself a crime, so Sir Roderic should never have died at all! Sir Roderic sees the point immediately: 'Then I'm practically alive!'[32] He is now free to marry Hannah; Robin will marry his Rose, and Richard, the honest British sailor, will be happy with the bread and cheese and kisses of Zorah, while Sir Despard and Margaret will toddle off to settle, far away from sin and sorrow, in Basingstoke!

Ruddigore seemed to have a jinx on it from the start. George

Grossmith, who was playing the part of Robin Oakapple, was taken ill
during the first week, but his indisposition gave a chance for his
understudy, Henry Lytton, who eventually succeeded him in all the
major Gilbert and Sullivan roles. Rutland Barrington recalled that on
the opening night the second act dragged so dreadfully that the
malcontents in the gallery were yelling out: 'Take it away – give us
back *The Mikado*!' However, there were highlights, or perhaps one
should say lowlights, for the moment when the ghostly figures came
out of their frames was most effective. It was, of course, an idea
Gilbert had used before in his play *Ages Ago* performed at the Gallery
of Illustration in 1869.

By general consent the performance of Jessie Bond as Mad
Margaret was the greatest achievement. Gilbert had written the part
specially for her knowing that she was thinking of leaving the
company in order to concentrate on straight acting parts, though she
was quite clearly best suited to comedy. François Cellier wrote that
the character of Mad Margaret was played with such conviction that
the famous authority on mental disorders, Mr Forbes Winslow,
wrote a congratulatory letter to Miss Bond and inquired where she
had found the model from which she had studied, and so faithfully
copied the phases of insanity.

Jessie Bond herself recalled strange occurrence while playing her part:

One night when *Ruddigore* had already been running some months, I had
the most extraordinary feeling that the man playing with me was not
Barrington, but another actor who was taking the part of Sir Despard
Murgatroyd in a provincial company that was playing in Newcastle that same
night. The illusion was to me so impressive that I spoke of it to others, and the
strangest thing of all was that the actor in Newcastle wrote to me that he had
had exactly the same experience, a vivid impression that I was playing the
part of Mad Margaret with him, instead of the actress who actually did so.[33]

This experience was much talked about, and led to a correspon-
dence in the press. It was, surely, one of 'the evil chances' of
Ruddigore.

Gilbert always considered the libretto to be one of his best, though
he agreed in later life that he had probably given it an unfortunate
name. A modern audience does not worry about that in the slightest,
and *Ruddigore*, the tenth Savoy Opera, still gives great delight, and it
was even performed with great gusto by the Oxford University
Gilbert and Sullivan Society in 1992.

10

The Merryman and his Maid

1887–1889

Ruddigore turned out to be much more successful than anyone had predicted, and it ran for 288 performances, far longer than either *The Sorcerer* or *Princess Ida*. In March 1887 it had become popular enough to be the subject of a burlesque presented at Toole's Theatre, the old Charing Cross Theatre renamed by its new owner, John Laurence Toole. This musical parody in one act was called *Ruddy George; or Robin Redbreast*, a pretty feeble show, but it was well received by those who had seen the original, and the characters of Sir Gilbert, Sir Arther and Sir Doyley(sic) Rougegorge caused some merriment, and their likenesses could be easily recognised in the portrait scene!

Nevertheless, a successor to *Ruddigore* was soon called for, and again the dreaded 'lozenge' loomed large in Gilbert's mind; he knew the audience would love the idea, but Sullivan was still having nothing of it, although he tried to placate Gilbert as far as possible. The problem was exactly the same as before: Sullivan, after setting ten of Gilbert's topsy-turvy librettos, however successfully, yearned for grand opera. In spite of the obvious delight he had given his audiences with his light pieces he felt he was not really doing what he should be doing, and such comedy was an abuse of his talent: he was not the only person who thought so. It would not be long before the Queen herself after attending a performance of *The Golden Legend* at the Albert Hall was wishing dear Sir Arthur would write a grand opera, he would do it so well.

There was another royal command. The year 1887 was the Queen's Jubilee, and Sullivan was asked by the Prince of Wales to set the poet laureate's 'Ode for the Opening of the Colonial and Indian Exhibition', a Jubilee Ode specially written by Tennyson, which might be performed as part of the ceremony in late June when Her Majesty would lay the foundation stone of the Imperial Institute, in South Kensington. Sullivan took great pains over the music to achieve the right balance between the spirit of majesty and the greatness of Empire; in this he felt he had been successful and the music was 'met with universal approbation', as the Prince of Wales expressed it when he wrote to say how much the Queen had been pleased with it. The Ode had been a short piece; it had taken him only four hours to compose, but such a grand theme had been preferable to Gilbert's 'lozenge', something Sullivan did his best at all times to forget.

No, there was no doubt in Sullivan's mind that his light opera days had come to an end. Almost any composer could produce such stuff. If only Gilbert could see things his way, Sullivan thought, and produce a more serious libretto. A switch of emphasis was what was needed.

Gilbert for his part considered himself, as always, the better judge of what the public wanted. While Sullivan might well know what pleased the people in the boxes and the stalls, Gilbert knew how to play to the gallery. If one were to compare the position of a dramatic author with a caterer who has to supply one dish of which all members of every class of society are invited to partake, it was no use giving everyone crème de volaille. It might please the epicure in the stalls, but irritate the costermonger in the gallery. 'If he supplies nothing but baked sheep's heads, the costermonger will be delighted, but the epicure will be disgusted.'[1]

Gilbert thought the most acceptable dish might be rump steak and oyster sauce, a capital thing in its way, and it may be taken as a type of the class of piece which would be most likely to succeed. 'It does not call for a very high order of merit on the part of the chef, but it requires a good deal of practical skill nevertheless'[2], he told a reporter from the *New York Tribune*.

By the summer there was still no definite new opera in sight. Instead D'Oyly Carte made plans to follow *Ruddigore* with a revival of HMS *Pinafore*, with more or less its original cast, although Rosina Brandram would now sing the part of Little Buttercup. Gilbert was keen to drill the cast, and he redesigned the sets and costumes, but about his next plot he remained intractable, quite determined to convince Sullivan of the sense in his decision. He revised the lozenge plot and read it out one evening after dinner. Sullivan recorded in his diary that the characters seemed to him to be mere puppets and not human at all. It was impossible to feel sympathy with a single person, and he could not see his way to setting the libretto in its present form; besides he was too ill to devote any time to it.

It was while this state of uncertainty prevailed that Gilbert's imagination was fired quite unexpectedly, and in a direction more to Sullivan's taste. He was waiting for a train on Uxbridge Station when he noticed an advertisement for the Tower Furnishing Company which showed the figure of a Beefeater dressed in the traditional Tudor costume with the Tower of London in the background. Gilbert immediately saw the possibility of using such a figure.

'I thought a Beefeater would make a picturesque central figure for another Savoy opera, and my intention was to give it a modern setting, with the characteristics and development of burlesque – and make it another *Sorcerer*, but then I decided to make a romantic and dramatic piece, and to put it back in Elizabethan times.'[3]

When Sullivan learnt that the lozenge-plot had once again been put away he was much relieved, and he was delighted when on Christmas morning Gilbert and Carte came to Queen's Mansions for a read-through of the plot. The working title at the time was 'The Tower of London'. Sullivan recorded his pleasure with the idea in his diary. It was a 'pretty story, no topsy-turvydom, very human and funny also'.[4]

This opera Sullivan would set, but it was going to take many months to complete. Nevertheless, with the plot decided, and with HMS *Pinafore* still running to respectably full houses, the three partners felt happy to stage two further revivals until the new piece was ready. In March 1888 *Pinafore* would be followed by *The Pirates of Penzance*, which ran for eighty performances, and in June *The Mikado* returned to play throughout the summer. It closed after 116 performances on 29 September, leaving three clear days to prepare the theatre for the new production to open on 3 October.

Gilbert took particular pains as usual to achieve authenticity. He spent many hours at the Tower making sketches of the building and the Beefeaters' uniform; he read as many books as he could about the period, particularly Harrison Ainsworth's *The Tower of London* published in 1840, a very popular historical novel. He had two of his own ballads in mind, and he borrowed a few ideas from William Wallace's opera *Maritana*. Some might agree with *Punch* that he borrowed more than a few.

'Had the opera been at the Saveloy Theatre instead of the Savoy

Theatre, and written by two unknown collaborateurs, say Sulibert and Gillivan, wouldn't the virtuously-indignant critics have been down on the librettist for not informing the public that the plot was founded on that of *Maritana*.'[5]

The similarity was obvious, but Gilbert's work was announced as 'new and original', and the result of all this careful borrowing and piecing-together was *The Yeomen of the Guard*, destined to be one of Gilbert's favourite pieces.

'I thought the *Yeomen* was the best thing we had done,'[6] he said, and many people would agree with him. However, less than a month before opening there was still doubt about the opera's title. On 13 September Gilbert wrote to Sullivan; 'The more I think of it, the more convinced I am that "The Beefeaters" is the name for the new piece. It is a good, sturdy, solid name, conjuring up picturesque associations and clearly telling its own tale at one.'[7]

He went on to say that 'The Tower' as a title would be nothing, and only a few knew that Beefeaters were called Tower Wardens. There is no doubt the title he did finally choose was the best, although it was strictly speaking inaccurate, just as he had been inaccurate in referring to Tower Warders as Wardens! The Yeomen of the Guard had been appointed in 1485 by Henry VII as members of the royal household to form part of the royal train at banquets and on other grand occasions. The Warders of the Tower were appointed later by Edward VI and because they wore the same uniform as the Yeomen they were known as Yeomen Extraordinary of the Guard. There is no reason to doubt Gilbert knew this and he was wise to leave out their extraordinariness.

The action of *The Yeomen of the Guard* is all set on Tower Green some time in the sixteenth century. Phoebe Meryll, the daughter of Sergeant Meryll, is sitting at her spinning wheel. She sighs as she spins, because she is in love, but not, it seems, with Wilfred Shadbolt, the Head Jailor and Assistant Tormentor, who approaches her. Shadbolt enjoys his professional duties, keeping the locks, chains, bolts and bars in good order, making sure the Little Ease is sufficiently comfortable, and the racks, pincers and thumbscrews all in good working order. He is particularly looking forward to the execution due to take place at half past seven that very evening. Colonel Fairfax, a handsome, bearded soldier of distinction, has been condemned to death for sorcery, for dealings with the devil. The previous night he had only just escaped death when there was a fire in the Beauchamp Tower. Phoebe, who had seen him every day during the past weeks taking his exercise on the Beauchamp Tower, is convinced of Fairfax's innocence, though aware he is a student of alchemy and science, and still hopes for a reprieve. She carries her spinning wheel away, leaving Wilfred in a fit of jealousy that turns his interior into boiling lead.

A crowd of men and women comes in, followed by Yeomen of the Guard: 'Tower Warders/Under orders,/Gallant pikemen, valiant sworders.'[8] These were all warriors once, but now in the autumn of their lives they rest in the 'ample clover' of the Tower, though should their loved land be invaded they are fully prepared to face 'a foreign foe/As in days of long ago'.

The crowd disperses and Dame Carruthers, the Housekeeper of the Tower, tells the Corporal she has been busy dealing with the chaos the fire has caused and how the prisoners had been crammed into a cell six feet square, but that now Fairfax is to be removed to the Cold Harbour to have his last hour alone with his confessor. The Corporal, who had served under Fairfax, vouches for his bravery, and Phoebe reveals that 'the bravest, the handsomest, and the best young gentleman in England'[9] has twice saved her father's life. Dame Carruthers also feels pity for the prisoner, but her loyalty to the Tower and its traditions knows no bounds, though she admits that if all who had dealings with the devil were beheaded, 'there'd be busy doings on Tower Green'.[10] She had been born in the old keep and she has grown grey in it, and there she hopes to die and be buried because 'there's not a stone in its walls that is not as dear to me as my own right hand'.[11]

> There's a legend on its brow
> That is eloquent to me,
> And it tells of duty done and duty doing.
>
> The screw may twist and the rack may turn,
> And men may bleed and men may burn.
> On London town and its golden hoard
> I keep my silent watch and ward![12]

When Phoebe is left on her own, she is joined by her father, Sergeant Meryll. There is one possible hope for Fairfax: Meryll's son, Leonard, who has already shown himself to be a soldier of exceptional ability, is due to join the Tower Warders, and may bring a reprieve with him from Windsor. However, the young man arrives empty-handed, and his father makes a quick decision. No one knows Leonard, and his arrival has hardly been noticed, so if he goes into hiding, and Phoebe can steal the cell key from Wilfred Shadbolt's belt, Fairfax could be dressed in a Yeoman's uniform and imperson-ate the new recruit, Leonard Meryll. A brilliant idea, yet the scheme is rash and may well fail. Leonard takes the money his father offers and, embracing him and his little sister, he hurries off to hide.

Fairfax is led in on his way to the Cold Harbour Tower. He is greeted by his old friend, Sir Richard Cholmondeley, the Lieutenant of the Tower, who is impressed by the prisoner's calm disposure. Fairfax says that he would rather have life than death, but death when it comes doth so in a punctual and business-like fashion. When he sees Phoebe's distress he comforts her and is pleased to see Meryll. 'We are soldiers, and we know how to die, thou and I. Take my word for it, it is easier to die well than live well – for, in sooth, I have tried both.'[13]

> Is life a boon?
>> If, so, it must befall
>> That Death, whene'er he call,
> Must call too soon.
>> Though fourscore years he give,
>> Yet one would pray to live
> Another moon![14]

On the other hand if life should be a thorn, then Man is well done with it.

Such bravery overpowers Phoebe and she is led away weeping. Fairfax asks Sir Richard for his help. He has been accused of sorcery quite falsely by his kinsman, Sir Clarence Poltwhistle, one of the Secretaries of State, in order that he might succeed to the Fairfax estate, which devolves to him should Fairfax die unmarried. This looks inevitable, unless Fairfax were to marry. The question is, to whom? Not that that would matter in his situation.

'Coming Death hath made of me a true and chivalrous knight, who holds all womankind in such esteem that the oldest, and the meanest, and the worst-favoured of them is good enough for him.'[15] Sir Richard says he will see what can be done, as Fairfax is led away. 'He is a brave fellow, and it is a pity he should die. Now, how to find him a bride at such short notice? Well the task should be easy!'[16]

It is even easier than Sir Richard thought, for at that moment Jack Point and Elsie Maynard, a strolling actor and singer, arrive on the scene hotly pursued by a crowd of men and women. The two are very frightened, although Jack Point assumes the appearance of self-possession. He explains that as they themselves are merry folk their wish is for all to be merry. 'For, look you, there is humour in all things, and the truest philosophy is that which teaches us to find it and to make the most of it.'[17]

The mob crowds round even more tightly and one man tries to grab Elsie, who swiftly rebuffs him with a 'Hands off!' Jack Point launches into a typically Shakespearian Fool's quibble on the words 'Hands off.' Then Elsie suggests that they entertain the crowd with the singing farce 'The Merryman and his Maid', which they proceed to sing and dance charmingly. The mobsters are so enthusiastic at the song's end that they wish for a kiss for the pretty maid, even 'a kiss all round'. Faced with this prospect Elsie draws a dagger to fend the men off. She is just about to be overpowered by one man when the Lieutenant arrives with the guard and the crowd falls back.

Elsie explains that their entertainment had been met with discourtesy. The Lieutenant commands the mob to be dispersed. Elsie and Jack introduce themselves. Elsie's mother, old Bridget Maynard, who usually travels with them, has fallen ill with a fever, and is in bed. The two of them had come to the Tower in the hope of picking up some silver, to buy an electuary for her. The Lieutenant sees that Elsie is exactly what he is looking for. He offers her a hundred crowns to be married to a 'worthy, but unhappy gentleman, who is to be beheaded in an hour on this very spot'. Jack is sceptical about this arrangement: he is not yet wedded to Elsie himself but hopes to be, for time works wonders. However, the hundred crowns is very tempting, and besides Elsie will be a widow after an hour of marriage, so he agrees.

> Though as a general rule of life
> I don't allow my promised wife,
> My lovely bride that is to be,
> To marry anyone but me,
>   Yet if the fee is promptly paid.
>   And he, in well earned grave,
>   Within the hour is fully laid.
>   My objection I will waive!
>   Yes, objection I will waive![18]

The Lieutenant whispers to Wilfred, who has entered, Elsie's eyes are bound with a handkerchief, and she is led off towards the Cold Harbour Tower. The Lieutenant then tells Jack he has need of a jester himself, and is prepared to take him on. Jack hopes that he will have better employment than his last, which had been as jester to the Archbishop of Canterbury, who had whipped him and set him in the stocks for 'a scurril rogue'. The Lieutenant takes Jack off to discuss the terms of employment, and Elsie is led back from the wedding. Wilfred removes the bandage from her eyes. She looks at the ring on her finger, reflecting that it has only brought her gold and sadness, and although she had not seen her husband he is surely too young and brave to die. She leaves the stage sadly.

Wilfred is alone for a while. It is an odd freak, he thinks, for a dying man and his confessor to be closeted alone with a strange singing bird. He would have spied through the keyhole, but someone had stopped it up. His keyhole!

Phoebe and Meryll creep in behind unnoticed. Phoebe comes forward and begins to charm Wilfred, while she surreptitiously steals the bunch of keys from his belt. She hands the keys to her father, who is still unseen by Wilfred. Phoebe continues her attentiveness and teases Wilfred into thinking he has a chance of marrying her. Soon Meryll returns with the keys, and once Phoebe has attached them back on to Wilfred's belt her manner changes immediately. She is not Wilfred's bride!

Meryll comes from the Tower cautiously. He marvels over Phoebe's subtlety. 'What a helpless ninny is a love-sick man! He is but a lute in a woman's hands – she plays upon him whatever tune she will.'[19] Fairfax enters wearing a Yeoman's uniform, and he is now clean-shaven. He thanks Meryll for the great risk he has taken, the latter checks the new recruit's uniform, his ruff, his sword, and hands him his halberd. He takes care to remind Fairfax that from now on he is Leonard Meryll!

The Yeomen of the Guard march in to greet their new companion. They have heard of Leonard's bravery on the battlefield. Phoebe rushes in and embraces Fairfax as though he were her brother. Fairfax is puzzled, but he soon realises that Leonard Meryll must have a sister. 'How you have grown! I did not recognise you!'[20] He also learns that Phoebe is rather less than more betrothed to Wilfred. Wilfred commends Phoebe to her 'brother's' fraternal care.

The bell of St Peter's begins to toll. The crowd enters; the block is brought on to the stage, and the Headsman takes his place. The Yeomen of the Guard form up. the Lieutenant enters, and tells off Fairfax and two others to bring the prisoner to execution.

> The prisoner comes to meet his doom;
> The block, the headsman, and the tomb.
> The funeral bell begins to toll –
> May heaven have mercy on his soul![21]

Fairfax and the two other Yeomen return from the Tower in great excitement. The prisoner's cell is empty! The prisoner free? Who could have helped him to escape? It must have been the work of enchantment! Elsie realises her own situation. 'Oh, woe is me! I am his wife, and he is free!'[22] Jack Point is likewise anxious:

> Whate'er betide
> You are his bride
> And I am left
> Alone bereft!
> Yes woe is me, I rather think![23]

Elsie faints into Fairfax's arms; all the Yeomen and the populace rush off in different directions to hunt for the fugitive, leaving only the Headsman on the stage, and Elsie insensible in Fairfax's arms.

It is the same scene two days later, but by moonlight. The women led by Dame Carruthers have gathered together to mock the Yeomen because the prisoner is still free, in spite of the most thorough search.

When all have departed Jack Point enters. He is in low spirits; he is finding it difficult to please his new master. Wilfred Shadbolt is also in low spirits, and is taunted by Jack as a 'jailor that jailed not, or that jailed, if jail he did, so unjailoryly that 'twas but jerry-jailing, or jailing in joke'.[24] Such jesting, it turns out, is just what Wilfred envies. He has the ambition to become a professional jester himself, and asks Jack to help him. Jack reveals the secret of Elsie's marriage to Fairfax and persuades Wilfred to swear that he has shot the escaping prisoner with an arquebus as he was crossing the river. He had seen Fairfax sink, but had seen no more. If Wilfred will swear to this, Jack will help him to become 'the very Archbishop of jesters, and that in two days time!' 'I will teach thee all my original songs, my self-constructed riddles, my own ingenious paradoxes; nay, more, I will reveal to thee sources whence I get them.'[25]

Wilfred agrees to the bargain. It will, of course, release Elsie from her marriage too, and leave her free for Jack to marry!

Fairfax, still disguised as Leonard Meryll, is pleased to have escaped death. Perhaps he should now run away altogether, but he is held back by the thought of his unknown bride. He is worried too about Elsie Maynard, but he does not as yet know she is his bride. He discusses the matter with Sergeant Meryll, and hears that Dame Carruthers has nursed Elsie in Meryll's quarters and has used the opportunity to pursue Meryll whom she has wanted to marry for years, the old witch. Meryll has shunned her like the plague. 'Another day of it and she would have married me! Good Lord, here she is again!'[26] Meryll begins to hurry off, but is intercepted.

Dame Carruthers is accompanied by her niece, Kate. Naturally thinking she is speaking to Leonard Meryll, she warns him to have nothing to do with Elsie Maynard, and reveals how the girl had spoken in her sleep about the marriage, the hundred crowns, and the husband who would die in an hour.

> Strange adventure! Maiden wedded
> To a groom she's never seen –
> Never, never, never seen!
> Groom about to be beheaded,
> In an hour on Tower Green!
> Tower, Tower, Tower Green!
> Groom in dreary dungeon lying,
> Groom as good as dead, or dying,
> For a pretty maiden sighing –
> Pretty maid of seventeen!
> Seven, seven, seventeen![27]

Fairfax now knows that Elsie is his wife – he might have done worse with his eyes open! Soon he is given the opportunity to test Elsie's true feelings, and he attempts to woo her. Surprised that the man she thinks to be Leonard should declare his love for her, Elsie, who is very much attracted by him, has to tell him her secret. 'My husband is none other than Colonel Fairfax!'[28] However, Fairfax continues to press his suit: 'We will be married tomorrow, and thou shalt be the happiest wife in England!'[29] Elsie is horrified.

'Master Leonard! I am amazed! Is it thus that brave soldiers speak to poor girls? Oh, for shame, for shame! I am wed – not the less because I love not my husband. I am a wife, sir, and I have a duty, and

– oh, sir! thy words terrify me – they are not honest – they are wicked words, and unworthy of thy great and brave heart! Oh, shame upon thee! Shame upon thee!'[30]

Fairfax has heard what he needed to know, and he is about to admit he has been testing her when a shot is heard. Sergeant Meryll rushes in. What can this mean? A shot from an arquebus from the wharf, and at such an hour? Is an enemy approaching? What danger is at hand? The Lieutenant arrives and Jack Point and Wilfred give their explanation. Fairfax has been shot, and it is certain that he's very, very dead! The Lieutenant orders the river to be dragged: the body must be found. Wilfred, the hero of the hour, is carried off shoulder-high.

All depart except Elsie, Jack, Fairfax and Phoebe. Jack assures the weeping Elsie that Fairfax was but a pestilent fellow, and as he had to die he might just as well have died by being shot as any other way. He had made a good death. How could Jack be sure the escaping man was Fairfax? Oh, he had seen him, and he had 'a plaguey, ill-favoured face too. A very hang-dog face – a felon face – a face to fright the headsman himself and make him strike awry.'[31]

On hearing this Phoebe and Fairfax laugh, and Fairfax vows that if he shall ever come to life again Jack Point shall pay for his remarks. Yet in Jack's lying book Elsie is free to marry him. When Fairfax sees Jack's clumsy attempts at wooing he pushes him aside and offers to give him a lesson in how it should be done. The effect is so passionate that Phoebe is smitten by jealousy, so much so that when she is left alone, and Wilfred arrives, she tells him that she loves Leonard Meryll, but that Leonard now loves Elsie and intends to marry her. Even Wilfred is not too dim-witted to see that something must be wrong. Leonard Meryll is surely Phoebe's brother, that is if he is not the accursed Fairfax! Phoebe has given the secret away, and Wilfred realises that she knows he has been lying about the shooting. The two make a bargain: each must remain silent, and to make sure of Wilfred, Phoebe consents to be his wife: 'Thou art a very brute,' she says, 'but even brutes must marry, I suppose.'[32]

At that moment the real Leonard Meryll arrives with the news of Fairfax's reprieve. The document had been signed two days earlier, but Secretary Poltwhistle had maliciously kept it back. It is now in the Lieutenant's possession. Phoebe is overcome with joy: the Colonel is free. She kisses Leonard, much to Wilfred's amazement. This is her brother? Another brother! Are there any more of them?

If there are she should produce them at once and let him know the worst! Phoebe admits she had been deceitful before, but now she will be Wilfred's 'very own' and marry him in a year, or two, or three. Surely that is enough for him? Sergeant Meryll hurries in excitedly, followed by Dame Carruthers who remains unobserved. Has Phoebe heard the brave news? He sees Phoebe's predicament: Wilfred has discovered the secret and she must pay the price for his silence. When Wilfred and Phoebe have gone Dame Carruthers comes forward; she has, of course, heard everything, with the result that Meryll must buy her silence also by giving her his hand in marriage!

The Yeomen and the women enter in the brightness of a summer morning. Elsie is dressed for her wedding to the man she still thinks is Leonard Meryll. She is sad at the prospect, but resigned. Phoebe and Dame Carruthers are with her. There is a flourish as the Lieutenant arrives with good news. Elsie's husband is alive: he is free, and has come to claim his bride that very day!

Fairfax enters, handsomely dressed and attended by other gentlemen. He sternly claims Elsie as his bride, but he is able to conceal his identity until the very last moment. When Elsie recognises him as 'Leonard', she is overjoyed. At this moment Jack Point enters. He makes a last vain attempt to win back Elsie's heart by singing the song of the Merryman and his Maid, but it is all too late. As Fairfax and Elsie happily embrace, Jack falls insensible at their feet.

The part of Jack Point was the last George Grossmith played at the Savoy, and it was generally thought to have been his best. We have no way of telling. Of course, a jester traditionally combined humour with pathos, and Gilbert and Grossmith were well aware of that, but the critics could not decide whether the opera was meant to be serious or funny, neither did it seem certain to the critic in *Punch* what the cast itself thought, with the result that with the exception of Jessie Bond, as Phoebe, and Rosina Brandram, as Dame Carruthers, none of the actors played with conviction:

'They seem uncertain as to the character of the piece – is it serious, or isn't it? And if it isn't, are they to keep the joke to themselves, or let the audience into the secret? Mr Grossmith, with an occasional wink at the house, seems to incline to the latter view, and no doubt when he has exaggerated his dances, developed his comic business, and made the part quite his own, it will go with roars.'[33]
Punch also thought the opera too long: 'My summary is this: Cut at

least twenty minutes out of the First Act; take a quarter of an hour out of the Second Act, so as to finish by eleven.'[34]

It was hoped that the actors might be given 'carte blanche ("a very D'Oyly Carte task", as the Jester would say) and go in for the old larks of Mikado & Co, and the Savoyards will feel themselves once more at home, and their kind friends in front will be satisfied with everybody generally at the House of Savoy.'[35]

Gilbert himself had been desperately worried right up to the opening. At the very last moment when the orchestral players were already assembled Gilbert pleaded with Sullivan to leave out one of the sentimental songs sung by Richard Temple as Meryll. Earlier in the day he had told Sullivan by letter that in his opinion unless Act I was cut considerably the success of the opera would be 'most seriously imperilled'. If this was a 'professedly comic opera', then the mood of the music for the first few songs was too sombre. Sullivan was not pleased, but he finally agreed after the first performance to leave out the Meryll song. It seems Gilbert was right about the length, and his apprehension understandable. In his anxiety to please Sullivan he had subdued his lyrics, though in several instances, as in 'Is life a boon?', he had produced something more sublime. *The Times* expressed the situation admirably: 'Mr Gilbert is in his way a man of genius, and even at his worst is a head and shoulders above the ordinary librettist. In the present instance he has not written a good play but the lyrics are suave and good to sing and, wedded to Sir Arthur Sullivan's melodies, they will no doubt find their way to many a home where English song is sung.'[36]

Jessie Bond has recalled how jittery Gilbert had been on that opening night:

I remember the first night of *The Yeomen* very well. Gilbert was always dreadfully overwrought on these occaisons, and this time he was almost beside himself with nervousness and excitement. He and Sullivan had both put their very best into the play, and he was more than usually anxious that all should go well. I am afraid he made himself a perfect nuisance behind the scenes, and did his best, poor fellow, to upset us all.

It will be remembered that the curtain rises on Phoebe alone at her spinning wheel; and Gilbert kept fussing about, 'Oh, Jessie, are you sure you're all right?' – Jessie this – Jessie that – until I was almost as demented as he was.

At last I turned on him savagely. 'For heaven's sake, Mr Gilbert, go away and leave me alone, or I shan't be able to sing a note!' He gave me a final frenzied hug, and vanished.[37]

In fact he left the Savoy altogether and hurried to the Drury Lane Theatre to sit through another historical piece, *The Armada*, but he was back with his own cast again in time for the final curtain, and yet another rapturous reception.

The ovation *The Yeomen of the Guard* received from the audience that night was something for Gilbert to remember, and it would perhaps provide some consolation for the depressing episode that took place in the following month when his four-act play *Brantinghame Hall* opened at the St James's Theatre. The thing was a complete flop, and it was viciously attacked by Clement Scott in the *Daily Telegraph*. Gilbert leapt to his own defence, but he was certainly unnerved:

'I will not disguise from you that your virulent attack upon my unfortunate play – an attack which has elicited dozens of letters of sympathy from absolute strangers – has had the effect of determining me to write no more for the stage.'[38]

He had tried to be honest and thorough in his determination to write original plays that should combine literary merit with an absolute freedom from coarseness and immorality, he said, and although he had certainly succeeded in the latter, it seemed he must have failed in the former. He was not prepared to expose himself to such insolent jibes in the future. He had written his last play. He was particularly upset for the cast: Rutland Barrington, who had now left the Savoy, Lewis Waller, and a young and beautiful actress, Julia Neilson, whose humiliation Gilbert considered worse than his own, as he told the newspaper's proprietor.

'If it be any additional satisfaction to you to know that in your determination to make your onslaught as thorough as possible, you have crushed the hope out of the life of a poor girl who, paralysed with nervousness, was appealing practically for the first time in her life – to the men who were to decide her destiny – you are most fully entitled to it.'[39]

If any good came out of the situation, it was that Barrington returned to the Savoy. Julia Neilson, of course, survived the onslaught, and Gilbert, although certainly hurt, was never a man to be silenced.

11

I am a Cypher in the Theatre

◦◦◦◦ 1889–1890 ◦◦◦◦

When Sullivan heard his music for *The Yeomen of the Guard* described as being on 'a higher plane', and as 'genuine English opera, the forerunner of many others', he was greatly encouraged. Here was indeed a breakthrough, and ironically he had Gilbert to thank for it, not that Sullivan himself thought of it quite like that. As far as he was concerned his part in the Savoy operas had been rather a hole-in-corner affair, the pieces had been hurried out for immediate financial advantage, and they were not in the same class as the grand designs he and Carte had already planned.

Even now Carte was overseeing two great building projects; the Savoy Hotel, adjoining the Savoy Theatre, which would open later in the year; and a completely new theatre on a site at the eastern end of Shaftesbury Avenue: this would be the Royal English Opera House, a building still in use today as the Palace Theatre, in Cambridge Circus. The foundation stone had been laid late in the previous year, 1887, by Carte's second wife, Helen. Sullivan was involved in many ways with all this: he was a director of both the hotel and the new theatre, and he had stood as Carte's best man at his wedding in the Savoy Chapel, when Carte, a widower, had married Helen Lenoir, for many years his most efficient and loyal secretary. Carte had promised Sullivan that if he were to compose a grand work, his would be the first to be performed at the new Opera House. The difficulty as ever seemed to be in making Gilbert share their point of view, since he was not involved in either of their building projects, though he was overseeing the building of a new theatre of his own.

On 9 January 1889 Sullivan called on Gilbert to explain his views about the future. He wanted to do some dramatic work on a larger musical scale, and he wished to do it with Gilbert if he would, but the music must occupy a more important position than in their other pieces. He told Gilbert he wished to get rid of the strongly marked rhythm, and rhymed couplets, and have words that would give a chance of developing musical effects. Furthermore he wanted a voice in the musical construction of the libretto. At the time Gilbert seemed to Sullivan to give his assent, but he had, in fact, given no definite commitment. He could not see why Sullivan could not write light and serious music at the same time as he had done in the past: both *The Martyr of Antioch* and *The Golden Legend* had been composed without forsaking light opera.

It was not long before Sullivan followed up his visit with a short letter telling Gilbert that he had now decided to devote all his energies to the composition of a grand opera, a work of dramatic and serious purpose, and this would have to be completed before he attempted anything else. He still hoped that Gilbert would write the libretto.

On 20 February Gilbert replied. He had thought carefully over Sullivan's predicament, and while he understood and sympathised with his desire to write Grand Opera, he did not believe such a piece would succeed at either the Savoy or at Carte's new theatre unless a much more powerful singing and acting company were got together than the company they now controlled. Moreover, to speak from his own selfish point of view, such an opera would afford him no chance of doing what he did best – the librettist of a grand opera is always swamped by the composer. No, anyone could write a good libretto for such a purpose, but Gilbert would be lost in it. He then went on to say he had doubted if the success of *The Yeomen of the Guard* was a justification for continuing in the same vein.

The success of the *Yeomen* – which is a step in the direction of serious opera – has not been so convincing as to warrant us in assuming that the public want something more earnest still. There is no doubt about it, the more reckless and irresponsible the libretto has been, the better the piece has succeeded – the pieces that have succeeded the least have been those in which a consistent story has been more or less consistently followed out. Personally, I prefer a consistent subject – such a subject as the *Yeomen* is far more congenial to my taste than the burlesque of *Iolanthe* or the *Mikado* – but I think we should be risking everything in writing more seriously still.[1]

Gilbert then makes a special plea: 'We have a name, jointly, for humorous work, tempered with occasional glimpses of earnest

183

drama. I think we should do unwisely if we left, altogether, the path which we have trodden together so long and so successfully.'²

However, if Sullivan was determined to write a serious work, Gilbert would not stand in his way, and he even suggested the name of a serious librettist, Julian Sturgis. Why not write a grand opera with him? There was also another important factor to consider: where in God's name would Sullivan find a grand opera soprano who could act?

Gilbert had argued the case as best he could. Surely the comic and the serious were not irreconcilable. He had seen how easily Sullivan seemed to have composed *The Martyr of Antioch* in the wake of *The Pirates of Penzance*. It would be madness to sever the connection with the Savoy: 'I can only say that I should do so with the profoundest reluctance and regret,'³ Gilbert wrote.

Sullivan did not reply to Gilbert's letter until 12 March: he was staying in Monte Carlo and had plans to visit Italy later in the month. He told Gilbert he had been greatly disappointed by the public's seeming indifference to *The Yeomen of the Guard*, since he had looked upon its success as opening out a large field for works of a more serious and romantic character. If this indifference meant a return to their former style of piece, he had to say, and with deep regret, that he could not do it. He continued:

I have lost the liking for writing comic opera, and entertain very grave doubts as to my power of doing it. You yourself have reproached me directly and indirectly with the seriousness of my music, fitted more for the Cathedral than the Comic Opera stage, and I cannot but feel that in very many cases the reproach is just. I have lost the necessary nerve for it, and it is not too much to say that it is distasteful to me. The types used over and over again (unavoidable in such a company as ours), the Grossmith part, the middle-aged woman with fading charms, cannot again be clothed with music by me. Nor can I again write to any wildly impossible plot in which there is not some human interest.⁴

Sullivan said he did not agree with Gilbert that the most successful of their ventures had been those in which the plot had been 'wild and irresponsible'. He considered *Patience* and *Mikado* to have had plots with a consistent story and mildly humorous, but worked out by human beings. However, the important thing was that they should make a decision and not argue. If Gilbert thought that in a serious opera he must more or less sacrifice himself, this was only what

Sullivan had been doing all the time and, what was more, he would have to continue doing so if they were to work on more comic operas, that is if they were to have any chance of success. This was because business and syllabic setting had to assume an importance which, however much they fettered the composer, could not be overlooked. He would be bound, in the interests of the piece, to give way.

What Sullivan wanted was to write a piece where the music was the first consideration – where words suggested music and did not govern it, and where music might intensify and emphasise the emotional effect of the words. Was it likely that Gilbert would agree? He still hoped so.

Now is there any 'modus vivendi' by which my requirements can be met, and which you can enter into willingly and without any detriment to your hearty interest in the piece? And will it not facilitate matters if you bear in mind that in September there will be very little of the old Savoy Company left? Grossmith goes; Barrington has gone. Temple wants to go, and Miss Ulmar must go ... Here, then we seem to be in an 'impasse', and unless you can solve the difficulty I don't see my way out of it.[5]

When he read thoughts like these Gilbert was filled with amazement and regret. He replied by return of post.

If you are really under the astounding impression that you have been effacing yourself during the last twelve years – and if you are in earnest when you say that you wish to write an opera with me in which 'the music shall be the first consideration' (by which I understand an opera in which the libretto, and consequently the librettist, must occupy a subordinate place) there is most certainly no 'modus vivendi' to be found that shall be satisfactory to both of us.

You are an adept in your profession, and I am an an adept in mine. If we meet, it must be as master and master – not as master and servant.[6]

Sullivan was now staying at the Hotel Danieli, in Venice. He had time to think. One thing must not be ignored and that was money. The financial advantage of writing another comic piece with Gilbert for the Savoy could not be denied. Although the present situation with Gilbert was disagreeable, it would hardly have arisen in the same way if the previous five-year contract between the three partners, whereby a new opera could be called for at six months' notice, had not expired. Besides, Sullivan knew that Gilbert was right when he said it was possible to compose serious and comic pieces at more or less the same time, so that a further Savoy opera would not hinder a more exalted venture. Nevertheless it was important to set out clearly to Carte what was passing through his mind and, if possible, gain his support in the argument: to this end he wrote at length on 26 March. It was a provocative letter, and Sullivan invited Carte to repeat its contents to Gilbert.

Gilbert had utterly ignored all his arguments and contentions, Sullivan said, and he had only written 'a few lines of huffy resentment at one or two of his sentences', with the result that they were no nearer a solution of the question than before. Neither did he feel he could reply to Gilbert's letter, because he might unwittingly say something which would again be misunderstood and raise fresh difficulties. He had hoped that Gilbert would have met his representations in a more friendly spirit, and that he would have condescended at least to have argued any points whereon he differed.

There was one point in Gilbert's letter on which there was agreement: 'If we meet it must be as master and master, not master and servant. If in future this could be carried out it would probably smooth many a difficulty, and remove a great deal of unnecessary friction.'[7]

Then Sullivan provided a reason, which was to have important repercussions: 'for excepting during the vocal rehearsals, and the two orchestral rehearsals I am a cypher in the theatre'.[8]

Once the stage rehearsals had begun Gilbert was supreme until the fall of the curtain on the last rehearsal, and Sullivan did not feel that the time was well spent.

With reference to rehearsing the piece I feel very strongly. Day after day everyone is called, and the chorus and others hang about for a couple of hours doing nothing whilst two people are rehearsing a long scene of dialogue. When the chorus begin they are tired, and then over and over again goes the music in order to get an exit or a bit of business right until the music gets sung so badly and so carelessly that it is impossible to put it right again. Gilbert of course has a right to call what rehearsals he likes – and anyone he likes and at any hour. This I am not questioning, my objection is that I am the sufferer by this kind of rehearsal, that my music gets cruelly murdered.[9]

If Gilbert could accept all Sullivan said as reasonable, there was an end of the matter, and if he were disposed to meet his views in all details, it would be possible to see about a new piece at once.

With this letter out of the way Sullivan decided on the following day to write to Gilbert. He explained he had delayed writing sooner because he had been so annoyed by Gilbert's abrupt letter. Yet he thought it was silly and unnecessary for the two of them to quarrel over a matter that could be so easily arranged, and he really did not think that his requests were unreasonable.

All I ask is that in the future, (1) my judgment and opinion should have some weight with you in the laying out of the musical situation, even to making important alterations after the work has been framed, because it is impossible sometimes to form a right judgment until one begins to work at the number or situation itself.

(2) That I should have a more important share in arranging the attitudes and business in all the musical portions, and (3) that the rehearsals should be arranged in such a way as not to weary the voices, and cause everyone to sing carelessly and without regard for tune, time or count.[10]

These requests did not, in Sullivan's view, trench on Gilbert's gound, or demand anything but what had to do directly with the music and its efficient representation. He attached great importance to them, particularly the first, the musical construction of the book. He felt that Gilbert would find the requests rational, and if they could be accepted in the spirit in which they were made, the two of them could go on smoothly as if nothing had happened, and, Sullivan hoped, successfully. If not, he would regret it deeply, but, in any case, Gilbert would hear no more recrimination on his part.

That was the end of the matter as far as Sullivan was concerned. In his diary that day he recorded: 'Wrote a long letter to Carte, stating my feelings on the subject of my position in the theatre as contrasted with Gilbert's, and also protesting against the manner the stage rehearsals were conducted by G. wasting everybody's time, and ruining my music. If Gilbert will make certain concessions to me in the construction and manner of producing the pieces, I will go on writing as merrily as ever.'[11]

When Gilbert read Sullivan's letter he was bewildered. He saw the requests as just and reasonable, but surely they amounted to no more involvement than Sullivan had always enjoyed in the past:

'They are requirements with which I have always unhesitatingly complied,' Gilbert replied, 'and indeed I have always felt, and fully appreciated, the value of your suggestions whenever you have thought it advisable to make any.'

If only Sullivan's letter to Gilbert stood alone, but Gilbert was also now aware of Sullivan's letter to Carte! Gilbert had been deeply hurt: the letter had teemed with unreasonable demands and utterly groundless accusations, the very least of which, if it had the smallest basis of truth, Gilbert thought, would bring the collaboration to an end. Had Sullivan no recollection of 'business' arranged and re-arranged to meet his reasonable objectives? Had he no recollection of any of his expressed wishes not acted upon 'without expostulation, argument or demur, upon the spot?' The idea was preposterous.

> You say that our operas are Gilbert's pieces with music added by you, and that Carte can hardly wonder that 12 years of this has a little tired you. I say that when you deliberately assert that for 12 years you, uncomparably the greatest English musician of the age – a man whose genius is a proverb wherever the English tongue is spoken – a man who can deal en prince with operatic managers, singers, music publishers and musical societies – when you, who hold this unparalleled position, deliberately state that you have submitted silently and uncomplainingly for 12 years to be extinguished, ignored, set aside, rebuffed, and generally effaced by your librettist, you grievously reflect, not upon him, but upon yourself and the noble Art of which you are so eminent a professor.[12]

Faced with this impasse between the two collaborators Carte decided to take immediate action. In the middle of April he travelled over to Paris to meet Sullivan and try to persuade him to make his peace with Gilbert. In this he was successful, and he was able to inform Gilbert of the result:

> Sullivan is prepared to write you at once another Comic Opera for the Savoy on the old lines, if you are willing also, and he says he will write to you today to this effect. As an inducement to this I have agreed with him that his 'Grand Opera' shall be produced at my New Theatre later on. I think this is not a bad arrangement.
>
> Sullivan says that he is ready to set to work energetically as soon as you give him the new material and I do hope therefore that you will find his letter to you such that you can see your way to write in reply clinching the matter, and then that you can proceed with the New Opera forthwith.[13]

Sullivan returned to England on 20 April and four days later was present for the opening night of Pinero's *The Profligate*, for which he had composed a special song. This was the first play to be performed at the 'new' Garrick Theatre in the Charing Cross Road, a theatre built largely through Gilbert's influence and money as an act of friendship towards the actor-manager, John Hare. Knowing he was bound to see Gilbert that evening he spent some time composing a suitably conciliatory letter.

You admit that my requirements are just and reasonable, although holding opinions they have always been met. Be this as it may, there should now be no difficulty in working harmoniously together in another piece, as we both thoroughly understand the position, and I am prepared to set to work at once upon a light or comic opera with you (provided of course that we are thoroughly agreed upon the subject).

I am enabled to do this all the more willingly since I have now settled to write an opera on a large scale (Grand Opera is an offensive term) to be produced next Spring. I have my subject of my own choice, and my collaborator; also an agreement with Carte to keep the new theatre for me for this purpose, and not to let it to anyone else before then. In this manner I can realize the great desire of my life, and at the same time continue a collaboration which I regard with a stronger sentiment than that of pecuniary advance. All this involves an immediate setting to work with the Savoy piece so as to get it finished by August or September. How will this fit in with your arrangements?[14]

Gilbert responded positively, and on 9 May he met Sullivan for a 'long and frank explanation; free and unspoken on both sides'.[15] The two shook hands and buried the hatchet. It seems they did not discuss their new project in any way other than expressing their mutual intent, because a few days later Sullivan was writing to Gilbert as follows:

'I understood from Carte some time ago that you had some subject connected with Venice and Venetian life, and this seemed to me to hold out great chances of bright colour and taking music. Can you not develop this with something we can both go into with warmth and enthusiasm, and thus give me a subject in which (like the *Mikado* or *Patience*) we can both be interested?'[16]

Gilbert was happy to develop his Venetian idea and the result was *The Gondoliers; or The King of Barataria*, which opened at the Savoy at the beginning of December. The quarrel had seemed to clear the air, and the collaborators worked closely together, although for each man it was a strain, for Sullivan because he was tired and ill, and for Gilbert because, like most sane and honest people who think they have been right in an argument, he felt guilty over his victory: he had dragged Sullivan back to topsy-turvydom.

*　　*　　*

The Gondoliers has the usual two acts, and the first is set in the
Piazzetta, in Venice, with the Ducal Palace on the right. The year is
1750. It is a bright, sunny day, and Fiametta, Giulia, Vittoria and
other attractive *contadine* are discovered: each is tying a bouquet of
roses. Each bouquet is tied with special care, and the girls envy the
roses because they are all offered in honour of two particular
gondoliers, Giuseppe and Marco Palmieri, for whom every maid in
Venice sighs, and who are coming ashore to choose their brides.
There are twenty-four girls in all, but as Fiametta explains:

> We have hearts for them, in plenty,
>> They have hearts, but all too few,
> We, alas, are four and twenty!
>> They, alas, are only two![17]

A hopeless situation, and one hardly to the liking of Antonio,
Francesco, Giorgio and the other gondoliers, all the merriest fellows
and equally passionate, who have entered unobserved by the girls.
Soon other Venetians arrive to swell the chorus.

After Antonio has tried to draw the girls' attention towards his
friends, Marco and Giuseppe appear in a gondola at the back of the
stage. They jump ashore, and the girls crowd about them to present
their bouquets, so many, in fact, that the two men can hardly hold
them. When it comes to choosing their brides there is little problem:

> As all are young and fair,
> And amiable besides,
>> We really do not care
>> A preference to declare.
> A bias to disclose
>> Would be indelicate –
> And therefore we propose
>> To let impartial Fate
>> Select for us a mate![18]

How will they manage this, the other men wonder. It is easily done
with a game of blind man's buff, and the girls prepare to bind the two
men's eyes, an operation which allows for much flirting and down-
right cheating. At last they are ready for the game and eventually
Marco catches Gianetta, and Giuseppe Tessa. The two girls try to
escape but in vain, and the men pass their hands over the girls' faces to

discover their identity. It comes as no surprise that these are the very girls they wanted, and each man kisses his partner!

> Fate in this has put his finger –
> > Let us bow to Fate's decree,
> Then no longer let us linger,
> > To the altar hurry we![19]

They all dance off two and two. There is a flourish as a gondola arrives at the Piazzetta steps, from which enter the Duke of Plaza-Toro, the Duchess, their daughter Casilda, and their attendant Luiz who carries a drum. All are dressed in pompous but old and faded clothes, and very much down-at-heel. They have just travelled from the sunny Spanish shore, and the journey has been difficult; nor is the Duke's reception what he is used to, and there is no sign of the Grand Inquisitor, the occupant of the Ducal Palace, but this is hardly surprising when the Plaza-Toro suite consists of only one drummer!

DUKE. Where are the halberdiers who were to have had the honour of meeting us here, that our visit to the Grand Inquisitor might be made in becoming state?

LUIZ. Your Grace, the halberdiers are mercenary people who stipulated for a trifle on account.

DUKE. How tiresome! Well let us hope the Grand Inquisitor is a blind gentleman. And the band who were to have the honour of escorting us? I see no band!

LUIZ. Your Grace, the band are sordid persons who required to be paid in advance.

DUCHESS. That's so like a band!

DUKE. Insuperable difficulties meet me at every turn![20]

There was only one thing for it: if style was to be maintained Luiz would have to tootle like a cornet-a-piston. Unfortunately the poor fellow can only offer to imitate a farmyard.

Luiz is commanded to announce the Duke's arrival at the Ducal Palace. Once the three members of the family are left alone the Duke reveals a secret to Casilda, a secret that for state reasons has been kept for twenty years, and one which should make Casilda the happiest young lady in Venice!

'When you were a prattling babe of six months old,' her father tells her, 'you were married by proxy to no less a personage than the infant son and heir of His Majesty the immeasurably wealthy King of Barataria![21]

Casilda thinks it a most unpardonable liberty that she had never been consulted, but she should consider her husband's extreme youth and forgive him, for it seems he might have had a difficult time, as the Duke relates:

Shortly after the ceremony that misguided monarch abandoned the creed of his forefathers, and became a Wesleyan Methodist of the most bigoted and persecuting type. The Grand Inquisitor, determined that the innovation should not be perpetuated in Barataria, caused your smiling and unconscious husband to be stolen and conveyed to Venice. A fortnight since the Methodist Monarch and all his Wesleyan Court were killed in an insurrection, and we are here to ascertain the whereabouts of your husband, and to hail you, our daughter, as Her Majesty, the reigning Queen of Barataria![22]

The 'reigning Queen' is somewhat perplexed to find her father and mother kneeling at her feet, and looks towards Luiz, now returned, for reassurance. She may be a Queen, but she has nothing suitable to wear, and the family is practically penniless. The Duke has thought of everything: although he is at the moment unhappily in straitened circumstances, his social influence is still something enormous, and a company, to be called the Duke of Plaza-Toro Limited, is in course of formation to work him. An influential directorate has been secured, and the Duke will join the board after allotment.

To Casilda this all seems degrading: what about the possibility of liquidation? A grandee of Spain turned into a public company! Such a thing was never heard of! The Duke reassures her that he does not follow fashions – he makes them. He always leads everybody. When he was in the army he led his regiment. He occasionally led them into action. He invariably led them out of it.

> In enterprise of martial kind,
>   When there was any fighting,
> He led his regiment from behind –
>   He found it less exciting.
> But when away his regiment ran,
>   His place was at the fore, O!
>   That celebrated,
>   Cultivated,
>   Underrated,
>   Nobleman,
>   The Duke of Plaza-Toro!

When, to evade Destruction's hand,
    To hide they all proceeded,
No soldier in that gallant band
    Hid half as well as he did,
He lay concealed throughout the war,
    And so preserved his gore, O!
        That unaffected,
        Undetected,
        Well-connected
            Warrior,
    The Duke of Plaza-Toro!

When told that they would all be shot
    Unless they left the service,
That hero hesitated not,
    So marvellous his nerve is.
He sent his resignation in,
    The first of all his corps, O!
        That very knowing,
        Overflowing,
        Easy-going,
            Paladin,
    The Duke of Plaza-Toro![23]

The Duke and Duchess go into the Ducal Palace, and no sooner have they gone than Luiz and Casilda rush into each other's arms, but this must be their last embrace because Casilda is married! Luiz informs her that his mother had been the nurse into whose care the safety of the young boy had been entrusted; nevertheless, he had been stolen by the Inquisition. Surely Casilda cannot accept the situation? No, but she must. Until ten minutes ago, she had loved Luiz with a frenzy that words are powerless to express, and now their love, so full of life, is but a silent, solemn memory!

Oh, bury, bury – let the grave close o'er
The days that were – O that never will be more!
Oh, bury, bury love that all condemn,
And let the whirlwind mourn its requiem![24]

The Duke and Duchess re-enter from the Ducal Palace accompanied by Don Alhambra del Bolero, the Grand Inquisitor. Queen

Casilda is not in the least anxious to meet the man who had so
thoughtfully abstracted her infant husband, now the young King,
and brought him to Venice. Is there any doubt as to His Majesty's
whereabouts? Casilda hopes there might be; perhaps Luiz and she
might be saved. Unfortunately there is no possible doubt whatever!
He is there in Venice 'plying the modest but picturesque calling of a
gondolier'. The Grand Inquisitor relates the events surrounding the
abduction of the young prince, of how he had brought him to Venice
and left him in the care of a highly respectable gondolier who
promised to bring him up with his own son of similar age and teach
him the trade. After a year the gondolier had died from 'a taste for
drink, combined with gout', but even in his last months alive had
been no reliable source of information.

> But owing, I'm much disposed to fear,
>   To his Terrible taste for tippling,
> That highly respectable gondolier
> Could never declare with a mind sincere
> Which of the two was his offspring dear.
>   And which was the Royal stripling![25]

So it is now not quite clear which of the two is the Royal Prince
Casilda had married. All very confusing, but the nurse who looked
after the infant is alive and is now the wife of a highly respectable and
old-established brigand, who carries on an extensive practice in the
mountains around Cordova. She is bound to know, and will establish
the King's identity beyond all question. This good woman is also, of
course, the mother of the musical young man who is the past-master
of the delicately modulated instrument, the drummer, Luiz. Already
the nurse has been summoned to appear, and should she find any
difficulty in making up her mind, the persuasive influence of the
torture chamber will jog her memory. For the moment there is no way
of telling which is the Prince and which the Gondolier!

The Ducal group goes back into the palace, and Luiz departs in a
gondola, just as the other gondoliers enter with the *contadine*, followed
by Marco, Gianetta, Giuseppe and Tessa, the bridegrooms with their
brides, and all the year is merry May. Don Alhambra enters behind
them. The gondoliers and *contadine* shrink from him, and gradually go
off, much alarmed. The four lovers alone remain, and when they see
the Grand Inquisitor's stern expression they assume he is an undertaker. When they inform him that they have just been married, only

ten minutes ago, he realises it has made a very awkward situation. Marco and Giuseppe obviously do not know who Don Alhambra is, and Giuseppe slaps him on the back, for he still thinks him to be an undertaker, an inferior mortal in comparison to their own important status, although such a comparison is against their principles.

'We are jolly gondoliers, the sons of Baptisto Palmieri, who led the last revolution. Republicans, heart and soul, we hold all men to be equal. As we abhor oppression, we abhor kings: as we detest vainglory, we detest rank: as we despise Venetian gondoliers – your equals in everything except our calling, and in that at once your masters and your servants.'[26]

On hearing this Don Alhambra declares loudly that one of these two must be the King of Barataria! However, it does not matter: as they are both republicans and hold kings in detestation, whichever one is the king is bound to abdicate at once!

Don Alhambra makes to leave, but Marco and Giuseppe stop him. The thought of abdication alarms the two girls. Perhaps there is some doubt as to what they really do believe; as Giuseppe admits, when they say they detest kings it is only bad kings they detest. They could conceive of an ideal king who would be absolutely unobjectionable. A king, for instance, who would abolish taxes and make everything cheap, except gondolas, and give a great many free entertainments to the gondoliers, and let off fireworks in the Grand Canal, and engage all the gondoliers for the occasion, and scatter money on the Rialto among the gondoliers. A king like that might be a blessing to his people. It seems therefore that their objections are not insuperable.

Don Alhambra suggests that as the country is in a state of insurrection the two should assume the reins of government at once, and until it is ascertained which one is the real king, they should rule jointly, so that no question can arise in the future as to the validity of any of their acts. This seems an admirable idea: they can give places at court to all their friends, and the girls are eager to get home to pack, but there is a shock in store: ladies are not admitted at court, and the kings must be separated from their wives after only half an hour of marriage! Don Alhambra assures them that the separation is only temporary, perhaps a few months.

Tessa and Gianetta have no alternative but to accept the situation, but each is happy to think that at least one day she may be a Queen, sitting on a golden throne with a crown instead of a hat on her head, and diamonds all of her own!

Oh, 'tis a glorious thing, I ween,
To be a regular Royal Queen!
No half-and-half affair, I mean,
But a right-down regular Royal Queen![27]

The gondoliers and *contadine* enter to find out the cause of such hilarity and jollity. It seems Giuseppe and Marco may have been adopted as gentlemen of quality. Quality indeed, and the two bid every man to join them in their kingdom, where in spite of the general objection to pavilions and palaces, republican fallacies will be respected. It is wondered how such republican fallacies may be respected? Quite simply because posts will be found for each one according to their frame of mind, even within formerly accepted classes of society. For example:

The Aristocrat who banks with Coutts,
The Aristocrat who hunts and shoots,
The Aristocrat who cleans our boots –
They all shall equal be![28]

Likewise the Lord High Bishop orthodox will be equal with the Lord High Vagabond in the stocks! Here is the ideal, though Giuseppe and Marco, anxious to get away to their island crown, are conscious of a great loss: conflicting feelings rend their combined soul apart. The thought of royal dignity may be elating, but the thought of leaving their brides behind breaks their heart. Tessa and Gianetta beg them to remember, whatever else they might forget, that they are married.

A *xebeque*, a small three-masted Spanish ship, lateen-rigged, but with some square sails, is hauled alongside the quay. The men begin to embark, and after embracing their brides, Marco and Giuseppe follow as the sails are hoisted. The girls wave a farewell to the men as the curtain falls.

Act 2 is set in a pavilion in the court of Barataria. Marco and Giuseppe, magnificently dressed, are seated on two thrones, occupied in cleaning the crown and sceptre. The gondoliers are also there, some dressed as courtiers or officers of rank, others as private soldiers or servants. After three months under their joint rule they are very happy and enjoying themselves without reference to social distinctions; some are playing cards or throwing dice, others are reading or playing games. Happiness is the very pith under 'a monarchy that's tempered with Republican Equality'.

> This form of government we find
> The beau ideal of its kind –
> A despotism strict, combined
> With absolute equality![29]

The sole desire of the monarch is complete happiness for all, to put each subject at his ease by doing all they can to please. All seems perfect, but there is one problem: the kings have agreed to rule jointly until it is finally known which of them is the real king, but they are receiving only one ration of food. Annibale, one of the gondoliers, suggests that an interim order for double rations might be made on their Majesties entering into the usual undertaking to indemnify in the event of an adverse decision, but they must work extra hard, and stick to it.

The joint monarch agrees to rise early in the morning and in return for the privilege of being addressed as 'Your Majesty', having their salutes returned by sentries, and for heading the subscription lists to all the principal charities, they will make themselves useful about the palace.

> Oh, philosophers may sing
> Of the troubles of a King,
> But of pleasures there are many and of worries there are none;
> And the culminating pleasure
> That we treasure beyond measure
> Is the gratifying feeling that our duty has been done![30]

A very pleasant existence, but there is something lacking, and that is the dear little wives they left behind three months ago. Yes, life is very dull without female society. They can do without everything else, but they cannot do without that. As Marco says, there is only one recipe for perfect happiness: a pair of sparkling eyes and a pair of rosy lips.

As if their thoughts had been read a chorus of *contadine* runs in, led by Fiametta and Vittoria. They are met by all the ex-gondoliers, who welcome them heartily. It seems the girls have crossed the seas at considerable risk, and have brought Tessa and Gianetta with them. There is an ecstatic moment as the two rush into the arms of the delighted Giuseppe and Marco; the girls are anxious to know every detail of how their husbands have spent their time. Are they fond of reigning, and is it a better life than gondoliering? They relate how they had persuaded old Giacopo to lend them his ship, but uppermost in each of their minds is the important question: who is the King and, therefore, which of them is the Queen? They are told it will not be known until the nurse arrives, so in the meantime let there be a banquet and a dance to celebrate the honeymoon.

> Dance a cachucha, fandango, bolero,
> Xeres we'll drink – Manzanilla, Montero –
> Wine, when it runs in abundance enhances
> The reckless delight of that wildest of dances![31]

The cachucha is in full swing, when it is suddenly interrupted by the unexpected appearance of Don Alhambra, who looks on in astonishment. Marco and Giuseppe appear embarrassed. The others run off, except for the Lord High Drummer Boy who is driven off by Don Alhambra.

The Grand Inquisitor is surprised to find that the monarchy has been remodelled on republican lines, that all departments now rank equally, and everybody is at the head of his department. It is certainly not what he had expected, he refuses an offer of macaroni and a rusk as sustenance after his journey, and he is suffering from gout. As far as he is concerned, in every court there should be distinctions that should be observed, otherwise when everyone is somebody, then no one's anybody.

Tessa and Gianetta enter quietly unseen by the three men; impelled by curiosity, they remain listening at the back of the stage. Don Alhambra announces some important news. His Grace the Duke of Plaza-Toro, Her Grace the Duchess and their beautiful daughter Casilda have arrived at Barataria. This means nothing to Marco and Giuseppe, but Don Alhambra explains that one of them is, in fact, married to Casilda, and therefore an unintentional bigamist. At that moment Tessa and Gianetta come forward and introduce themselves as Marco and Giuseppe's wives. Oh dear, this is very unfortunate. If the man who is King is already married, then neither of the girls will ever be Queen. However, there is not long to wait before the truth will be known, because the old lady who nursed the royal child is at present in the torture chamber waiting for Don Alhambra to interview her, although there is no hurry to relieve her discomfort as she is quite all right: she has all the illustrated papers to look through.

The situation is very entangled: two husbands have managed to acquire three wives; three wives – two husbands. That is two-thirds of a husband to each wife!

The orchestra strikes up a march, and a procession of retainers enters, heralding the approach of the Duke, the Duchess and Casilda. All three are now dressed with the utmost magnificence. Casilda, Barataria's high-born bride, has come to claim the royal hand, and, as her parents point out, at the age of twenty-one, she's excelled by none! The Duchess tries to encourage Casilda by relating the circumstances of her own courtship, and her marriage to the Duke; she had exercised such tact and patience that she had managed to tame his volcanic temper. Casilda is hardly encouraged, and her only hope is that when her husband sees what a shady family he has married into he will repudiate the contract altogether. Shady? How can a nobleman be shady, who can look back upon ninety-five quarterings, who has been urgently applied for long before he was registered under the Limited Liabilities Act, and has helped so many towards preferment.

When Marco and Giuseppe enter they introduce themselves, and the Duke presents them to the young lady to whom one of them is married. The Duke takes the monarchy to task for the poor reception he received on his arrival, no guard of honour, no town illuminated, no refreshment provided, no triumphal arches erected, and no bells ringing, except the bell he had to ring himself. Giuseppe apologises and explains his upbringing as a gondolier has meant his ideas of politeness are confined to taking off his cap to his passengers when they give him a tip. This is not enough for the Duke; a royal salute for his daughter would have cost so little, not that Casilda would have wanted it. The Duke gives Giuseppe and Marco a few lessons in deportment, and after dancing a gavotte, he and the Duchess depart leaving Casilda alone with Marco and Giuseppe. Casilda tells them that not knowing she had been married in infancy, she is now over head and ears in love with somebody else: this is the men's case exactly.

Tessa and Gianetta enter, Casilda's sisters in misfortune. The three decide to arrive at some satisfactory arrangement, or everything will get hopelessly complicated.

> Here is a fix unprecedented!
>> Here are a King and Queen ill-starred!!
> Ever since marriage was first invented
>> Never was known a case so hard![32]

How can moralists call marriage a state of unity, when excellent

husbands are bisected, and wives divisible into three? Don Alhambra
arrives with the Duke and Duchess. The Prince's foster-mother has
been found, she will declare, to silver clarion's sound, the rightful
King – let him forthwith be crowned. Don Alhambra brings forward
old Inez, who reveals startling news.

> The Royal Prince was by the King entrusted
> To my fond care, ere I grew old and crusted;
> When traitors came to steal his son reputed,
> My own small boy I deftly substituted!
> The villains fell into the trap completely –
> I hid the Prince away – still sleeping sweetly;
> I called him 'son' with pardonable slyness –
> His name is Luiz! Behold his Royal Highness![33]

A sensation! Luiz ascends the throne, crowned and robed as King.
Casilda rushes into his arms. Marco, Gianetta, Giuseppe and Tessa
are left with mixed feelings, they are united to those they adore,
though on one point they are rather sore, but on the whole delighted!
One thing is certain: pure and patient love has been rewarded.

> Then hail, O King of a Golden Land,
> And the high-born bride who claims his hand!
> The past is dead, and you gain your own,
> A royal crown and a golden throne![34]

All kneel as Luiz places a crown on Casilda's head. Once more the
gondoliers are content to ply their honourable trade: so goodbye,
cachucha, fandango, bolero, for all are left with feelings of pleasure!

When *The Gondoliers* opened on the evening of 7 December 1889 it
was realised at once that Gilbert and Sullivan were in top form. This
opera deserved to rank immediately after *The Mikado* and *Pinafore*
bracketed, declared *Punch*, and the *Daily Telegraph* was equally excited: the opera conveyed the impression of having been written *con
amore*. The piece was so brilliant to eye and ear that there was never a
dull moment on the stage or off it. For Sullivan everything went with
immense 'go' and spirit, right up to the end. Gilbert and he got a
tremendous ovation, and they had never had such an enthusiastic
house and such a brilliant first night. Surely the island of Barataria, a
title Gilbert had borrowed from Cervantes' *Don Quixote*, was in for a
long run! Sullivan was so confident he went off happily to the

Portland after the performance.

As usual Rutland Barrington and Jessie Bond, as Giuseppe and Tessa, carried the audience with them by sheer exuberance of spirit; they were the life and soul of the piece. The part of the Duchess had been specially written for Rosina Brandram, and Geraldine Ulmar played Gianetta. There were also two newcomers to the company: Frank Wyatt, who played the 'Grossmith' part of the Duke of Plaza-Toro, and Decima Moore, a young actress of eighteen, who was Casilda. W.H. Denny, who had made such a success of the part of Wilfred Shadbolt in *The Yeomen of the Guard*, was Don Alhambra, and Courtice Pounds, who had been Colonel Fairfax in the previous opera, Marco.

Sullivan had been right, the opera was destined to run for 554 performances, and Gilbert was equally optimistic. He had put a great deal into the production, at a time when he was frequently in great pain through gout. He had made Don Alhambra complain of such pain in the text. He had also been particularly anxious not to upset Sullivan, who in the end had excelled himself. One would never have thought such exuberant music could have been composed by a man also so often in pain. On the morning of 8 December he thought he would tell Sullivan how indebted he felt towards him.

'I must thank you again for the magnificent work you have put into the piece. It gives one the chance of shining right through the twentieth century with a reflected light,'[35] he wrote.

One may see how prophetic Gilbert was here. *The Gondoliers* has remained one of the favourites. Sullivan appreciated the tenderness of the note, and he was equally magnanimous. There was no need to talk of reflected light:

'In such a perfect book as *The Gondoliers* you shine with an individual brilliancy which no other writer can hope to attain. If any thanks are due anywhere, they should be from me to you for the patience, willingness, and unfailing good nature with which you have received my suggestions, and your readiness to help me by according to them.'[36]

Here were the two gondoliers, like Giuseppe and Marco, seated on one throne, ruling as one individual, and *Punch* published a cartoon of Gilbert and Sullivan so seated, with the caption 'Once upon a time there were two Kings.' The problem was that in Carte, there was a third king, and Carte and Sullivan were about to launch into a project together that excluded Gilbert, and, although he was pretty certain their project would fail, Gilbert felt a sense of loss: the result was catastrophic.

12

The Flowers of Progress

The many performances of *The Gondoliers* ran consecutively except for one night, 6 March 1891. Then the Savoy Theatre was dark and empty, no blazing arc lights illuminated the crowded Strand, and bills were pasted up outside the theatre to announce the closing for one night. The reason was the whole production had been taken down to Windsor to play a command performance before the Queen. A special train had left Paddington at midday to convey the two hundred or so actors, musicians and stage hands, together with all the costumes, props and scenery. Carte was in his element on such an occasion, one that did the company so much honour. A special stage had been erected in the Waterloo Chamber, and curtained cubicles for dressing rooms had been set up in the Throne Room. Because the stage was necessarily much smaller than the one the cast was used to, there had to be intense rehearsing on arrival. The performance would begin at 9 p.m. and the ladies and gentlemen of the Household would be present, together with many of the princes and princesses.

This was the first theatrical entertainment the Queen had allowed to take place at the castle since she had been widowed in 1861. Even after thirty years she was still dressed in black and wore a widow's cap at the performance. The Royal Family and their chief guests were separated from the stage by a bank of flowers and foliage; on a table beside the Queen were beautifully bound copies of the score and the libretto, and a jewelled opera-glass. The music was familiar to Her Majesty, and she recorded in her diary her fondness for it, and her joy that it was on that night so charming throughout and so well acted and sung. She was seen often to beat time to the rhythm with her fan. The singers were naturally a little nervous, particularly Barrington who had to sing of the 'troubles of a king', and when they came to the quartet, 'A Right-down, Regular Queen', they were apprehensive of how it might be received, but they need not have worried, for those songs amused the Queen greatly! However, in spite of the obvious enjoyment, the applause was subdued at the end, the rowdiness of the gallery was sorely missed by the players, and there had been only one encore throughout the evening, and that for Jessie Bond as Tessa, when she sang 'When a Merry Maiden Marries' in Act 1.

Nevertheless the cast felt triumphantly happy when the performance was over, and they took one final curtain call at which the Queen bowed to them before she left the room. Afterwards the members of the company were presented to her in the drawing-room, but the Queen only remained with them for a short while. It was by then after midnight, the cast changed and took supper, and caught their special train to London, and, as Jessie Bond remembered, they arrived at Paddington 'in the cold light of dawn, tired to death, but happy beyond words'.[1]

But things had not been at all happy for Gilbert for at least a year, almost since the opera had opened, though once he had seen that the new piece promised to be a success, he had set sail with Kitty on a cruise to India lasting for about three months. When he arrived home in the first week of April 1890, he was surprised to find, on opening his first royalty cheque from the Savoy, that his share of the proceeds was far lower than expected. He had heard *The Gondoliers* had been playing to packed houses, hundreds had been turned away from the door, and seats were booked up for months in advance. This called for an explanation, so Gilbert decided, as was his perfect right, to look at the books: he was in for a shock. When Carte produced the accounts it was obvious there were many deductions for expenses, and Carte annoyed Gilbert by saying that it was owing to his insistence that the production of this opera had cost so much more than any of the others. However, there was one item of expenditure that particularly angered Gilbert, the cost of renewing the carpet in the theatre lobby. Thus the infamous carpet quarrel began.

Gilbert had as much an eye for detail as Carte, and it was, if anything, more acute; from his early legal experience he knew how small particulars might well turn out to be of great significance, and he had also been meticulous over the smallest detail in his opera productions. It was true, however, as Carte pointed out to him that in the production of *The Gondoliers* he had tended to order items without first obtaining an estimate. Such details, when it came to accounts, were insignificant to Sullivan. How his heart must have sunk when he read Gilbert's letter written on 22 April 1890, which arrived the day after Sullivan had enjoyed a day in the Prince of Wales's party at the Epsom races.

Gilbert related at length how he had had trouble with Carte. He had been appalled to learn from him that the preliminary expenses for *The Gondoliers* had amounted to the stupendous sum of £4,500. These Gilbert then proceeded in part to break down, itemising some of those he considered needless: Miss Moore's second dress which had cost £75, when her first dress had cost only £50, and £100 for Miss Brandram's second dress; this costly garment had now, he said, for some occult reason, been sent on tour! Then there was £450 for the carpenters' wages during the time they were engaged on the scenery, and the gondola, built by Lubhart, together with a sailing boat, the two columns and the two chairs and fountain for Act 2 had cost £460; £112 for timber, £120 for ironmongery, £95 for canvas and so forth. At last he came to the most surprising item of all: £500 for new carpets for the front of the house!

I pointed out to Carte that we (you and I) were, by our arrangement, liable only for 'repairs incidental to the performances' – that new carpets could not possibly be 'repairs' – and that carpets in the lobbies and on the staircases in front could not, by any reasonable latitude of construction, be considered as 'incidental to the performances' – except in a sense that would include everything of every kind belonging to every part of the theatre.[2]

Gilbert continued in much the same vein. Carte had angrily maintained that Gilbert and Sullivan were jointly liable with him for all upholstery in front, and had emphatically declared that nothing would induce him to adopt any other view. Gilbert had then asked him why, if Sullivan and he had to bear two-thirds of the expense, they had not been consulted as to the advisability or necessity of spending so enormous a sum on goods which at once became his property. Carte had declined to go into the question, and Gilbert had become so angry he had told him that if he adhered to his contention he would not commence another piece for the Savoy unless a fresh agreement were drawn up. Carte had replied that the only alteration he would agree to make would be to increase the rent of the theatre to £5,000 instead of £4,000, and that if Gilbert were dissatisfied with the existing state of things he had only to say so. Gilbert repeated that he was still dissatisfied, and Carte had said: 'Very well, then; you write no more for the Savoy – that's understood', or words to that effect.

'I left him with the remark that it was a mistake to kick down the ladder by which he had risen – a sentiment which I hope will meet with your approval on general principles and also singularly apposite to the case in point.'[3]

Gilbert ended by quoting in full the terms of the agreement the two of them had with Carte, and apologised for bothering Sullivan with such a long letter. He felt sure that Sullivan would agree that it was absolutely necessary that a distinct understanding should be arrived at, if the two of them were ever to work with Carte again.

In fact Gilbert had grossly exaggerated the sum involved in the carpet purchase: the actual sum had been £140, as Carte had been pleased to point out as a fair example of the general inaccuracy of Gilbert's letters during the row.

Of course, Gilbert knew perfectly well that Sullivan had every intention of working with Carte, and very soon too: he was busily engaged in the composition of *Ivanhoe*, scheduled to open at Carte's new theatre in the January of the following year, but Gilbert had not been prepared for the readiness with which Sullivan sided with Carte over the matter of the carpet. He should have foreseen this was likely to happen, since Sullivan was at that particular time very much under Carte's control.

The reports of the events that followed, and the many letters that were bandied to and fro between the three men, make very depressing reading. It all seems so incredibly petty-minded, but there is little doubt Gilbert had a point, however fine: replacing a carpet was not a repair, neither was it incidental to any particular performance. Gilbert also knew on the testimony of Carte's wife, Helen, that it was her husband's practice, whenever a new piece was produced, to purchase whatever might be wanted for the front of the house, and add the amount to the preliminaries. Gilbert had not revealed this fact to Sullivan, as he was anxious through courtesy to leave Helen Carte out of the argument. If only the matter could have been left at that, but it was not to be.

Gilbert certainly felt that Carte had persuaded Sullivan to take his side, and that the two had ganged up against him; he confided to his friend, the playwright Brandon Thomas, author of *Charley's Aunt*, that Carte and Sullivan had made an agreement to exclude him from any future ventures, and were merely using the carpet affair as a means of forcing him to sever his connection with the Savoy. This was not strictly true, though Carte had written to Sullivan to seek his absolute backing.

On 5 May Gilbert informed Sullivan that the time to end their collaboration had at last arrived. 'I am writing a letter to Carte (of which I enclose a copy) giving him notice that he is not to produce or perform any of my libretti after Christmas 1890. In point of fact, after the withdrawal of *The Gondoliers*, our united work will be heard in public no more.'[4]

Gilbert had decided to find out exactly what accounting had been done at the Savoy over the past years, and he instructed his solicitors accordingly. At the same time he called upon Sullivan to support him. Sullivan did not quite know how to react to this. He had no grievance himself, no dispute, and he had raised no question which would justify him at this juncture in supporting the demand that the Savoy accounts should be kept in a different manner. Should a new contract ever be drawn up, he said, there were various points that he would urge strongly, if not insist upon, but the chance of such a contract ever being needed seemed more remote than ever. However, to call in lawyer and accountant was a deplorable step in his view. He would do nothing that might fuel the fire, and he wished to remain aloof from taking part in such an unhappy dispute.

Carte reacted to Gilbert's withdrawal of his libretti from the Savoy by witholding £2,000 from Gilbert's July royalty cheque, with the result that Gilbert issued a writ for its recovery. Furthermore Gilbert's solicitors discovered a serious discrepancy in the recent accounts, an error of £1,400 in four months, and advised their client to apply for £1,000 more. Again he was grieved when Sullivan sided with Carte. The result of this situation was that the case of *Gilbert* v. *Carte and Sullivan* came before Mr Justice Lawrence in court on 3 September 1890, later than had been hoped by the defendants because Gilbert had been over in Carlsbad for the treatment of his gout. There was no doubt in the judge's mind, and the case was summarily discharged in Gilbert's favour. Carte was ordered to pay Gilbert £1,000 immediately.

Quite seriously Gilbert thought that now he had been proved right Sullivan, Carte and he might all become friends again, in spite of the fact that he had brought a further action against Carte, an application for the appointment of a receiver at the Savoy Theatre. As he had been proved right, he intended to keep the upper hand, with the result that his letters refused to let the legal argument rest. He was still anxious for Sullivan and Carte to admit that he had been right. As Hesketh Pearson expressed it: 'Gilbert's olive branch was not without a thorn or two.'[5]

On receipt of a letter from Gilbert a day or two after the case was heard, Sullivan replied:

My old personal regard for you as a friend pleads very strongly to let the past five months be blotted out of our years of friendship as if they had never been lived through – as if the pain and suffering I (and I honestly believe you also) have endured had been only a nightmare. But I am only human and I confess frankly that I am still smarting under a sense of the unjust and ungenerous treatment I have received at your hands.[6]

Sullivan did not reject the idea of reconciliation outright. He wrote:

If there is to be a reconciliation let it be a thorough one with confidence restored all round, not merely a patched up truce. But confidence cannot be restored whilst you still contend that no other course was open to you but to take the action which was an injury and humiliation to me. And you are doing yourself and your nature a gross injustice in pleading this. I would much rather believe, as I solemnly vow I do believe, that you plunged without forethought into these disastrous proceedings in a fit of uncontrolled anger greatly influenced by the bad health you were suffering from. I will never believe that except for this you would have turned round upon your colleagues, charging one with dishonesty, the other of practically abetting him, bad faith and supineness – putting the whole force of the law into motion in order to settle a wretched dispute over a small sum of money; as if you cared one rap for a few hundred pounds; it's not your nature. But what you unfortunately did care for was to show your resentment in the most forcible manner and in such a form as to have given me the greatest pain and worry.[7]

Sullivan could not possibly agree to sit down and discuss the original dispute calmly. No, he wanted a thorough and loyal reconciliation. It was no exaggeration, he continued, to say that he had been made physically and mentally ill over the whole wretched business. He had not yet got over the shock of seeing 'our names coupled, not in brilliant collaboration over work destined for worldwide celebrity, but in hostile antagonism over a few miserable pounds'.[8]

Gilbert was incensed by the suggestion that he had acted through ill health. He was certain there was some shady dealing, and this was a matter of honesty. He would not, as Sullivan had suggested, drop the case against Carte, it was important to get to the bottom of the matter, the accounts for the whole of the time the contract had been running must be gone through with a toothcomb, and the accounts were as much his, as a partner, as the scenery, dresses and properties in the theatre.

Sullivan was right to think the sum was to Gilbert a 'few miserable pounds'. During the trial it was revealed that Gilbert had received as much as £90,000 in royalties since the partnership had begun, but this was a matter of principle: there seemed to be sums that Carte had no more right to than Gilbert's watch and chain.

There was no doubt Gilbert had done very well financially, as the transcript of the trial confirmed, but the transcript confirmed something else that was to worry Gilbert deeply: it was quite clear that in his affidavit to the court Sullivan had lied. The fact that it had been at Carte's insistence in an attempt to discredit Gilbert did not matter. Several times during the coming years Gilbert would plead with Sullivan to admit that he knew the statements in his affidavit were false, but Sullivan never would admit it, and Gilbert never forgave him.

In his plot-book for *Utopia, Limited*, in an early draft, Gilbert has one character say: 'I have explained nothing. I have done better – I have made an affidavit that what you suppose to be happiness was really unspeakable misery – and they are furious! You know you can't help believing an affidavit.'[9]

He might have added, 'unless it has been sworn by Sir Arthur Sullivan'.

The only person to have remained calm throughout this affair was Helen D'Oyly Carte; she admired Gilbert's talent immensely, and the two had always thoroughly understood and appreciated each other in the past; she knew how sensitive he was by nature; she had certainly received nothing but courtesy from him, but she realised too that his excitability could easily get the better of him. She had done her best in the early stages of the row to smooth matters over. She wrote to Gilbert telling him she had been very grieved by the altercation in her husband's office at which she had been present. It really should never have taken place.

'You seemed so different from your usual self and it all came so suddenly and was really so entirely unprovoked,'[10] she said.

The two men had each said many things in anger on the occasion, and each had been very insulting, but she was anxious to emphasise there had been an unequal balance in this.

'Anything in the conversation that might be considered insulting was certainly in some things you said to Mr Carte, not in anything he said to you, although he was of course more or less excited towards you because of the conversation.'[11]

Helen Carte also wished to insist that at no time did her husband use the words: 'Then you write no more for the Savoy', or anything to that effect. Gilbert must have imagined it.

It was not surprising, in view of Gilbert's high regard for Helen Carte, that it was to her that he turned after the court case. Although she did not agree with his idea of bringing in 'a legal person' as an arbitrator over the Savoy's financial affairs, she did agree to meet him on 15 September 1890 at her home. During that private meeting at No. 4 Adelphi Terrace Gilbert admitted his fuss about the carpet had been made because he was exceedingly angry, but nevertheless he did think it would be wise if the Savoy accounts were carefully examined right back to the start of the partnership. This was something Helen Carte could not personally agree to, she would have to consult her husband. She told Gilbert how upset her husband had been over the whole affair, and how bad for business the court case had been, coming just at a time when he was trying to raise funds on mortgage for a new opera house. Above all he was distressed that Gilbert took the view that Sullivan and he had made Carte's fortune, since they had made their own as well.

When Carte himself heard of Gilbert's request, he took the line that if Gilbert wished to open the past eleven years' accounts and deduct all repair expenses, then all incidental profits, drinks, advertisements and small items like those should be deducted as well. He had always, he said, divided all profits three ways, even the profits from those items which by right, as owner of the theatre, he was entitled to keep. He also put in writing to his wife a special hope, assuming that she would tell Gilbert: 'I shall be very glad when the day comes, if it does come, when Gilbert and I can shake hands and forget all this ever occurred.'[12]

Gilbert remained unhappy about the accounts, but although he still knew he had reason to be suspicious, he shelved his idea about an arbitrator; besides, he had many other matters on his mind, for it was at this time that he and his wife moved away from London to live at Harrow Weald. The place they had bought, Graeme's Dyke, though the Gilberts changed the name to Grim's Dyke, was a large mock-Tudor house designed by Norman Shaw, and built originally for the artist Frederick Goodall RA. It stood in 110 acres of wooded farmland, but there were extensive lawns and a large kitchen garden. Gilbert took great pains over the years to develop the grounds, and among his many innovations were tennis courts and a small lake deep enough for bathing. Grim's Dyke would be Gilbert's home for the rest of his life.

Sturgis and Sullivan's *Ivanhoe* opened at the Royal English Opera House on 31 January 1891. It was a very grand occasion. The Prince and Princess of Wales, the Duke of Edinburgh and other members of the Royal Family were present, but there was no sign of Gilbert. Sullivan had sent him tickets for the stalls, explaining that as the 'Royalties' had taken two boxes out of six, there was no box left. 'The enclosed stalls are not what I should have liked to send you,'[13] he wrote.

Gilbert declined the tickets, because he was still smarting over Sullivan's affidavit. He would have been happy to be present if he had received from Sullivan an admission that the statements of which Gilbert complained were made under misinformation. However, he did attend a performance of *Ivanhoe* about a month later, and admitted to having enjoyed it. As he told Helen Carte: 'I am, as you know, quite unable to appreciate high-class music, and I expected to be bored – and I was not. This is the highest compliment I ever paid to grand opera.'[14]

Although *Ivanhoe* ran for 155 nights with two full casts singing alternate performances, and therefore could be described as a success, Gilbert had been right all along: the whole English opera venture, on which Sullivan and Carte had staked their reputation and much of their fortune, was in the end a failure. There are several causes for this; for one thing the future repertoire had not been carefully thought out. Everything had depended on Sullivan's opera having a particularly long run, but the main cause was that Sullivan, however brilliant he might have appeared at the time, was just not able to rise to the occasion. There were certainly fine melodies in the piece, as one would expect from Sullivan, and the song 'Ho, Jolly

Jenkin' became popular, but the general effect was one of dullness. His fellow composer, Hubert Parry, had gone to a performance expecting to be pleased, but was thoroughly disappointed, and found most of the piece 'flat, characterless, and inadequate'.[15]

When the audiences began to dwindle Carte became alarmed, since there was nothing organised to take its place so soon. The opera he had commissioned from Frederick Cowen was not anything like ready. In the end a production of André Messager's *La Basôche* was brought in to follow *Ivanhoe*, and when this ran for only two and a half months Carte was not prepared to risk anything further, so he sold the theatre.

It was a bitter blow, but neither Carte nor Sullivan was ruined by it: there was still the Savoy to fall back on, and, although *The Gondoliers* had come to the end of its run on 20 June 1891, a new and original comic opera *The Nautch Girl*, by George Dance and Frank Desprez, with music by Edward Solomon, had opened ten days later. The same Savoy stalwarts, Barrington and Bond, put all they had into this exotic Indian tale, with Barrington as Punka, the Rajah of Chutneypore, and Bond as Chinna Loofa. Other characters were Suttee, Baboo Currie, Pyjama and Hollee Beebee, while Courtice Pounds played the part of Bumbo, an idol. This was the kind of thing the Savoy audiences loved, and would do for two hundred nights; some thought Gilbert could hardly have done better, others that the piece was not so subtle. There could be no Gilbert at the Savoy, however, not even in revival, because Gilbert had withdrawn his consent, though this only applied to England; the operas were still being enjoyed in America and Australia, and had played in Germany, Austria and France besides.

No Gilbert. Not unless one went to the Lyric Theatre. On 4 January 1892 *The Mountebanks*, an opera with a Sicilian setting, opened with music by Alfred Cellier. There was sadness about the event, because Cellier had died during the week before opening, but it seems the dear man had not been in the least put off by the lozenge plot. Perhaps because the lozenge had been watered down to a liquid!

In *The Mountebanks* Gilbert is in his element; as if to rival the culinary characters in *The Nautch Girl* he introduces Giorgio Ravioli, Luigi Spaghetti, Elvino di Pasta and Risotto, whose bride is Minestra. The plot revolves round the Tamorras, a secret society, led by Arrostino Annegato, whose members are living disguised as Dominicans in a monastery perched on a steep rock. They chant in dog Latin, and plan to waylay a duke and duchess and hold them to ransom. All their efforts are thwarted by the love-affairs in which different members of the society are involved in the village. One of the girls, Ultrice, is in love with, and detested by, Alfredo, a young peasant. She is incensed by his obvious love for Teresa, a flirtatious village beauty, very much in love with herself. Ultrice procures a potion from a troupe of mountebanks, which charms all those who drink it. The effect is that all the members of the society are changed into what they pretend to be; thus the members of the society really become friars, the young Minestra disguised as an old woman finds real wrinkles on her brow, and so on. Only a change of heart by Ultrice can restore things by burning the label of the wicked bottle.

It is all topsy-turvy, and truly Gilbertian. But what strikes one immediately on reading the libretto is that here Gilbert is really as good as his best: the lyrics are particularly polished, and the whole is very funny. The reason for this is easy to understand: Gilbert had done considerable work on the idea in the past, and much of it was written during happier days. It was only Sullivan's own intransigence that had prevented him from setting the opera.

In the previous year Gilbert had presented *Rosencrantz and Guildenstern*, a skit on *Hamlet*, at a public matinee at the Vaudeville Theatre, and in *The Mountebanks* he makes Pietro, the showman, present two waxwork figures of Hamlet and Ophelia to the enthusiastic onlookers of the village.

> Now all you pretty villagers who haven't paid, stand you aside,
> And listen to a tragic tale of love, despair and suicide.
> The gentleman's a noble prince – a marvel of ventriloquy –
> Unhappily afflicted with a mania for soliloquy.
> The lady is the victim of the God of Love tyrannical –
> You see it in her gestures, which are morbidly mechanical;
> He's backed himself at heavy odds, in proof of his ability
> That he'll soliloquize her into utter imbecility.
> She wildly begs him to desist – appeals to his humanity,
> But all in vain – observe her eyes a-goggling with insanity.
> He perseveres, improving the occasion opportunatic –
> She sticks straws in her hair – he's won the wager – she's a lunatic.[16]

There is another song about Ophelia in the opera, when Bartolo the Clown and Nita the Dancing Girl have become Hamlet and Ophelia, and clockwork for life, it seems, through the power of the potion:

Ophelia was a dainty little maid,
  Who loved a very melancholy Dane;
Whose affection of the heart, so it is said,
  Preceded his affection of the brain.
    Heir-apparent to the Crown,
      He thought lightly of her passion.
    Having wandered up and down,
      In an incoherent fashion,
  When she found he wouldn't wed her,
  In a river, in a meadder,
  Took a header, and a deader
      Was Ophelia!

Ophelia to her sex was a disgrace,
  Whom nobody could feel compassion for;
Ophelia should have gone to Ely Place
  To consult an eminent solicitor.
    When such promises as these
      Breaks a suitor, rich and regal,
    Why, substantial damages
      Is the panacea legal –
  From a jury – sons of Adam,
  Though as stony as Macadam,
  Maid or madam, she'd have had 'em,
      Would Ophelia!

There is a third verse in much the same vein: Bartolo says if Nita is Ophelia, then not a moment will he tarry: 'Off I'll carry and I'll marry / Poor Ophelia!'[17]

With lyrics of this sort, it was not surprising that *The Mountebanks* was immediately popular, and it showed quite clearly that Gilbert could be just as successful without Sullivan, even if he could feel no compassion for Ophelia, though this would be hard to believe since Gilbert was invariably courteous to most women, and particularly so to the women in the chorus in his operas. During the run of *The Mountebanks*, the manager of the Lyric, Horace Sedger, dismissed eighteen members of the chorus in an attempt to cut costs. Immediately Gilbert took up their cause, and supported their appeal to the law, although it was against his own financial interest: the action was unfair, because the women had been employed for the whole run. The women won their case, and they had Gilbert to thank for it.

We shall remember with pleasure the kindness and consideration you bestowed on us during the rehearsals, and could wish no better than always to be in your productions, to be ever under your surveillance.

Wishing you a long and most successful run with *The Mountebanks* and hoping you will have a most enjoyable holiday after all your hard work and anxiety.'[18]

The letter was signed by all the chorus ladies.

It began to look as though Sullivan might not be successful on the opera stage without Gilbert. The public was about to find out, for Sullivan was engaged in setting a libretto by Sydney Grundy for the Savoy. This was *Hadden Hall*, based on the legend of Dorothy Vernon. Sullivan had composed much of the piece in Monte Carlo under great difficulty during 'days of violent struggle against the recurring onslaughts of pain',[19] often dragging himself to his desk. He had indeed been very seriously ill, and at one time it was thought he might not get better. *Hadden Hall* did eventually open on 24 September 1892, after *The Nautch Girl*'s successor, *The Vicar of Bray*, revival of another of Grundy's pieces set by Solomon, had run from January to June. By this time Gilbert had mounted a second opera *Haste to the Wedding*, at the Criterion Theatre.

Sullivan's music for *Hadden Hall* received a cheery welcome, and was considered very much better than *Ivanhoe*. One critic in the audience on the opening night was Bernard Shaw: he wrote: ' I contend that Savoy opera is a genre in itself: and that *Hadden Hall* is the highest and most consistent expression it has yet attained.'[20] Its 'highest and most consistent expression' achieved without Gilbert! Shaw was only one voice, but there were many voices murmuring the current rumour that Gilbert had made it up with Sullivan, and the two were planning another opera together, a wild rumour, perhaps, but true.

The fact was the two missed working with each other. Tom Chappell, the publisher of the words and music, who had stood to lose by the rift between the pair, had, with Gilbert's prompting, brought about a reconciliation. It is said that it only took him two weeks from the time he decided to attempt it, but Gilbert was still anxious for Sullivan to come clean about the affidavit. On 4 October 1891, Sullivan had written to Gilbert:

'Tom Chappell tells me that you propose that you and I should submit the matters which have been the cause of our rupture to a third party, and, according to his decision, that one or the other of us should confess himself in the wrong, and therefore we could renew our old friendly relations.'[21]

Sullivan must have known exactly what Gilbert was after, but he was not prepared to play into his hands. The matter originally in dispute was really all settled and forgotten, it would be a great mistake to reopen it now. No, Sullivan wished to forget the past, and he was quite ready to let bygones be bygones. He was happy to meet Gilbert at all times in the most friendly spirit, provided the disagreeable events of the past eighteen months were never alluded to, or at least never discussed.

'I say this in good faith,' he concluded, 'and I hope you will meet me in the same spirit.'[22] The result was that the two did meet for two hours at Queen's Mansions on 7 October, and a modus vivendi was decided upon which made progress possible. As one writer has put it: 'there was fire in the embers of the old friendship, but little flame; light, but only a grateful suggestion, now and then, of the warmth with which the old Savoy – for it, too, was ageing – once had glowed.'[23]

The new spring took many months to burgeon, but when it did finally blossom, it burst forth with *Utopia, Limited; or the Flowers of Progress*, 'an original Comic Opera in Two Acts', which opened at the Savoy on 7 October 1893, after the short run of a very dreary piece by J. M. Barrie and Arthur Conan Doyle to Ernest Ford's music, called *Jane Annie; or, The Good Conduct Prize*. The members of the Savoy Company, and especially Richard D'Oyly Carte, breathed a sigh of relief. It was all too good to be true: G and S were back!

Part III

The Wicked World

13

Utopia, Limited

✦ 1893–1896 ✦

Gilbert wrote the libretto of *Utopia, Limited* in six and a half months.
'I have finished the piece,' he informed Sullivan on 17 July 1893.
During the writing he and Sullivan had conferred frequently by post,
with Gilbert sending a few pages at a time, often supplying alternative
lyrics in case one was more suitable for Sullivan to set. Towards the
end of May Sullivan visited Grim's Dyke, where he found Gilbert
looking ill: he was suffering from gout and sciatica, but he had still
been able to carry on with his work.

Throughout the summer while Sullivan was staying at his house in
Weybridge, the letters travelled to and fro. Sullivan had been
insistent that there should be no comedy at the expense of Rosina
Brandram as an 'elderly ugly lady' in the piece: 'I thought "Katisha"
was to be the last example of the type,'[1] he wrote, when it looked as
though the character of Lady Sophy was another chip off the elderly
block. Gilbert accordingly changed Lady Sophy into a more dignified
figure, but he was equally insistent that a new protégée of his, a young
American soprano, Nancy McIntosh, should sing the leading part of
Princess Zara. In fact, Gilbert had altered the original plot to give
Princess Zara greater importance.

'She sings up to C (whatever that means)' he informed Sullivan,
'and I am told that she is never out of tune. Miss McIntosh was keenly
alive to the advantage of seeing you and she said she would gladly
attend any appointment you might make.'[2]

Nancy McIntosh was 'rather tall, extremely fair – very nice
looking, without being beautiful – good expressive face – no appre-
ciable American twang', and Gilbert was anxious to help her in any
way he could. Now that Jessie Bond had left the company, he needed

another 'daughter'. However, in Nancy's case the relationship was permanent, because the Gilberts adopted her as their daughter, and she went to live with them at Grim's Dyke.

When Sullivan eventually auditioned Nancy he was a little disappointed, but Gilbert had promised her the part, and that was that, though she turned out to be much better that Sullivan had first thought.

By the third week of July Sullivan was well on with the music. He had played through the finale to Act 1 to Gilbert in London, who thought it the best finale Sullivan had done. It was hoped to begin rehearsals in September, but Gilbert's gout was still causing him great anxiety. 'I am so afraid of being incapacitated by gout during rehearsals if I don't go and clear it out of my system first,'[3] he told Sullivan on 17 July. In seeking treatment he decided to visit a specialist in Homburg, and he was out of the country for a month, but he continued to correspond with Sullivan, for it was very important that the collaboration should go smoothly. When Sullivan had suggested that Gilbert might remain in Homburg for an extra week, he declined: 'If three weeks of this place have no effect on me, I am not likely to benefit by four. I am extremely anxious about Act 2, and long to get home to tackle it [the revision]... I know that your difficulties must be increased by my absence at such a crucial time.'[4]

The rehearsals began on 4 September, with Gilbert reading through the libretto to the entire cast and management. He was still in considerable pain, and there were some days when a bath chair was needed to move him about. As the weeks progressed it became obvious that *Utopia, Limited* promised to be the most elaborately staged production Gilbert had ever mounted, and the cost of it all was almost twice that of *The Gondoliers*. What also struck those who had worked with Gilbert in the past was how much more patient he was. When Barrington unavoidably turned up half an hour late for the first rehearsal, Gilbert took it all in good heart. Nancy McIntosh referred to this quality when she was interviewed after the dress rehearsal.

'Each rehearsal was a pleasant experience. But that, I must confess, was greatly owing to Mr Gilbert who is the most delightful and painstaking stage-manager possible. I never knew so patient a man. After you have done a thing wrong twenty times, he will put you right on the twenty-first as amiably as if he were telling you quite a new thing.'[5]

Those who had worked with Gilbert in the past would have found all this hard to believe, but he was changed, there was no doubt.

*　　*　　*

Utopia, Limited is, like its predecessor, a satire on monarchy, and limited liability, but all that England held dear in the last years of Queen Victoria's reign is also held up to scrutiny. Here is another King whose one desire is to make his people happy, though the barb is put from a different angle. The satire was much sharper in Gilbert's original version, but in his anxiety to comply with Sullivan's wishes he was forced to leave some excellent things out.

The scene opens to reveal a Utopian palm grove in the gardens of King Paramount's palace, showing a picturesque and luxuriant tropical landscape, with the sea in the distance. Salata, Melene, Phylla and other maidens are discovered lying lazily about the stage and thoroughly enjoying themselves in lotus-eating fashion. All are languorous and lying in a dream of nothingness; they have no need to take opium, for visions come from Poppydom direct at their command. But there is an alternative: to live the life of Lazyland, in open idleness, lulled by music or, as Phylla suggests, the simple joys of birdsong, rippling water, or the languid loves of the turtle dove. All such simple joys are at hand.

Calynx, the Utopian Vice-Chamberlain, arrives to announce the good news that His Majesty's eldest daughter, Princess Zara, is returning after five years in England, 'the greatest, the most powerful, the wisest country in the world', after taking a high degree at Girton. The Princess has achieved a complete mastery over all the elements that have tended to raise that glorious country, England, to her present pre-eminent position among civilised nations!

Salata is excited that in a few months Utopia may hope to be completely Anglicised. Calynx assures her that this will be so. Melene thinks everything is better left as it is.

'Life without a care – every want supplied by a kind and fatherly monarch, who, despot though he be, has no other thought than to make his people happy – what have we to gain by the great change that is in store for us?'[6]

Silly girl! Has she not thought about English institutions, English tastes and, oh, English fashions! England has made herself what she is, because everyone there thinks for himself. In Utopia there is no need to think, because their monarch anticipates all their wants, and their political opinions are formed for them by the journals to which they subscribe. In England the conversation of the very meanest is 'a coruscation of impromptu epigram!'[7]

Suddenly Tarara, the Public Exploder, rushes on in an angry rage, gabbling away in the Utopian language. The girls all stop up their ears, and Calynx admonishes Tarara for disobeying the King's order that the Utopian language be banished from the court and all communications shall henceforth be made in English.

Tarara says he is well aware of the fact, but suddenly produces an explosive 'cracker'. He explains the reason: he has recently been appointed Public Exploder to His Majesty, but because of his nervous disposition he has to accustom himself to the startling nature of his duties by degrees. His job is alarming in the extreme: it is quite simply to blow up the King with dynamite should he ever be ordered to do so by the two Wise Men, Scaphio and Phantis, who watch the King day and night to see if he commits any act of political or moral indiscretion. Should he do so Tarara must perform his grisly operation, and inherit the throne himself, whereupon another Public Exploder must be appointed. Tarara says he has had to let off steam in Utopian because in English, the language of that pure and great nation, 'strong expressions do not exist'. Consequently, as he had been prompted by the situation to utter expletives, there was nothing for it but to say: 'Lalabalele molola lililah kallalale poo!'

Calynx understands the situation perfectly: 'After many unhappy experiments in the direction of an ideal Republic, it is found that what may be described as a Despotism tempered with Dynamite provides, on the whole, the most satisfactory description of a ruler, – an autocrat who dares not abuse his autocratic power.'[8]

This is all right in theory, but how in practice does it work? Has Calynx ever read the *Palace Peeper*, a 'society' paper, Tarara asks. Calynx has never even heard of it, but this is hardly surprising, since the King's agents usually buy up the whole edition. However, Tarara has a copy he has obtained from his aunt who works in the publishing department, and its contents reveal some shocking truths.

'Well, it actually teems with circumstantially convincing details of the King's abominable immoralities! If this high-class journal may be believed, His Majesty is one of the most Heliogabalian profligates that ever disgraced an autocratic throne! And do these Wise Men denounce him to me? Not a bit of it! They wink at his immoralities!'[9]

A guard marches in, escorting Scaphio and Phantis, the two Wise Men, each the pride of Utopia in his mental fertility:

> O they never make a blunder.
> And no wonder,
> For they're triumphs of infallibility.[10]

Scaphio and Phantis set out their task in exact detail:

> Our duty is to spy
>   Upon our King's illicities,
> And keep a watchful eye
>   On all his eccentricities.
> If ever a trick he tries
>   That savours of rascality,
> At our decree he dies
>   Without the least formality.
> We fear no rude rebuff,
>   Or newspaper publicity;
> Our word is quite enough,
>   The rest is electricity.
> A pound of dynamite
>   Explodes in his auriculars;
> It's not a pleasant sight –
>   We'll spare you the particulars.[11]

It is therefore not surprising that the despot is imbued with 'virtues quite delectable', and is the very paragon of the polite tyrant. No one had ever met an autocrat so delightfully bland to the least in the land.

When Scaphio and Phantis are alone, Phantis, who is fifty-five years old, reveals how much he is in love with Princess Zara; he does not know whether his love is returned, but neither man has any doubt that Zara will be his, because her father must consent if they but say the word. However, Phantis is fearful of the effect five years in England might have had, for 'she returns from a land where every youth is a Greek god'.[12] Scaphio is eleven years older and wiser, but he has no experience of love; nevertheless he promises to help Phantis to fulfil his harmless whim, and put the screw on the King if necessary. Phantis goes into a dance of happiness.

> Your friendly aid conferred,
>   I need no longer pine.
> I've but to speak the word,
>   And lo! the maid is mine![13]

Then Scaphio breaks into a dance of unselfishness, and they dance off together.

King Paramount, 'a despot whose tyrannic will is law', marches in, attended by guards and nobles, and preceded by dancing girls. The

King wonders what it must feel like to be contradicted, but he will probably never know how a thwarted monarch feels. He issues a solemn decree in accordance with his people's wishes:

> My subjects all, it is your wish emphatic
> That all Utopia shall henceforth be modelled
> Upon that glorious country called Great Britain –
> To which some add – but others do not – Ireland.[14]

It seems this process of Anglicisation has already commenced: the King's younger daughters, the twin princesses, Nekaya and Kalyba, have been 'finished' by a good and grave English lady. The two girls are to be exhibited daily in the market-place between the hours of ten and four, so that all may recognise English maidenly perfection.

Nekaya and Kalyba appear; they are about fifteen years old; they are very modest and demure in their appearance, dress and manner. They stand with their hands folded and their eyes down: 'How English and how pure!' They do not relish their task, particularly as it cuts into their lunch, but they accept their duty to set an example:

> Then all the crowd take down our looks
> In pocket memorandum books.
>   To diagnose
>   Our modest pose
>   The Kodaks do their best:
> If evidence you would possess
> Of what is maiden bashfulness,
> You only need a button press,
>   And we do all the rest.[15]

Perhaps some young ladies, they think, will need to concentrate harder than others:

> Oh, maids of high and low degree,
> Whose social code is rather free,
> Please look at us and you will see
> What good young ladies ought to be![16]

The King leads on Lady Sophy, an English lady of mature years and extreme gravity of demeanour and dress, carrying a lecturer's wand in her hand. The King obviously has great regard and admiration for her. Today the girls will illustrate a course of maiden courtship, from the start to the triumphal matrimonial finish. As Lady Sophy delivers the lecture, the princesses follow and illustrate in gesture. When the lecture is ended Lady Sophy leads the girls off to repeat the illustration in ten minutes' time in the market-place.

King Paramount confronts Scaphio and Phantis. The *Palace Peeper*, to which the King is forced to contribute scurrilous articles about himself, is particularly crammed with scandal in the current issue: 'Another Royal Scandal', by Junius Junior, and 'Ribald Royalty', by Mercury Major, and many others: all quite the funniest things in the King's opinion. He may be a bad King, but he is a good subject: he has written a comic opera: *King Tuppence, or A Good Deal Less than Half a Sovereign*. Then there have been stinging little paragraphs about his Royal goings-on with a Royal Second House-maid – delicately sub-acid! It is particularly important that Lady Sophy must never see a copy of the *Palace Peeper*, neither must Princess Zara when she arrives. Unfortunately Lady Sophy has already seen a copy given to her by Tarara.

As things stand King Paramount is able to achieve little. During the day thousands tremble at his frown, but during the night, between eight and eleven o'clock, thousands roar at it. As Scaphio explains to him:

'During the day your most arbitrary pronouncements are received by your subjects with abject submission – during the night they shout with joy at your most terrible decrees. It's not every monarch who enjoys the privilege of undoing by night all the despotic absurdities he's committed during the day.'[17]

The King is sure it must have its humorous side, but it makes life a complete farce. You are born and you die, and Time has had his little joke! Scaphio and Phantis leave the King to his own thoughts, but he is soon joined by Lady Sophy, that blameless type of perfect womanhood, and she has a copy of the *Palace Peeper*. She confronts him over its scandalous revelations, but the King denies them. He could not have danced with the Second Housemaid, because she has only one leg. Lady Sophy upbraids him with other scandals and says the writer of the articles must be punished. The King says he is waiting until there is a punishment suitable to fit the crime; he is in constant communication with the Mikado of Japan, who is a leading authority on such points. He manages to distract Lady Sophy's mind from the issue by saying how afflicted he is by her heavenly gaze: his brain is turned completely, but she insists that something must be done about the lying writer. She executes a dance of repudiation and departs, followed by the King.

The orchestra strikes up a march as the whole court heralds the arrival of Princess Zara, who is escorted by Captain Fitzbattleaxe, and four troopers, all in the full uniform of the First Life Guards. There is no fear that the Princess, this maiden rich in Girton's lore, might have been in danger on her journey with such formidable protection, in spite of the storm they had encountered.

> On the Royal Yacht,
>   When the waves were white,
> In a helmet hot
>   And a tunic tight,
> And our great big boots,
>   We defied the storm:
> For we're not recruits,
>   And his uniform
> A well-drilled trooper ne'er discards –
> And we are her escort – First Life Guards![18]

The Princess presents 'the pride and boast of their barrack-yards' to the court. They have taken, she says: 'O! such care of me!' The court imagines they will be missed at home by the Knightsbridge nurse-maids, but they answered stern duty's call and had to leave them. It soon becomes clear that there has been more than protection going on between the Princess and Captain Fitzbattleaxe.

The King, the Princesses Nekaya and Kalyba, and Lady Sophy enter. The four troopers present arms. The Princess welcomes her father and sisters, and is anxious to present the Captain, who has taken such care of her during the voyage. The troopers move to the four corners of the stage, and they are surrounded by an admiring group of young girls of whom they take no notice: this is nothing new to them, because they get a good deal of that sort of thing, standing sentry at the Horse Guards. The King is anxious about the ladies' behaviour, but the Captain assures him that it is a particularly English sight. Princess Zara once again commends the devoted care she has received from the Captain, and the two quietly agree to conceal their love for the time being.

When the King and court have gone, Phantis is alarmed to find that Scaphio, far from helping his cause, is now a rival for Zara's hand; they begin to bicker, but are interrupted by Captain Fitzbattleaxe and Zara herself. At the sight of her the two Wise Men come straight to the point 'We don't know how we are to settle which of us is to marry you.'[19] This is all very awkward for the Princess and she appeals to the Captain for guidance. Why not settle it in the English fashion he suggests. What is that?

It is very simple. In England, when two gentlemen are in love with the same lady, and until it is settled which gentleman is to blow out the brains of the other, it is provided, by the Rival Admirers' Clauses Consolidation Act, that the lady shall be entrusted to an officer of the Household Cavalry as stakeholder, who is bound to hand her over (on the Tontine principle) in a good condition of substantial and decorative repair.[20]

This solution is accepted by the rivals, and the Princess says she has no alternative under the terms of the Act, and she and the Captain reassure each other they are on fairly safe ground, since both Scaphio and Phantis prefer survival.

Later Zara finds herself alone with her father for the first time. She has Lady Sophy's copy of the *Palace Peeper*, and she cannot see anything humorous in it. Why does her father, the despotic King of his country, permit such scandalous insinuations? The King has to admit that he is not altogether a free agent; he is controlled. He is nominally a despot, but he is really the helpless tool of two unscrupulous Wise Men, who insist on his falling in with all their wishes and threaten to denounce him for immediate explosion if he remonstrates.

In confessing this to his daughter the King breaks down completely, but Zara is able to come up with the ideal solution to her father's problem. With a view to remodelling the political and social institutions of Utopia, she has brought with her six representatives of the principal causes that have tended to make England the powerful, happy, blameless country which the consensus of European civilisation has declared it to be. Zara advises her father to place himself unreservedly in the hands of these gentlemen. and they will reorganise his country on a footing that will enable him to defy his persecutors.

The King cannot thank Zara enough. The court must be assembled at once, so that these six 'Flowers of Progress' may be introduced. The courtiers are surprised at the King's unaccustomed lack of courtesy, but they answer the summons. The King explains that his daughter has brought the types of all the causes that have made England so great, and he hands over the proceedings to Zara, who speaks frankly:

> Attend to me, Utopian populace,
>   Ye South Sea Island viviparians;
> All in the abstract, types of courtly grace,
> Yet when compared with Britain's glorious race,
>   But little better than half-clothed barbarians![21]

The Utopian populace heartily agrees with this assessment. The Flowers of Progress enter, led by Captain Fitzbattleaxe, and the Princess introduces them in order. First the Captain, who represents a military scheme/In all its proud perfection. Secondly, she presents Sir Bailey Barre, QC, MP, a complicated gentleman, a great arithmetician who can demonstrate with ease that two and two are three, or five, or anything you please;

> An eminent Logician who can make it clear to you
> That black is white – when looked at from the proper point of view;
> A marvellous Philologist who'll undertake to show
> That 'yes' is but another and a neater form of 'no'.

Sir Bailey concurs to all this: he is able to scout all preconceived ideas on any subject:

> And demonstrate beyond all possibility of doubt,
> That whether you're an honest man or whether you're a thief
> Depends on whose solicitor has given me my brief.[22]

The third and fourth Flowers of Progress are Lord Dramaleigh, Lord High Chamberlain, and Mr Blushington of the County Council. These two, Zara explains, are the types of England's physical and moral cleanliness; the Lord High Chamberlain will cleanse the Utopian court from moral stain, and purify the stage, while the County Councillor will purify all the streets and squares, and keep a modest eye on 'wicked music halls'. Blushington can hardly wait to get going:

> In towns I make improvements great,
> Which go to swell the County Rate –
> I dwelling-houses sanitate,
> And purify the Halls![23]

The next to be presented is Mr Goldbury, a company promoter. To speculators he supplies a grand financial leaven/Time was when two were company – but now it must be seven. Mr Goldbury is very ready to explain.

Stupendous loans to foreign thrones
   I've largely advocated;
In ginger-pops and peppermint drops
   I've freely speculated;
Then mines of gold, of wealth untold,
   Successfully I've floated,
And sudden falls in apple-stalls
   Occasionally quoted:
And soon or late I always call
   For Stock Exchange quotation –
No schemes too great and none too small
   For Companification.[24]

The Utopians are greatly excited by all these prospects of improvement and they show their enthusiasm in their own language with 'Ulahlica! Ulahlica! Ulahlica!'

The sixth and last Flower of Progress is a welcome figure from earlier days, though now much exalted: Captain Sir Edward Corcoran, RN, Great Britain's proudest boast, who protects that island's sea-girt coast from the blows of foreign foes, and he will show the Utopians how to protect their own. The Royal Navy has seen many changes since Corcoran first joined the service in the days of sail.

CAPT.   Though we're no longer hearts of oak,
       Yet we can steer and we can stoke,
       And thanks to coal, and thanks to coke,
         We never run a ship ashore!
ALL.   What never?
CAPT.   No, never!
ALL.   What never?
CAPT.   Hardly ever!
ALL.   Hardly ever run a ship ashore![25]

The Flowers of Progress go into action immediately: the army will be increased, the court purified, the navy must get up steam and cut its canvas short, the rulers must learn to speak on both sides of an argument, and the thoroughfares must be widened and the drains flushed out. Mr Goldbury says that Utopia's much too big for one small head: he'll float it as a company limited! A company limited? What on earth does that mean, King Paramount wonders; the term is new to him. Mr Goldbury explains the form:

Some seven men form an Association
　(If possible, all Peers and Baronets),
They start off with a public declaration
　To what extent they mean to pay their debts.
That's called their Capital: if they are wary
　They will not quote it at a sum immense.
The figure's immaterial – it may vary
　From eighteen million down to eighteen pence.
　　I should put it rather low;
　　The good sense of doing so
Will be evident at once to any debtor.
　　When it's left to you to say
　　What amount you mean to pay,
Why, the lower you can put it at the better.

They then proceed to trade with all who'll trust 'em,
　Quite irrespective of their capital
(It's shady, but it's sanctified by custom);
　Bank, Railway, Loan, or Panama Canal.
You can't embark on trading too tremendous –
　It's strictly fair, and based on common sense –
If you succeed your profits are stupendous –
　And if you fail, pop goes your eighteen pence.
　　Make the money-spinner spin!
　　For you only stand to win,
And you'll never with dishonesty be twitted,
　　For nobody can know,
　　To a million or so,
To what extent your capital's committed!

If you come to grief, and creditors are craving
　(For nothing that is planned by mortal head
Is certain in this Vale of Sorrow – saving
　That one's Liability is Limited), –
Do you suppose that signifies perdition?
　If so you're but a monetary dunce –
You merely file a Winding-Up Petition,
　And start another company at once!
　　Though a Rothschild you may be
　　In your own capacity,

As a Company you've come to utter sorrow –
But the Liquidators say,
'Never mind – you needn't pay,'
So you start another Company tomorrow!'[26]

King Paramount has listened intently. The whole business strikes him at first sight as dishonest, but if it is good enough for virtuous England, the first commercial country in the world, then it is good enough for Utopia. Scaphio, Phantis and Tarara remind the King he has not consulted them in the matter. The King inquires of Goldbury whether Great Britain is governed upon the joint stock principle: Goldbury says it has not quite come to that yet, but it is rapidly moving in that direction, the date's not distant. Well, says the King, Utopia shall be the leader in the field.

We'll go down to Posterity renowned
As the First Sovereign in Christendom
Who registered his Crown and Country under
The Joint Stock Company's Act of Sixty-Two.[27]

Ulahlica! The people are delighted, but it is by no means certain whether their King will go up or down to Posterity in Utopia, Limited.

Act 2 is set in the Throne Room in the palace. It is night, and Captain Fitzbattleaxe is singing to Zara. He is so overcome by her beauty that he finds it difficult to sing: he cannot do himself justice. Zara is unconcerned, for who thinks slightingly of the coconut because it is husky? All part of her Girton training. Matters in Utopia have developed rapidly. The sister-services have been so thoroughly remodelled by Corcoran and Fitzbattleaxe that the South Pacific trembles at the name of Utopia! It had all been very much easier than expected without the interference of the Admiralty and Horse Guards. Freed from the trammels imposed upon them by idle Acts of Parliament, the others have given their natural talents full play and introduced reforms which, even in England, were never dreamed of!

Mr Goldbury has been just as busy and has applied the limited liability principle to individuals, and every man, woman and child is now a limited company with liability restricted to the amount of his declared capital. 'There is not a christened baby in Utopia who has not already issued his little Prospectus!'[28] How marvellous, says

Captain Fitzbattleaxe, is the civilisation which can transmute, by a word, a limited income into an income limited!

Neither has reform stopped there; now all Utopians are wearing the 'tasteful fashions of England', and the first drawing-room under the new state of things is to be held in the Throne Room that very evening, not in the afternoon as is usual in England, for, as Zara says: 'We all look so much better by candle-light.' As her own court train has just arrived she must hurry away to change, but not before she and the Captain once again declare their love for one another.

King Paramount enters dressed as a Field Marshal; he is finding the uniform a little cramping. He asks the Captain if it is not, in fact, a practical joke to dress anyone up like this. The meeting of the First Statutory Council of Utopia Limited will take place before the Drawing-Room, so Lord Dramaleigh, Captain Corcoran, Sir Bailey Barre, Mr Blushington and Mr Goldbury enter from different directions. The King, who is unfamiliar with the forms of an English Cabinet Council, invites the Lord Chamberlain to set out the chairs, with due regard to the solemnity of the occasion. There is nothing simpler, and the six men range their chairs across the stage, the King in the middle, like Christy Minstrels. Is this in accordance with the practice at the Court of St James's, the King asks, somewhat bewildered. Lord Dramaleigh assures him it is in accordance with the practice of St James's Hall!

At the meeting between those who signed the Articles of Association all the reforms are listed, and it is soon noticed how much more perfectly Anglicised Utopia has become than England itself. All the evil courses that once demoralised Utopia have been expunged: the police courts are empty and divorce is abolished, whereas in England divorce is only 'nearly obsolete'. No peeress at a Utopian Drawing-Room before the Presence passes/Who wouldn't be accepted by the lower middle-classes./Each shady dame, whatever be her rank, is bowed out neatly.

> In short, this happy country has been Anglicized completely!
>> It really is surprising
>> What a thorough Anglicizing
> We have brought about – Utopia's quite another land;
>> In her enterprising movements,
>> She is England with improvements,
> Which we dutifully offer to our mother land![29]

The city has been beautified, and all that isn't Belgrave Square is Strand and Piccadilly, and there are no slummeries, either there or in England. The labour question has been solved, poverty is obsolete and hunger is abolished: it is thought that they are going to be abolished in England! The Chamberlain has purged the stage of all 'risky' situations and indelicate suggestions, and the peerage has been remodelled on an intellectual basis, which is rather rough on the hereditary races, but it is going to be remodelled in England, so that brewers and cotton lords no longer seek admission, and literary merit will be met with proper recognition, as literary merit does in England.

Who knows but we may count among our intellectual chickens,
Like you, an Earl of Thackeray and p'r'aps a Duke of Dickens –
Lord Fildes and Viscount Millais (when they come) we'll welcome sweetly –
In short, this happy country has been Anglicized completely![30]

The men rise and replace their chairs. As marching music begins, the Royal Household processes in, including, besides the Lord Chamberlain, the Vice-Chamberlain, the Master of the Horse, the Master of the Buckhounds, the Lord High Treasurer, the Lord Steward, the Comptroller of the Household, the Lord-in-Waiting, the Groom-in-Waiting, the Field-Officer in Brigade Waiting, the Gold and Silver Stick and the Gentlemen Ushers. These are followed by the three princesses, their trains carried by pages of honour, Lady Sophy and the ladies-in-waiting.

The King warns his daughters of the solemnity of the occasion, so there must be no giggling. He takes his place in front of the throne, the Princess Zara on his left, the two younger princesses on her left. The revels may now commence, and His Majesty must kiss each of the debutantes much to Lady Sophy's chagrin, and the King's apprehension that this might be more jam for the *Palace Peeper*.

The ladies attending the drawing-room enter formally, and their cards are handed from official to official until they reach the Lord Chamberlain who calls out the names. The ladies curtsy in succession to the King and princesses, and pass out. When all the presentations are accomplished, the King, the princesses and Lady Sophy come forward, and all the ladies re-enter. The King explains the ceremonial has copied all Great Britain's courtly ways, though 'lofty aims catastrophe entail/We'll gloriously succeed or nobly fail!'[31]

When all have left the Throne Room, Scaphio and Phantis arrive dressed as judges in red and ermine robes and undress wigs. They are furious at the whole proceeding. The Englishmen must be forced to leave Utopia, and the King once more brought into their power. The King himself enters and has to face their complaints, but he is defiant. 'If you will be so good as to formulate a detailed list of your grievances in writing, addressed to the Secretary of Utopia Limited, thay will be laid before the Board, in due course, at their next monthly meeting.'[32] Scaphio and Phantis know they have been defied, and they are now helpless. When the King has left them they plot a course of action with Tarara's connivance to raise a revolution, repeal the Act of Sixty-Two, reconvert the King, and insist on his immediate explosion, and if this doesn't work, they must think up another plot. There is not a moment to spare.

When Lord Dramaleigh and Mr Goldbury are alone, they talk about the two younger princesses, pretty little girls but timid. Just then Nekaya and Kalyba enter, showing just how timid Lady Sophy has taught them to be. The two men proceed to undo all Lady Sophy's good work, and Mr Goldbury tells them 'an English girl of the highest type is the best, the most beautiful, the bravest, and the brightest creature that Heaven has conferred upon this world of ours. She is frank, open-hearted, and fearless, and never shows in so favourable a light as when she gives her own blameless impulses full play!'[33]

The girls are shocked at the thought, but Mr Goldbury illustrates how active an English girl's life really is: following the hounds, playing cricket, running, golfing, punting, rowing, swimming, and dancing till the small hours:

> At ball or drum, till small hours come
>   (Chaperone's fan conceals her yawning)
> She'll waltz away like a teetotum,
>   And never go home till daylight's dawning.
> Lawn-tennis may share her favours fair –
>   Her eyes a-dance and her cheeks a-glowing –
> Down comes her hair, but what does she care?
>   It's all her own and it's worth the showing![34]

The princesses are happy to think they may now sing and play, and laugh and shout, and Mr Goldbury has something even more important to tell them:

Whatever you are – be that:
Whatever you say – be true:
Straightforwardly act –
Be honest – in fact,
Be nobody else but you.[35]

The two girls dance off delighted that they no longer have to be prim to be truly English, for Art is wrong and Nature right!

Lady Sophy soliloquises: she confesses that at the age of fifteen she had vowed only to unite herself to some spotless king, such as she had read of in fairy-tales. The King enters quietly behind her and overhears what she is saying. She has searched in vain, and has had to learn that there is no such thing as a pure and spotless king, and even King Paramount's angelic grace is but 'a mask on nature's face'.

The King is pleased that Lady Sophy loves him, but when he confronts her, she hastily produces a copy of the *Palace Peeper*. While the rumours about the King's private life remain uncontradicted, she considers him a degraded and repulsive thing. The King admits that he has written the offending paragraphs himself, which is why he has not brought the author to book and boiled him on the spot. Lady Sophy is so full of 'rapture unrestrained' at this 'candid retraction', and the King too that his proposal is now accepted, that they dance with each other gracefully.

While this is going on Lord Dramaleigh enters unobserved with Nekaya, and Mr Goldbury with Kalyba. They are followed by Zara and Captain Fitzbattleaxe. The two girls deflect Zara's attention to the King and Lady Sophy, who are still dancing affectionaltely together. At this point the King kisses Lady Sophy, which causes the princesses to make an exclamation. The King and Lady Sophy are at first much confused at being detected, but eventually throw off all reserve, and the four couples break into a wild tarantella, and at the end depart.

There is great excitement as the people of Utopia hurry in, led by Scaphio and Phantis, and Tarara. Reform has become remorseless, and it is all the fault of those hated Flowers of Progress. So down with them! The King, his daughters, Lady Sophy and the six 'Flowers' arrive. What is all this uproar, the King demands. Is this the way to show gratitude? Scaphio begins a tirade of complaints. These so-called boons have brought Utopia to a standstill! The army and the navy have been so reconstructed, and remodelled upon so irresistible called boons have brought Utopia to a standstill! The army and the navy have been so reconstructed, and remodelled upon so irresistible a basis, that all the neighbouring nations have disarmed – and war's impossible! The County Councillor has passed such drastic sanitary laws that all the doctors dwindle, starve and die! The laws, remodelled by Sir Bailey Barre, have quite extinguished crime and litigation: the lawyers starve, and all the jails are let as model lodgings for the working classes! In short, Utopia, swamped by dull prosperity, demands that these detested Flowers of Progress be sent about their business, and affairs restored to their original complexion!

The King is taken aback. What is to be done, he asks Zara. Zara thinks they must have omitted something. Sir Bailey Barre whispers in Zara's ear. Of course! Now Zara remembers. Why, she had forgotten the most essential element of all! And this is?

Government by Party! Introduce that great and glorious element – at once the bulwark and foundation of England's greatness – and all will be well. No political measures will endure, because one Party will assuredly undo all that the other Party has done; and while grouse is to be shot, and foxes worried to death, the legislative action of the country will be at a standstill. Then there will be sickness in plenty, endless lawsuits, crowded jails, interminable confusion in the Army and Navy, and, in short, general and unexampled prosperity![36]

Ulahlica! Ulahlica! Phantis is baffled, and Scaphio warns that 'an hour will come!' It not only 'will come', it has come already. Scaphio and Phantis are led off into custody. The King decrees that from this moment government by party is adopted, with all its attendant blessings; and henceforward Utopia will no longer be a monarchy limited, but, what is a great deal better, a limited monarchy!

ZARA.   There's a little group of isles beyond the wave –
        So tiny, you might almost wonder where it is –
    That nation is the bravest of the brave,
        And cowards are the rarest of all rarities.
    The proudest nations kneel at her command;
        She terrifies all foreign-born rapscallions;
    And holds the peace of Europe in her hand
        With half a score invincible battalions!
KING.   Oh, may we copy all her maxims wise,
        And imitate her virtues and her charities;
    And may we by degrees acclimatize
        Her Parliamentary peculiarities!

By doing so, we shall, in course of time,
   Regenerate completely our entire land –
Great Britain is that monarchy sublime,
   To which some add (but others do not) Ireland.
     Such, at least, is the tale
     Which is born in the gale,
      From the island which dwells in the sea.
     Let us hope for her sake,
     That she makes no mistake –
      That she's all she professes to be![37]

For the first time Gilbert allowed the press to be present at the dress rehearsal, as well as the first night, so that when the reviews appeared the critics had had a double chance of taking in the full shock of what he had given them, and it was a shock. Unlike the previous operas, *Utopia, Limited* has very little plot, and, as *Punch* noted, it would be difficult to name a single telling 'situation' in the whole piece, but the satire is far more searing than anything Gilbert had written before; now he was angry and bitter, and the humour was 'dark humour'. For the first time, with Scaphio and Phantis, he had presented really evil, merciless people – the Mikado was a tame joker, in comparison. There was also something new in the character of King Paramount, who, without any fault of his own, is a pawn in the hands of the two unscrupulous Wise Men. Gilbert has placed his King in a similar position to his own over the past three years, for he had considered himself as a pawn in the hands of Carte and Sullivan. It was not surprising that Sullivan had failed to rise to the occasion with his music: he did not share Gilbert's darkened view of life, and he was worn out. Something the critic from the *Daily Telegraph* noticed: 'It would be altogether unreasonable to expect the musician of more than a dozen comic operas to go on producing strains new in character and expression.'[38] It would have been much to ask, but it was Sullivan's misjudgement that he applied to Gilbert's highly developed satire a musical setting more atune to the earlier whimsical days of *The Pirates of Penzance* and *Patience*, than with *The Yeomen of the Guard*. Whereas Gilbert had undoubtedly moved forward, and had 'grown sager, soberer', as *The Theatre* expressed it, Sullivan had suffered from his journey in pursuit, and had stood still.

14

The Grand Duke

Gilbert had been very distressed to read that Nancy McIntosh had not fared very well in the reviews: her singing was just acceptable, but she had a great deal to learn about acting before she could be taken seriously. The *Gazette* was particularly harsh: 'Even when the nervousness of a first night and the inadequacies of the part are allowed for liberally, it is impossible as yet to guess whether she has any gift for acting.'[1]

Sullivan had quietly decided to himself that he would not include her in another production, but he had his own wounds to lick. There were various changes to be made if the Utopians had any chance of a decent run. Gilbert wanted the music to the finale rewritten, something Sullivan agreed to do in return for Gilbert's excluding several lines of dialogue.

In spite of the high hopes Gilbert had had for *Utopia, Limited* it was pretty obvious by Christmas it was not likely to make a very long run, though it did manage to continue until the beginning of June 1894 when it was withdrawn after 245 performances.

As soon as he saw something would be needed to take its place, Gilbert set to work immediately on a successor. Sullivan, who had spent much of the winter out in Germany, was not completely opposed to the idea, provided he could have firm assurance from Gilbert that whatever the state of their relationship, his previous resort to litigation would not be repeated.

However, with the best will in the world, it would be impossible to have another opera written and composed by the summer, so Gilbert and Carte decided to follow *Utopia, Limited* with a revival of *The Mikado*. Gilbert enthusiastically suggested that Nancy should play the leading part of Yum-Yum, but he had not reckoned on Sullivan's hostile reaction to the idea. Sullivan would have none of it, and he refused permission for his music to be performed if Nancy was to be Yum-Yum. Gilbert counteracted by continuing to withhold his words, thus forcing the distracted Carte to make other plans. The two protagonists went for a while their separate ways.

Carte had to keep the Savoy open if possible, and his plan was this: *Utopia, Limited* would be followed by *Mirette*, another of Messager's operas, a story of love among the gypsies based on the French libretto by Michael Carré, and adapted for the Savoy by two undistinguished writers, Frederick Weatherly and Harry Greenbank. When their version failed after a few weeks, Carte invited Adrian Ross to produce a new version with new lyrics, which was little better, but the piece ran from July to October. Richard Temple had returned to the company to sing the part of the Baron Van den Berg, and he remained with it to play in the next opera, *The Chieftain*, which was a reworking by Sullivan and F.C. Burnand of their much earlier *The Contrabandista*, written for the German Reeds in 1867. This too turned out to be merely a stop-gap, running for ninety-six performances.

Meanwhile Gilbert had been very busy at the Lyric Theatre, where his new opera *His Excellency*, set to music by Dr Osmund Carr, had opened on 27 October under George Edwardes's management. He had brought many of his good friends into the production: George Grossmith, Rutland Barrington and Jessie Bond, together with Alice Barnett, who had played the Queen of the Fairies in *Iolanthe*, and, as might be expected, Nancy McIntosh as Christina, a picturesque street singer, who accompanied herself on the guitar, a part Gilbert had written specially for her.

In *His Excellency*, as in *The Mountebanks*, Gilbert is very much his old self, and it is ironic to think that Sullivan might very well have been the composer but for his low opinion of Nancy McIntosh.

Gilbert, still with thoughts of *Hamlet* in his mind, sets the opera in Elsinore, Denmark, in the year 1801. Act 1 takes place in the marketplace. The theme is practical joking. George Griffenfeld, the Governor of Elsinore, has an insatiable habit of playing practical jokes. At first this is at the expense of Erling Sykke, a young sculptor whose statue of the Prince Regent has been erected in the square, and a young physician, Dr Tortenssen, both of whom are led to think they have received important royal appointments, and are to be raised to

the peerage. Thinking their future prospects are now assured, the
men propose marriage to Griffenfeld's two daughters, Nanna and
Thora, but the girls are in the know about their father's part in the
matter, and enjoy the joke. Neither is this Griffenfeld's only practical
joke, for he has got engaged to Dame Hecla Cortlandt, a sixty-year-
old lady of property who wears a wig, and the soldiers of the King's
Hussars, garrisoned in the town, are made to behave as girl ballet-
dancers every day at certain hours.

> Oh you may laugh at our dancing schoolery –
>   It's all very well, it amuses you,
> But how would you like this dashed tomfoolery
>   Every day from ten to two?[2]

Meanwhile Christina, a street ballad singer, has fallen in love with the
face and figure of the statue, and when later the Prince Regent himself
comes on the scene disguised as Nils Egilsson, a strolling player, she
is immediately struck by the similarity of his features to the statue.
The Prince is very attracted by Christina: of all the maids he has ever
met, she is the fairest, the most winning, and the most original, 'like
the breath of a hay-field after a season of hot ball-rooms!'[3]

The people have become sick and tired of the Governor's practical
jokes, in which he and his daughters take such delight.

> Oh what a fund of joy jocund lies hid in harmless hoaxes!
>   What keen enjoyment springs
>   From the cheap and simple things!
> What deep delight from sources trite inventive humour coaxes
>   That pain and trouble brew
>   For every one but you![4]

There is such great variety to choose from: putting gunpowder into
Havana cigars, throwing the organ boys red-hot coppers, smearing
butter on doorsteps, setting stringy snares across the stairs: 'A good
spring gun breeds endless fun, and makes men jump like rockets –
Then hornets sting like anything, when placed in waistcat pockets.'[5]
But what are such as these when compared with easy chairs whose
seats are stuffed with needles?

> And treacle on a chair
> Will make a Quaker swear!
>   Then sharp tin tacks
>   And pocket squirts –

And cobbler's wax
  For ladies' skirts –
And slimy slugs
  On bedroom floors –
And water jugs
  On open doors –
Prepared with these cheap properties, amusing tricks to play,
Upon a friend a man may spend a most delightful day![6]

When Griffenfeld sees Nils Egilsson, he too is struck by the remarkable resemblance to the statue and thinks he can pass off the greatest practical joke of all by paying him 'five golden Freidrichs' to impersonate the Prince, distribute largess to all, titles, honours, and supposedly chastise the Governor for causing his people such misery; then at a strategic moment the imposture will be exposed.

Act 1 ends with Nanna and Thora pleading for mercy for their father: 'Ah, don't be hard on one whose passion ruling/Was, from his birth, a taste for April fooling!'[7] The Prince Regent will have to decide, and the scene ends with the people rushing off to find out, except for Christina who is laughing up-stage, and Griffenfeld, Nanna and Thora, exhausted with laughter, sinking on to the seat at the foot of the statue.

In Act 2, set in the courtyard of the castle, the tables are predictably turned upon the joker, Griffenfeld is humiliated, and reduced to the rank of private; Sykke and Tortenssen each receive their royal appointments, and Nanna and Thora, tired of practical joking, give their consent; Dame Hecla finds happiness with Mats Munck, the Syndic of Elsinore, and Christina consents to the Prince Regent's proposal.

What of Griffenfeld? Although reduced to the lowest rank, and now on sentry duty at the castle, he is mocked in only the mildest terms: 'You little roguey poguey!'[8] Griffenfeld stamps to attention: 'Sir!!!' and the Regent and Christina remain on-stage as the other couples dance off together towards the castle; all wave farewell to Griffenfeld, who presents arms as the curtain falls.

Certainly Gilbert had put much of himself into the character of Griffenfeld. The satirist, like the practical joker, will frequently find himself ostracised by the very folk who have laughed so heartily at his jokes. 'This time he has gone too far!' So the Prince of Wales thought when he saw Rutland Barrington dressed as a field marshal and wearing the Order of the Garter regalia as King Paramount in *Utopia, Limited*: he felt mocked.

In *His Excellency* Gilbert was able to keep up the pace, the jokes still kept flowing, but sooner or later the mind must rebel, the flow of wit slow down and become a trickle only. Eventually, the laughs the humorist is able to raise become hollower and hollower, his situations crueller and crueller, until an audience can barely wrinkle up a smile, looks on bewildered, and are finally repelled.

> Quixotic is his enterprise, and hopeless his adventure is,
>   Who seeks for jocularities that haven't yet been said.
> The world has joked incessantly for over fifty centuries,
>   And every joke that's possible has long ago been made.
> I started as a humorist with lots of mental fizziness,
>   But humour is a drug which it's the fashion to abuse;
> For my stock in trade, my fixtures, and the goodwill of the business
> No reasonable offer I am likely to refuse.
>   And if anybody choose
>   He may circulate the news
> That no reasonable offer I am likely to refuse.[9]

His Excellency was a success for Edwardes, who had formerly been Carte's business manager at the Savoy, and he went on to greater things, not only at the Gaiety Theatre, but also at Daly's, which he leased. Shows like *The Shop Girl* and *The Gaiety Girl* became extremely popular, as did *The Geisha*, *San Toy* and *The Merry Widow*. Soon Edwardes had outpaced the D'Oyly Carte Company altogether. Nevertheless, he would only work with Gilbert on the one occasion, as the two fell out over taking *His Excellency* to America. It was partly over whether Nancy McIntosh would travel with the company, and play the part of Christina.

At this juncture it is necessary to stress that Gilbert's championing of Nancy was something fully shared by his wife. In the mores of today, where prurience pervades, it is perhaps difficult to accept that there was no affair going on between Nancy and Gilbert despite all the pointers. That they were very close and very fond of each other is quite obvious; that Nancy was an attractive girl may be seen from her photograph, but Gilbert was a man of his time, a gentleman, and his attentions are likely to have been fatherly and protective, with a little flirting but no more, and all with the full approval of Kitty Gilbert, with whom Nancy used regularly every Sunday to attend church.

In the summer of 1895 Gilbert and Sullivan had come together again for what was to be their last opera, and Gilbert, in order to placate Sullivan, had agreed that Nancy would not appear this time. He also rescinded his ban on revivals, which cleared the way for *The Mikado* to play at the Savoy, while the new piece was being prepared. *The Mikado* opened on 6 November, with Barrington, Temple, Brandram and Bond playing their original parts, and it ran to very full houses until 4 March 1896.

The new opera, which opened three days later, was *The Grand Duke or The Statutory Duel*. Gilbert had concocted his plot from several sources, but there was a main one: 'The Duke's Dilemma', a short story that had appeared originally in *Blackwood's Magazine* in 1852, and the musical version based on it, *The Prima Donna*, set by Tito Mattei, and performed in 1889. This more than suggested to Gilbert an opera set in a small German Grand Duchy.

Act 1 of *The Grand Duke* is set in the market-place of Speisesaal, in the Grand Duchy of Pfennig Halbpfennig. There is a well, with decorated ironwork. Gretchen, Bertha, Olga, Martha and other members of Ernest Drummkopf's theatrical company are seated at small tables, enjoying a repast in honour of the nuptials of Ludwig, the leading comedian, and Lisa, his soubrette. Ludwig and Lisa arrive, and wonder whether they are good enough for each other, but they soon sit down to join the rest. The notary, Dr Tannhäuser, enters and is surprised the wedding breakfast is in progress before the wedding. What can have happened? It is soon known that the members of the company are all involved in a conspiracy to dethrone the Grand Duke, and that it is impossible to have the wedding because there is no parson. Why should this be? Parsons are three a penny. That 'little imp' the Grand Duke has selected this very day to hold a convocation of all the clergy in the town to settle the details of his own approaching marriage to the enormously wealthy Baroness von Krakenfeldt. Therefore no parson will be free until the evening, at a time when the actors will be performing their magnificent revival of *Troilus and Cressida*. This is why they have been forced to eat the wedding breakfast before the wedding!

No one has a good word to say of the Grand Duke, and Gretchen calls him 'the meanest, the cruellest, the most spiteful little imp in Christendom'.[10]

However, the Duke's tyranny will not last much longer, and tomorrow the despot will be dethroned. Ludwig warns everyone to remember the secret sign of their conspiratorial association, the eating of a sausage-roll!

> It's a greasy kind of pasty,
> Which, perhaps, a judgement hasty
> Might consider rather tasty:
>   Once (to speak without disguise)
>   It found favour in our eyes.[11]

Maybe so, but these conspirators have been eating the beastly things for six months, and they have been found 'very bilious on the whole', and 'it's no ill-breeding/If at these repulsive pies/Our offended gorges rise!'[12]

Martha has already given the sign six times that day, and she cannot eat her breakfast as a result. Ludwig, a martyr for the cause, proceeds to eat a sausage-roll with great difficulty, and Lisa helps him get it down with a swig of brandy. One thing seems certain: Ernest Drummkopf, the leader of their troupe, is almost certain to be elected the next Grand Duke.

Drummkopf arrives hurriedly. It is almost certain he will be elected, as two of the other candidates have been arrested for debt, and the third is a baby in arms, so, if the company votes solid, he is cocksure of election. However, he must remember his promise to his actors: each will be provided for for life; every man will be ennobled, and every lady will have unlimited credit at the court milliners, and all salaries shall be paid weekly in advance. What vision! No, there is nothing to it: a man who for ten years has managed a theatrical company can rule anything: ruling a Grand Duchy is only a question of management. Instead of playing Troilus of Troy for a month he will play the Grand Duke of Pfennig Halbpfennig for a lifetime! Such a prospect should surely make any man happy, but Drummkopf is miserable because the lovely British comedienne, the beautiful Julia, whose dramatic ability is so overwhelming that the audiences forgive even her strong English accent – that rare and radiant being treats his respectful advances with 'disdain unutterable!' And yet, who knows? She is haughty and ambitious, and it may be that the splendid change in his fortunes may work a corresponding change in her feelings towards him.

Julia Jellicoe comes into the square, and she wishes to speak to

Drummkopf on a purely professional matter. She understands that the conspiracy is to develop tomorrow, and as Drummkopf is almost certain to be elected to the throne, and all the posts about the court are to be filled by members of the troupe according to their professional importance, she is alarmed that as leading lady, she will be expected to become the Grand Duchess and therefore Drummkopf's wife. Drummkopf is delighted at the prospect, but he wonders if Julia is up to playing such a strongly emotional part, involving such long and repeated scenes of rapture, tenderness, adoration, devotion – 'all in luxuriant excess, and all of the most demonstrative description.'[13] Julia assures him that she is a true professional, and throughout her career she has made it a rule never to allow private feelings to interfere with her professional duties. However distasteful she might find the part, once she had taken it she would consider herself professionally bound to throw herself into it with all the ardour at her command.

> The role I'm prepared to endow
> With most delicate touches,
> By the heavens above us, I vow
> I will be your Grand Duchess![14]

Drummkopf feels himself to be the happiest man alive.

Suddenly there is alarm in the square. People crowd in, and Ludwig and Lisa are with the notary; all are greatly agitated, for in all innocence Ludwig has betrayed the association and revealed the plot to the Grand Duke's own detective, to whom he had given the sausage-roll sign. The man had seemingly replied by eating three with obvious relish for the simple reason that he liked them, but it was too late, and Ludwig made him a confidant. The notary smiles placidly as Drummkopf and Julia upbraid Ludwig for his careless-ness, because he has a way of resolving the problem. The two men must fight a statutory duel. A statutory duel? No one has ever heard of such a thing. The notary explains.

'It is true that the practice has fallen into abeyance through disuse. But all the laws of Pfennig Halbpfennig run for a hundred years, when they die a natural death, unless, in the meantime, they have been revived for another century. The Act that institutes the Statutory Duel was passed a hundred years ago, and as it has never been revived, it expires tomorrow. So you're just in time.'[15]

In a statutory duel each man draws a card from the pack and the one who draws the lowest card dies a social death: he loses all his civil rights, his identity disappears, his name is expunged from the list of voters, and the winner takes his place whatever it may be, discharges all his functions, and adopts all his responsibilities. Furthermore the winner, or survivor, will go straight to the Grand Duke and denounce the dead man as the moving spirit of the plot. He is accepted as a King's witness, and, as a matter of course, receives a free pardon. As the law expires tomorrow the loser will be able to come back to life, and have his name restored to the list of voters.

Julia is cynical: once the loser comes to life again he will be at once arrested, tried and executed on the evidence of the informer. But, the notary assures her, a man may only die once. 'Death expunges all crime, and when he (the loser) comes to life again, it will be with a clean slate.'

> Sword or pistol neither uses –
> Playing card he lightly chooses,
> And the lower simply loses![16]

In the draw Drummkopf draws a king, but Ludwig an ace. Amid great excitement the notary agrees to keep Julia and Lisa in trust, and they hurry off.

The seven chamberlains of the Grand Duke Rudolph march in.

> The good Grand Duke of Pfennig Halbpfennig,
> Though, in his own opinion, very very big,
> In point of fact he's nothing but a miserable prig
> Is the good Grand Duke of Pfennig Halpbfennig!
>
> Though quite contemptible, as every one agrees,
> We must dissemble if we want our bread and cheese,
> So hail him in a chorus, with enthusiasm big,
> The good Grand Duke of Pfennig Halpbfennig[17]

Grand Duke Rudolph enters, he is a small man, meanly and miserably dressed in old and patched clothes, but blazes with a profusion of orders and decorations. He is very weak and ill from low living, for he is a man who has an extravagant respect for tuppence-ha'penny, and all courtly ceremonial whenever it can be practised inexpensively. The chamberlains hand him his snuff-box and his handkerchief with due ceremony, as each item passes down the line from the Junior to the Senior Chamberlain.

The Duke is to be married to the wealthy Baroness Caroline von

Krakenfeldt tomorrow. A great festive occasion paid for by public expense, and wedding presents are expected to be on a scale of extraordinary magnificence. However, the Grand Duke does not feel comfortable about this, the first little treat he has allowed himself since his christening, but there are definite advantages.

'Caroline's income is very considerable, and as her ideas of economy are quite on a par with mine, it ought to turn out well. Bless her tough old heart. She's a mean little darling!'[18]

The Baroness arrives for her appointment on time, and she brings the detective's secret report with her, which happens to be wrapped in a newspaper. She chances to read an account of Rudolph's life headed 'Our Detested Despot!' in which it is revealed he had been betrothed to the Princess of Monte Carlo in infancy. Surely this must put her own marriage in jeopardy? The Grand Duke tells her there is nothing to fear, as the Prince of Monte Carlo is stony broke and has been unable to leave his house for years for fear of arrest by his creditors. On numerous occasions the Prince has pleaded with Rudolph for help, even to send the money to enable the Princess to come to Germany, but in vain. The Princess comes of age at two tomorrow, when the terms of the betrothal cease, and Rudolph will be a free man. This is why he has arranged his wedding to Caroline for two o'clock. How happy they will be living their life of strict economy.

When the Baroness has departed Rudolph turns to his detective's letter; he reads of the conspiracy to depose him, and the plot is to explode tomorrow! Why had the detective been so convulsed with laughter that he had failed to arrest the conspirators? What can he do? Rudolph does not know. He ought to keep cool and think, but how can he think when his veins are full of hot soda-water, and his brain fizzing like a firework, and all his faculties are jumbled in 'a perfect whirlpool of tumblification'? He breaks down completely in a fit of weeping. He is going to be ill, very ill indeed!

> When you've got a beehive in your head,
>   And a sewing machine in each ear,
> And you feel that you've eaten your bed,
>   And you've got a bad headache down here –
>   When such facts are about,
>   And these symptoms you find
>   In your body or crown –

> Well, you'd better look out,
>   You may make up your mind
>   You had better lie down![19]

As he sinks exhausted and weeping at the foot of the well, Ludwig enters eager to make his confession and obtain a full pardon. He is surprised to find the Grand Duke in such low spirits, but he is unable to report the death of Drummkopf and the collapse of the plot. Because Rudolph is so upset, he is looking for a suitable way to put an end to his life, seeing it would probably come to an end tomorrow anyway. Ludwig persuades him that he can avoid the catastrophe of being blown up by dynamite if he resorts to fighting a statutory duel, and Ludwig offers to be the survivor by cheating to make sure he draws the higher card. Thus Ludwig would be Grand Duke for a day only, and Rudolph can evade the threat of deposition. Rudolph is anxious: 'You won't go tipping people, or squandering my little savings on fireworks, or any nonsense of that sort?'[20] Ludwig gives his assurance.

In order to seem convincing the two decide to have a mock row publicly which will result in the duel. The people, who have already been watching from their windows, hurry in; they are all trembling, with faltering feet, and muscles all a-quiver, under the impression that they are to be arrested for their complicity in the conspiracy. Ludwig and Rudolph begin to row:

> When two doughty heroes thunder,
> All the world is lost in wonder;
>   When such men their temper lose,
>   Awful are the words they use![21]

The duel soon takes place and goes according to plan. Rudolph is subjected to general ridicule, and he goes off furious. Just let them all wait till tomorrow afternoon!

As soon as Ludwig takes over the reins of state he is swift to act: 'A very great deal may be done in a day!' He immediately signs an order renewing the law against duels for a further hundred years. This makes him Grand Duke for life. Besides, Ludwig announces he will give out court appointments to each and all according to professional position. This, much to Julia's horror and Lisa's alarm, means Julia, the leading lady, if she is to do her duty, must become his Grand Duchess.

> Our duty, if we're wise,
>   We never shun.
> This Spartan rule applies
>   To every one
> In theatres as in life,
>   Each has her line –
> This part – the Grand Duke's wife
>   (Oh agony!) is mine!
> A maxim new I do not start –
> The canons of dramatic art
> Decree that this repulsive part
>   (The Grand Duke's wife)
>   Is mine![22]

Lisa is heart-broken, but there can be no mercy. As the notary explains, though marriage contracts are very solemn, dramatic contracts are even more so! Lisa walks off weeping. Ludwig decides that the court dress from now on shall be the brand-new costumes the company possesses.

> Henceforth our Court costume
>   Shall live in song and story,
>   For we'll upraise
>   The dead old days
>   Of Athens in her glory![23]

This will be a jolly court indeed! Ludwig is carried round the stage and placed on the ironwork of the well. Julia stands by him, and the rest group round them.

It is the next morning, and the scene is the entrance hall of the Grand Ducal Palace. The members of the theatrical company enter, all dressed in their costumes for *Troilus and Cressida*; they carry garlands, play on pipes, citharae and cymbals, and are heralding the return of Ludwig and Julia from their marriage ceremony, which has just taken place. Ludwig announces that he intends to revive the classic memories of Athens at its best, for the company possesses all the necessary dresses and a course of quiet cramming will supply them with the rest. He confides to the audience that the whole thing is a sham, only 'classical pretension', and he promises them it is not their intention to dance a dithyramb, which might display a lot of stocking/Which is always very shocking. In fact, not everything Athenian is suitable for performance.

> Yes, on reconsideration, there are customs of that nation
>> Which are not in strict accordance with the habits of our day,
> And when I come to codify, their rules I mean to modify,
>> Or Mrs Grundy, p'r'aps, may have a word or two to say.
> For they hadn't mackintoshes or umbrellas or galoshes –
>> And a shower with their dresses must have played the very deuce,
> And it must have been unpleasing when they caught a fit of sneezing,
>> For, it seems, of pocket-handkerchiefs they didn't know the use.
> They wore little underclothing – scarcely anything – or nothing –
>> And their dress of Coan silk was quite transparent in design –
> Well, in fact, in summer weather, something like the 'altogether'.
> And it's there, I rather fancy, I shall have to draw the line![24]

The chorus leaves, and Ludwig is left alone with Julia and Lisa. Lisa begs Julia to be very gentle with Ludwig who is so highly sensitive and sentimental, and she departs weeping. Julia then sets about deciding exactly how she will play the part of the Grand Duchess. Ludwig advises her not to make it one of her 'hoity-toity vixenish viragos', but rather 'a tender, gentle, submissive, affectionate (but not too affectionate) child-wife – timidly anxious to coil herself into her husband's heart, but kept in check by an awestruck reverence for his excited intellectual qualities and his majestic personal appearance'. This will not do for Julia: she must have scenes of justifiable jealousy to fit in with her temperament, and she proceeds to act out the part, which 'calls for the resources of a high-class art'.

The members of the company hurry on in a state of great excitement to tell Ludwig the Baroness von Krakenfeldt has arrived at the door. The Baroness sweeps in furiously. She has been slighted, and she is ready to explode with rage! Ludwig has no idea who she is, as she demands that Rudolph be produced at once, but Ludwig explains that Rudolph has expired quite unexpectedly!

The Baroness is dumbstruck. She was to have been married today! Seeing the state of the assembly she wonders whether it is court mourning or a fancy-dress ball. It is, Ludwig explains, intended both to express inconsolable grief for the decease of the late Duke and ebullient joy at the accession of his successor – the Grand Duke had died in a statutory duel. But the Baroness knows all about statutory duels. 'But that's only a civil death! – and the Act expires to-night, and then he will come to life again!'[25]

Unfortunately not: the law has been revived for a further hundred years. Ludwig expects the Baroness to be distressed but she is ecstatic. She tells him that when he killed Rudolph he adopted all his overwhelming responsibilities, and she, Caroline von Krakenfeldt, is the most overwhelming of all. There is no doubt the law is on her side, and in spite of his only just having married Julia, Ludwig dances off to be married yet again, leaving Julia amazed that 'To-day is a day of illusion and sorrow'. Soon she departs sadly.

Ernest Drummkopf enters, unable to wait any longer to know what is going on. What is Ludwig up to? He sees a wedding procession winding down the hill, with everyone dressed in his *Troilus and Cressida* costumes. Ludwig must be marrying Lisa. No, Lisa is suddenly standing beside him, but she has not seen him: when she does, she is terrified and runs away. Perhaps Ludwig is marrying Julia, but Julia too enters. She is similarly transfixed when she sees him, and begins to run off, but Drummkopf catches her. He is only technically dead, he explains, and physically he is as much alive as ever he was in his life. Julia tells him what has happened, that Ludwig is now the Duke and the law extended, which means that Drummkopf must remain technically dead. He pleads with Julia to defy the law and marry him and run away to England, where he will play broken-English in London as she plays broken-German here. Julia says legal technicalities cannot be defied: she cannot be his wife, and at best she could only become his widow. That would be better than nothing, but Julia is certain as a widow she would be bound to get married again within a month! A situation Ernest Drummkopf has to accept.

> My offer recalling
> Your words I obey –
> Your fate is appalling,
> And full of dismay.
> To pay for this scorning
> I give you fair warning
> I'll haunt you each morning,
> Each night and each day![26]

When the two have departed in opposite directions, the wedding procession returns dancing. The Baroness is very happy as she and Ludwig are toasted in a 'magnum of merry champagne'.

In the midst of this celebration a march is heard, and a herald enters to announce that the Prince of Monte Carlo has arrived bringing his beautiful daughter. Ludwig is ignorant of the Prince and his principality, but he decides that everyone will conceal themselves when he arrives.

To a pompous march the Prince and Princess of Monte Carlo enter attended by six theatrical-looking nobles and the court costumier. The nobles are members of the Theatre Monaco, and the costumes are all hired for the day; nor may the nobles remove their gloves, because their nails are not presentable, and the Duke in order to account for their shortcomings explains, in a whisper bated, 'they are wealthy members of the brewing interest/To the Peerage elevated'.[27]

The Prince has been able to leave Monte Carlo because he suddenly made a fortune, having spent his enforced incarceration inventing the game of roulette. He was able to pay off all his debts, and just managed to bring his daughter to Pfennig Halbpfennig by train de luxe in time to marry the Grand Duke according to the terms of the marriage contract: another hour and they would have been too late.

The Princess begins to think that Rudolph's absence is a sign that he wishes to get out of the marriage because he thinks she is poor. He is such a miserly little wretch. Suddenly the Princess is aware of something moving behind the curtain. The curtains fly back and the court give a wild yell and rushes on to the stage dancing wildly. The Prince, Princess and nobles are taken by surprise at first, but eventually they join in the reckless dance at the end of which all fall down exhausted.

Ludwig explains the wildness as the 'official ceremonial for the reception of visitors of the very highest distinction', and if the ceremony for saying 'goodbye' were called for, it also was performed with the foot. Ludwig does not know anything about Rudolph's marriage contract, and the Princess naturally takes Ludwig to be Rudolph. She is horrified to learn he not only already has a Grand Duchess, but has three Grand Duchesses! The Princess wishes to leave, this is not a respectable court; her father on the other hand thinks collecting wives a 'pretty hobby' and wishes he could collect a few himself; perhaps Rudolph could provide him with a catalogue of the museum. The Princess retorts that she could never let Rudolph keep a museum. At the name 'Rudolph' Ludwig realises the muddle and reveals that he is Ludwig, the new Grand Duke. Rudolph is dead: he died quite suddenly of a cardiac affection, or, rather, a pack-of-cardiac affection. He fought a statutory duel and lost, and Ludwig has taken over all his engagements. The Princess insists she is a prior engagement, and has been engaged for twenty years. There is no time to lose and Ludwig must marry his fourth Duchess in twenty-four hours.

They are just going to leave, when Rudolph, Drummkopf and the notary arrive. All kneel in astonishment. Rudolph denounces Ludwig as an impostor, a 'tuppeny rogue'. He never was, nor ever will be, Grand Duke of Pfennig Anything! Dr Tannhäuser explains that there had been a serious mistake in the rules of the duel, and that according to the Act it is expressly laid down that the ace shall count invariably as the lowest card! This means the statutory duels fought are now null and void, and Rudolph and Ernest Drummkopf will come to life again. So Rudolph may marry the Princess, Ernest may marry Julia, and Ludwig and Lisa are together at last, and 'each shall have a pretty wedding!'

Following the precedent set when *Utopia, Limited* opened, Gilbert agreed to the press being present at the final dress rehearsal of *The Grand Duke*. The next day, the opening was a great success, and *The Theatre* pronounced the piece from first to last a delightful entertainment. Besides the expected praise for Barrington and Brandram, as Ludwig and the Duchess, there was great interest in Mme Ilka von Palmay, the Hungarian soprano and countess who played Julia. Gilbert had seen that her English, spoken with a strong Hungarian accent, would be suitable for Julia, an English girl supposedly speaking German. Unlike Nancy McIntosh, Palmay was experienced on the stage, and had sung in *Der Vogelhandler* at Drury Lane that summer. Her part in *The Grand Duke* made up somewhat for Sullivan's objection to her playing Nanki-Poo in a Berlin production of *The Mikado*.

However, once the gorgeous spectacle of it all, the magnificent set designed by W. Hereford, the lavish costumes and Gilbert's careful movement and grouping, had been taken in, many felt there was something deeply lacking, and there were dissonant voices. The dialogue seemed tiresome, and Gilbert had 'lost all his gaiety and nearly all his old brilliance'.[28] This was not entirely true, but it was true that Gilbert was worn out after all his effort and the gout was still plaguing him; Sullivan had left for Monte Carlo and had virtually collapsed on arrival. 'Another week's rehearsal with W.S.G. and I should have gone raving mad,'[29] he wrote to Burnand.

Perhaps the time had come at last to drown the book.

15

Fallen Fairies

⚜ 1897–1911 ⚜

The Grand Duke was indeed the last Gilbert and Sullivan opera, and after only 123 performances, the briefest run since *Thespis*, it was taken off on 19 July 1896 to be succeeded by *The Mikado*. At the re-appearance once again of its favourite the public began to flock back to the Savoy and the opera managed a further 226 performances, including its thousandth, an event celebrated about a month later when the theatre was festooned with 'bunting of Japanese silk, Japanese lanterns shading the electric lights, and chrysanthemums'.[1] Gilbert and Sullivan came on stage to take their bow, but Carte was absent through illness.

From now on the collaboration would continue only in the form of revivals, and there were many of these, interspersed with the odd original piece by other authors, none of which came to very much. One problem for Carte was that he had Ilka von Palmay on a three-year contract and she needed suitable parts. There was no question of her being Yum-Yum, because Florence Perry was particularly good, as was Emmie Owen as Peep-Bo, and Jessie Bond had returned as Pitti-Sing. Katisha was a contralto part, and besides Rosina Brandram was firmly situated there, so there was nothing in *The Mikado* at all for Palmay, the girl whom the *Illustrated London News* announced had 'achieved at one bound a great London reputation'.[2]

When *The Mikado* was replaced on 20 February 1897 with *His Majesty*, a comic opera written by Burnand, Lehmann and Ross, and set to music by Sir Alexander Mackenzie, Palmay sang the small part of Felice, a woodsman's daughter, but her position in the company was not resolved until she was given the leading part of Elsie Maynard in the revival of *The Yeomen of the Guard*, which ran through that summer under the personal direction of the author and composer, though the two were barely on speaking terms. For this production Gilbert, after making a special visit to the Tower, had completely redesigned the set for Act 2, which showed the wharf but without the Tower in the background, and this sort of minor alteration became common to the many revivals that were mounted during the following years. At least it gave the author the happy feeling he was involved, and made the audience aware it was not merely seeing the same old thing over again: all good for business.

One feature of this time at the Savoy was the arrival in the first company of Henry Lytton, who played Jack Point in the *Yeomen* revival. From now on he would play all the leading 'Grossmith' parts, most of which he had already played on tour, until he was succeeded by Martyn Green in 1934. It may be remembered Lytton had on one occasion taken over the part of Robin Oakapple from Grossmith at very short notice in *Ruddigore*. Lytton, like so many who worked under Gilbert, admired him greatly. He saw Gilbert as the pattern of the fine old English gentleman, and it was only those who knew him superficially who thought him a martinet. It was true, Lytton said, that under the stress of directing the operas Gilbert was excitable and could be cutting and cantankerous, but that failed to do justice to the innate gentleness and courtesy which were his great and distinguishing qualities.

'Upright and honourable himself, one could never imagine,' Lytton said, 'that he could ever do a mean, ungenerous action to anyone, nor had any man a truer genius for friendship.'[3]

Lytton recalled Gilbert's miniature stage on which he had so carefully plotted out every move in the operas. This was now set up at Grim's Dyke, where the master was spending more and more time, though he was active, as far as his gout allowed, in many matters locally, quite unnconnected with the theatre. He was a Justice of the Peace on the Edgware Bench, and eventually became Deputy Lord Lieutenant for Middlesex. Those who came up before Gilbert were sometimes severely dealt with, though sternness was more often tempered with kindness, and he was known to pay the fines of those who were too poor to pay. 'I can't bear to think of that poor devil going to prison for a month on nulla bona,' he wote to the Clerk of the Court on one such occasion, enclosing a cheque.

Towards any kind of misfortune he was lenient, but in cases of cruelty, particularly those involving children or animals, he gave the severest sentence possible, taking little or no notice of any plea of mitigation. It is said old offenders learnt to dread Gilbert's lash, and cowards trembled when they were brought before him.[4] Yet if there were anything in the evidence which amused, Gilbert would sometimes make a quick observation, which showed his wit was as sharp as ever. When an elderly husband and wife came up before him to seek a separation order Gilbert tried to persuade them to stay together on the grounds that they had been together for so long, but the wife remonstrated with him. 'Well, but he's a nasty old man, he beats me, and he's got an abscess on his back.' Gilbert was heard to reply half-audibly, 'Not a case of abscess makes the heart grow fonder.'[5]

In 1898 Gilbert appeared in court himself when he brought a libel action against the weekly paper, *The Era*, which reported theatrical news. It was a ridiculous business which had its origin in the subject of blank verse and the way it should be delivered by the actor, though it was a tour of Gilbert's last prose drama, *The Fortune Hunter*, under the management of the actress, May Fortescue, that sparked it all off.

After opening at the Theatre Royal, Birmingham, on 27 September 1897, the play was moved to Edinburgh where Gilbert decided to follow and do what he could to promote the piece, seeing the Birmingham reviews had not done it justice, and some had been hostile. He spent a night at the Windsor Hotel, an old-fashioned and rather dingy establishment, where, as he informed Kitty, he had only a 'fair sitting-room and a ghastly bedroom'.[6] It was therefore a very indignant Mr Gilbert who confronted the reporter from the Edinburgh *Evening Dispatch*, who asked for an interview. In the course of this Gilbert spoke of many matters: he said he had put more of himself into his blank-verse plays than any other, that *The Yeomen of the Guard* was the best of the Savoy operas and *Gretchen* and *Broken Hearts* his best plays. The reporter asked him if the number of adaptations performed indicated a scarcity of British dramatists. Gilbert replied:

No, it does not. The fact is managers cannot judge a play when they see it in manuscript. If Pinero writes a play and sends it to Sir Henry Irving, it is accepted, not because it is a good play but because it is Pinero. If a stranger who may be a clever dramatist sends Sir Henry or Mr Tree or anybody else a play, it is not accepted, however good it may be, because they can't judge. Your manager nowadays crosses to France, sees a play that goes well, and how it can be slightly watered down to suit our censorious society, and immediately transplants it.[7]

Gilbert said he had no time for translations, the English should leave the French stage alone: Sardou's plays elaborate character to such an extent that they might be pages out of Thackeray turned into French.'[8]

Then came the sentence that would ultimately lead Gilbert into trouble. Gilbert said that French actors could so speak and deliver speeches as to claim the attention of the audience. What of English actors?

Why, we have no actor who can make a thirty-line speech interesting! Whoever heard in this country 'All the world's a stage' declaimed by a Jacques who did not in every line make it plain he had learnt it off by heart. There is always the same dull monotony of delivery. Every living actor – Sir Henry Irving, Beerbohm Tree, George Alexander, excellent though they be otherwise – have that dull monotony of delivery. They keep to one note through the sentence, and finish a semi-tone higher or a semi-tone lower as the case may be.[9]

Then Gilbert went on to say the dramatic taste of the day lay in the direction of musical comedy, and bad musical comedy at that, 'in which half-a-dozen irresponsible comedians are turned loose upon the stage to do exactly as they please. These are our popular pieces.'[10]

However, Gilbert said he thought the theatre was as strong as ever, despite a dearth of original pieces, and he blamed the press for this because it drew no distinction between the production of an original play and the translation of a French one. It was a monstrous injustice to equate Pinero, who wrote original pieces, at his best in *The Magistrate* and *Dandy Dick*, with Sydney Grundy who was only a translator, though he did not wish to decry Mr Grundy in any sense.

Did Mr Gilbert have any further work in progress?

No! I will write no more plays. I mean to retire now. I am disheartened by the erroneous point of view from which criticisms are written in London. They never seem to dissociate the play from the author of the play. I am not complaining of bad criticisms. I have had plenty, and have learned much from them. But there is such a tendency to look upon the author of a bad or an unsuccessful play, not as a poor devil who has tried his best, but as a man who has committed an outrage against nature. The critics attack him as if he were a scoundrel of the worst type, and they go on at it week after week. I don't feel disposed to put myself forward as a cock-shy for these gentlemen. I think it better to refrain from writing as I am obliged to write. I prefer to work in a different groove where anything I may do will stand upon its own merits.[11]

Gilbert went on to speak of *The Fortune Hunter*. It had its faults as every play has, but it was very well acted, and Miss Fortescue had got together a good cast. He wanted to take Edinburgh opinion before the play moved to London. He had not seen the play from the front, and he did not intend to: he had not seen a play of his own from the auditorium for twenty-one years, save a performance of *The Mikado* played in German at Carlsbad seven years earlier.

'Some of my characters I hardly recognized, save for five minutes at a time, when they would go into the adaptor's bypath, and I became profoundly interested in what would happen next. Pooh-Bah, in fact, quite interested me.'[12]

The interview concluded with Gilbert's admission that he had written seventy-five dramatic pieces in the past thirty years, and *The Fortune Hunter* was the only one which had been on his hands.

When the interview appeared it was picked up by almost every newspaper in the country, and its more outspoken passages were quoted, often out of context, so that Gilbert felt obliged to write explanatory letters to the three actors he had mentioned by name, and to Sydney Grundy. He had been grossly misrepresented, he said, and as far as blank-verse speaking was concerned he had merely implied that the current fashion was, in his view, the wrong one.

It was the report of the interview published in *The Era* that Gilbert thought was unacceptable. *The Era* had suggested that Gilbert's abnormal self-esteem had with advancing years developed into a malady. 'In his own estimation he is a kind of Grand Llama or Sacred Elephant of dramatic literature. The mildest criticism of his work, the most gentle disapproval of one of his plays, is a crime of lèse-majesté for which, if it were in his power, he would punish the culprit severely.'

The article had continued by saying it was a significant fact that one of the first things Mr Gilbert had done when he retired from business was to become a JP and that had we lived under a more despotic dispensation he would commit all the London critics for contempt of court.

'Mr Gilbert's career has been a succession of combats with the object, alas! unattained, of vindicating the Gilbert theory of the universe against sceptics and rebels ... his real kindness and good-nature have simply been obscured by the abnormal protuberances of his bump of self-esteem.'[13]

Gilbert demanded £1,000 damages for the Grand Llama insult,

and the case was heard in the Queen's Bench Division before Mr Justice Day with Marshall Hall appearing as leading counsel for Gilbert, and Edward Carson for the defendant.

The transcript of the trial shows Gilbert in the witness-box, like Oscar Wilde, a match for his adversary's searching examination. The laughter aroused annoyed Carson greatly, and in his summing up he delivered such a scathing attack on the plaintiff's character that Gilbert walked out of the court. Just a snatch of Gilbert's wit during the trial must suffice: Carson asked Gilbert to name one bad musical comedy. Gilbert replied:

'Well, take the pantomime at Drury Lane Theatre with the great Dan Leno.' (Loud laughter.)

'But that only goes on a short time in the year.'

'It goes on for a long time in the evening.' (Laughter.)

'Do you really describe a pantomime as a bad musical comedy?'

'No, but I would describe a bad musical comedy as a pantomime.' (Great laughter.)

Later Gilbert was asked about translations; he said he had often translated Greek dramatists when he was at school, but he had never therefore claimed to be the author:

'I have always given Sophocles the credit for his share of the work in them.' (Laughter.) 'I once translated a French play, sitting up all night to do it, and got £3,000 out of it.'

'That was better than the bar?'

'It is better than my experience of it.' (Laughter.)

'There is a passage here [in *The Era*] in which you are described as Gilbert the Great, to which you take exception?'

'Yes, I do not feel I deserve the compliment.' (Laughter.)[14]

The jury were retired for two and a half hours but they could not agree, so each side had to pay its own costs. Gilbert felt he had made his point, and soon departed with Kitty and Nancy for a holiday. From Sorrento on 12 April 1989, he wrote to Berbohm Tree's wife, Maud.

I have not worried myself at all about the trial. I resolved not to look at a newspaper, and, in short, I determined to clear my mind of it altogether. After all I have done what I wanted to do. I was charged with having made an unworthy and malicious attack on a body of men, many of whom I hold in high regard, and it was (as it seemed to me) incumbent upon me to refute the charge. The only way of doing this was to bring an action. The case would have been mine but for the judge who was simply a monument of senile incapacity. To the very last he hadn't the faintest notion as to what the trial was about. My case was comparatively trivial, but it is fearful to think that grave issues in which a man's fortune or a woman's honour may be involved, are at the mercy of an utterly incompetent old doll.[15]

Gilbert went on to say that Carson had conducted his case in the spirit of a 'low-class police court attorney', but he had done no harm. Then Gilbert came to the main point in his letter to Maud Tree.

'I was particularly impressed with your husband's kindness in trying to make peace. As one of the men whom I was represented as having pointed at, it showed no little magnanimity on his part and one does not forget such things.'[16]

One does not forget such things, and many were those who would not forget similar acts of kindness from Gilbert himself.

While Gilbert was in Italy Sullivan was in England preparing his new opera, *The Beauty Stone*, for the Savoy, a piece for which Pinero and Comyns Carr had written the libretto. Comyns Carr had travelled to the Riviera to confer with Sullivan and found him often in considerable pain, but in spite of this 'the brightness of his disposition constantly asserted itself', and his enthusiasm at the gambling tables continued unabated, where Carr noticed his 'superstitious behaviour, and his feverish exhilaration'.[17]

In the past few years much had happened besides the constant sparring with Gilbert. The year 1897 had seen the Queen's Diamond Jubilee, and Sullivan had once again composed special music in celebration. In May his ballet, *Victoria and Merrie England*, 'a piece intended to reflect the life of Britain',[18] was danced at the Alhambra Theatre, and in June, as part of the official celebrations, his Jubilee Hymn, a setting of words by Bishop Walsham Howe, the Bishop of Wakefield, was performed. In recent years Sullivan's involvement with the Royal Family had become closer than ever. In the August of 1896 he had stayed at Engadine, in Switzeland, and spent almost every day in the company of the Duchess of York and her mother, the Duchess of Teck, walking and dining with them. Prince Francis of Battenberg was also there, and Mr and Mrs Leo Rothschild. After Engadine, Sullivan went on to Munich and Vienna, and at Nauheim

on the way home he had received a telegram from the Empress
Frederick of Germany, Queen Victoria's eldest daughter, now a
widow, inviting him to stay.

In April 1897 Sullivan was staying in Cimiez for Easter, where he
played the harmonium for the Easter Day service in the chapel of the
Regina Hotel in front of the Queen and other members of the Royal
Family. The Queen presented him with 'a lovely pocket-book as a
souvenir of the day'.[19] Sullivan was particularly pleased to be once
again in the company of his friend Prince Alfred, the Duke of
Edinburgh, who was now ruler of Saxe-Coburg-Gotha, and married
to Princess Marie of Russia.

In July the Queen invited Sullivan to stay at Windsor, where he
had twenty minutes' conversation with her alone, and after they
parted she sent him the Jubilee Medal; then Sullivan stayed up
playing billiards and smoking with members of the Household till
bedtime. However, Sullivan saw more of the Prince of Wales than
any other member of the Family. For one thing they shared a
passionate interest in racing, and Sullivan was usually in the
Prince's party at Newmarket and Epsom. But in August the two
were in a musical setting, at Bayreuth. Sullivan attended performances of *Parsifal* and the four operas of the Ring Cycle. Of
Rheingold he wrote, 'It is difficult to know how Wagner could have
got up any enthusiasm or interest in such a lying, thieving,
blackguardly set of low creatures as all the characters in his Opera
prove themselves to be.'[20]

Siegfried was 'intolerably dull and heavy, and so undramatic'.[21]
Only the last act of *Götterdämerung* came in for any praise, and he
thought it 'fine and impressive. The Leit Motiven seemed all natural
and not dragged in, and the whole act is much more dramatic, and
musically finer than all the others.'[22]

Sullivan, unlike Wagner, did not write his own words, and he
found the libretto of *The Beauty Stone* tedious to set. He resorted to
borrowing from *The Golden Legend* for some of the music, but despite
the difficulties it was all completed, rehearsed and ready to open on 28
May 1898.

The story tells how Laine, an ugly crippled girl, becomes beautiful
through the power of the Beauty Stone, and wins a beauty competi-
tion. She is pursued by Philip, Lord of Mirelemont, in Flanders, but
this does not go very smoothly because Mirelemont had returned
from imprisonment in Cephalonia with Lady Saida. Finally Laine

loses the stone and returns to her real self, and Mirelemont, returning blind from battle, never sees her, but the two live happily ever after. It is hardly surprising the opera failed to impress, and it ran for only fifty performances, to be followed by a revival of *The Gondoliers*. This was in turn followed by *The Sorcerer*, which celebrated its twenty-first anniversary, an occasion at which Sullivan not only conducted but also appeared with Gilbert at the final curtain call for the last time, though the two did not speak. The next time Gilbert saw Sullivan approaching in the street he cut him dead. 'I survived it,' Sullivan told Helen Carte, 'but I am not going to, wittingly, indulge him in a similar pleasure if I can help it.'[23]

By now Sullivan was working on Basil Hood's libretto of 'Hassan', which under the revised name of *The Rose of Persia* or *The Story-teller and the Slave*, was the last opera he would complete. Captain Hood, a descendant of Thomas Hood, had recently retired from the army and was making his way in the theatre; his words were very much more to Sullivan's taste than those of Comyns Carr, and the Eastern atmosphere and the romance of the story, Hassan bored by his twenty-five wives, the Sultan and Sultana in disguise as a dervish and a dancing girl, appealed particularly to him.

Some of the music was composed while Sullivan was in Switzerland, where he had happy memories of two years earlier when for a brief period he had fallen madly in love with a twenty-year-old girl, Violet Beddington, to whom, at the age of fifty-four, he had proposed marriage. Sullivan told her he probably had only two years to live. Could she not give him two years of her life? Could she find the love that would renew him? After that – she should still have her own life before her. He would leave her all he possessed, but he said it would have to be a secret wedding. Violet thought this all over and decided it would not do, but she had returned his affection. 'To what are you looking forward?' he had asked her, and she had replied. 'Only this day being with you ... to have a perfect day with you.'[24]

Hood came out to Switzerland to discuss the opera, and Sullivan enjoyed his company, finding him in every way helpful: 'He is such a nice fellow and so pleasant to work with,'[25] he wrote. However, most of the composition of this new work was completed back in England at the house he had rented at Wokingham. When the opera opened on 29 November 1899, following a revival of *Trial by Jury* and HMS *Pinafore*, it was considered a worthy successor to Gilbert's work, though Hood was rather unfairly accused of writing Gilbertian pastiche. In fact, the words owed as much to Fitzgerald's 'Omar Khayyam' as to Gilbert, and Hood was a punster in his own right. Sullivan had risen to the occasion and composed some delightful music. The *Daily Telegraph* was pleased to note the music was 'quite after the pattern that became familiar in the Savoy's palmiest days'.[26] Sullivan had felt confident enough, after conducting the first performance, an experience at which he confessed to feeling 'hideously nervous', to pronounce the piece a great success, something unusual for him recently. The *Daily Telegraph* also raised his spirits considerably by saying, 'The musician is once again absolutely himself.'[27] Sullivan felt this to be true, though physically he was still intermittently suffering dreadful pain. It seemed in Hood he had found the ideal replacement for Gilbert, and it was natural to think of a further Hood and Sullivan venture.

The small world of theatres and operas was for a while eclipsed by what was happening in the world at large. England was once again at war! The Boer War had begun in October 1899. In December during what came to be known as 'Black Week' three British armies were defeated at Tugele River, Magersfontein and Colenso. The country was horrified. Kipling had written his poem 'The Absent-Minded Beggar', in November, and the *Daily Mail* asked the great Sir Arthur Sullivan to set it to music. The result was Sullivan was rehearsing the song at the Alhambra Theatre and his Persian opera, as he called it, at the Savoy at the same time. The song was first heard on the evening of 13 November. Sullivan noted in his diary: 'Packed house – wild enthusiasm. All sang chorus!' He had stood on the stage and conducted an encore.

'Your splendid words went, and still go every night with a swing and an enthusiasm which even my music cannot stifle. It has been a great pleasure to me to set words of yours,'[28] he wrote to Kipling after a few days.

Indeed 'The Absent-Minded Beggar' became the rage, and drove 'all other songs from the barrel-organs'.[29] It was the most popular song of its kind since 'We don't want to fight, but, by Jingo, if we do'. Tens of thousands of copies were printed under the auspices of the *Daily Mail*, and sold for the benefit of soldiers' families, and if the average Englishman had never heard of Paul Kruger before, he certainly had now. The Queen wrote to Sullivan asking for a copy of the music and the stirring words!

When you've shouted 'Rule Britannia', when you've
    sung 'God save the Queen',
  When you've finished killing Kruger with your mouth,
Will you kindly drop a shilling in my little tambourine
    For a gentleman in *khaki* ordered South?
He's an absent-minded beggar, and his weaknesses are
    great –
  But we and Paul must take him as we find him –
He is out on active service, wiping something off a slate –
  And he's left a lot of little things behind him!
Duke's son – cook's son – son of a hundred kings –
  (Fifty thousand horse and foot going to Table Bay!)
Each of 'em doing his country's work
  (and who's to look after their things?)
Pass the hat for your credit's sake,
          and pay – pay – pay![30]

The last line of the stanza came as a refrain, but Kipling's hold of the metre was a little shaky, and it is not surprising Sullivan found it very difficult to set.

At this time Richard D'Oyly Carte's health was failing, and he approached Sullivan with the idea of his taking over the Savoy Theatre. At first this seemed attractive, but although Sullivan was definitely feeling a little fitter himself, he declined. He just did not want the responsibility, and besides, Helen Carte was well able to organise things: she had been doing so for many years. Yet writing for the Savoy was another matter, and Sullivan and Hood were already considering another opera with an Irish theme. The scheme of *The Emerald Isle* was ready by the end of June. It was good and up to the mark, Sullivan thought, when he read some of the lyrics for Act 1. However, work would not begin immediately, because Sullivan was busily setting a special 'Te Deum' in anticipation of a British victory in Africa. While at the Epsom races with the Prince news had come through that Roberts was at Johannesburg: it was only a matter of time.

Then on 30 July 1900 Sullivan heard the sad news that Prince Alfred had died. He was dreadfully upset: 'one of my oldest and best friends', he wrote in his diary. Within a matter of weeks two other close friends died. 'They go with cruel rapidity,' he wrote in his diary. If he was going to make any headway with the new opera, which, it was hoped, would be ready for November, he must get away. He returned to Switzerland, but he found his usual hotel full of 'howlng and shrieking Germans'. At Thusis towards the end of August he composed the first notes of *The Emerald Isle*. During the following three weeks he worked away sporadically, but was held up for a while because he ran out of scoring paper. On some days he sufffered from neuralgia, and after calling on the Duchess of York he was caught in a rainstorm and developed a throat infection that 'almost robbed him of his power of speech'.[31]

Although he began to wonder if he would ever see his home again, he arrived back in London on 19 September with something of the opera written, but it was a question of whether he could manage what he always had in the past, a last-minute rush right up to the first rehearsal. Hood was doing his part, but could he?

Sullivan knew his health was not recovering. He tried to work, but it was almost impossible. Tunbridge Wells might be the answer. 'Felt very seedy all day – pain from kidney trouble. Awfully nervous and in terror about myself,'[32] he recorded on the day he travelled down to Kent. When he had arrived he could not stand up, so a doctor was called, who got him in bed and injected him with something. Sullivan knew it was not morphine, but it relieved the pain directly and gave him a good night's rest.

The following day he felt well enough to get up and go for a short walk. Perhaps he could even work, but a week or so passed and he found work virtually impossible.

'Have been here just a fortnight, and what have I done? Little more than nothing, first from illness and physical incapacity, secondly from brooding and nervous terror about myself. Practically I have done nothing for a month.'[33]

The following day, 15 October, was a bright and sunny autumn day. 'I am sorry to leave on such a lovely day,'[34] he wrote in his diary. He returned to London in the care of Louis Jager, his valet, and his maid Clothilde Raquet. He struggled on for another month, and Mary Ronalds, helped by his servants, did her best to keep him in good spirits, but Sullivan never recovered, and he died in his nephew Herbert Sullivan's arms a little after six o'clock in the morning of 22 November 1900.

A revival of *Patience* had opened at the Savoy on 7 November, but Sullivan had been too ill to come to the theatre. Gilbert was not at all well himself, suffering from rheumatic fever contracted while he was clay-puddling the lake in the grounds at Grim's Dyke. Nevertheless when he heard Sullivan was seriously ill, he wrote him a letter which reached him ten days before the end.

I would be glad to come up to town to see you before I go, but unfortunately in my present enfeebled condition a carriage journey to London involves my lying down a couple of hours before I am fit for anything, besides stopping all night in town. The railway journey is still more fatiguing. I have lost sixty pounds in weight, and my arms and legs are of the consistency of cotton-wool. I sincerely hope to find you all right again on my return, and the new opera running merrily.[35]

Gilbert, like so many others, had not realised Sullivan was dying. As his letter indicates, he was out of the country when Sullivan died, so he did not attend the funeral, nor was he aware of what seemed such a terribly sudden death until some days afterwards. From Helouan he wrote to Herbert Sullivan apologising for the delay in expressing his personal sorrow and sympathy:

'It is a satisfaction to me to feel that I was impelled, shortly before his death, to write to him to propose to shake hands over our recent differences, and even greater satisfaction to learn, through you, that my offer of reconcilation was cordially accepted. I wish I had been in England that I might have had the opportunity of joining the mourners at the funeral.'[36]

The funeral was not exactly what Sullivan intended. His wish had been to be buried in the same grave as his mother in Brompton Cemetery. The grave had already been opened when news came that the Queen had intervened, and Sir Arthur was to receive a more fitting obsequy. The first part of the service would take place at the Chapel Royal, where Sullivan had been a chorister so many years before: then the funeral would proceed formally through the streets to St Paul's Cathedral, where Sullivan's body would be laid in the crypt, near to those of his fellow composers Maurice Green and William Boyce.

One of Sullivan's wishes during the days of his last illness had been, as he told Helen Carte, 'to bury the hatchet and smoke a pipe of peace' with Gilbert. Both hatchet and pipe could be found in the property-room at the theatre, he joked, and if the result was to relieve Gilbert of that awful gout, he would be well pleased. At the first night of the revival of *Patience* there had been some plan for Gilbert, Sullivan and

Carte, all of whom were ill, to appear on the stage in wheel chairs to take the final curtain, but Sullivan had felt too weak to manage it.

'It's not a question of taking a chill if I come out, but of ever getting out at all again. I am regularly bowled over – kidneys and throat.

Pray tell Gilbert how very much I feel the disappointment.

Good luck to you all. Three invalid chairs would have looked very well from the front.'[37]

It was not many months before Richard D'Oyly Carte also died. Gilbert himself had only narrowly escaped death in a train crash out in Egypt, but it was given to him to live another eleven years, years in which he enjoyed the peace and tranquillity of his beautiful home, oversaw revivals of many of the Savoy operas and the production of three new works: an opera and two plays. Gilbert had been very fortunate in his choice of a wife. Lucy, or Kitty as he always called her, was devoted to him, and organised their very large household, a task in which Nancy McIntosh was always a great help. There were twenty on the staff at Grim's Dyke, and it is one of the marks of this remarkably happy couple that they evinced great loyalty from their servants; the Gilberts' butler, for instance, had been with them for twenty-six years.

The rooms at Grim's Dyke were very large and finely furnished. The great drawing-room, which had formerly been Frederick Goodall's studio, had large ecclesiastical-looking windows, and it was full of treasures. In this room Gilbert had himself designed the massive fireplace, some fifteen feet high, carved in Cornish alabaster.

A visitor to the house noticed how, scattered among the many works of art and curios of all kinds, were interesting souvenirs from Gilbert's plays and operas.

In the billiard-room is the block and axe so long used in *The Yeoman of the Guard*. Here too are 250 drawings from the 'Bab Ballads' framed. In the hall – wherein is a fine suit of steel armour – is a huge model of a full-rigged ship. It rests on a sea of green glass, and is fourteen feet long. It is a facsimile of one of the old three-deckers of a hundred and ten guns sent to the Black Sea in the Crimean War – the *Queen*.[38]

Here was, of course, the model for HMS *Pinafore*, the deck and rigging of which when imitated on the stage had so impressed Lord Jellico. 'Not a rope wrong,'[39] he said.

At Grim's Dyke Gilbert lived the life of the gentieman he was.

There was nothing in the least nouveau riche about either the furnishings or the manner in which Kitty and he lived, though they entertained frequently and their garden parties were famous for their liberality and always beautifully hosted. Kitty Gilbert was a talented flower arranger, so that the house was always exquisitely decorated from their own hothouses and gardens, and Gilbert wore a red flower in his button-hole every day. Over the years the number of animals they kept increased. Besides the dogs – two Pekes, a Scotch terrier, a collie and a French poodle who all ate with the family in the dining room where a special tablecloth for each was laid on the floor – there were two blue Persian cats, horses – 'Bryant and May, the perfect match' – and the many animals on the farm; there was also a menagerie of more unusual creatures, monkeys, parrots, Siberian cranes and the lemurs, in which Gilbert took such pride, only rivalled in his affection by a pet fawn and a donkey, named Adelina after Adelina Patti because it had a high voice.

Gilbert was very fond of the fawn, a fallow deer, which he used to take for walks with the donkey along the country lanes. His affection was reciprocated and the young hind became so fond of him that it would not leave him alone, only happy if its nose was resting in Gilbert's hand, and four times one afternoon in search of such bliss it disturbed him at work in the library. When the fawn grew larger Gilbert decided it might be more sensible to send it to Bentley Park, where there was a herd of deer. This seemed an admirable idea and appeared to have been successful, but after four years, and now fully grown, it found its way back to Grim's Dyke. Gilbert liked to tell the story of how after the fawn had been gone a year he had happened to be walking through the park and given the particular whistle he had once used as a call, and the animal left the herd immediately and trotted up to lay its nose in his hand as though they had never been apart.

'Deer-stalking would be a very fine sport if only the deer had guns,'[40] Gilbert once said. He abhorred all blood-sports, but he was not against killing in any form, provided he was not the one to do the killing. 'It is not humanity on my part. I am perfectly willing that other people should kill things for my comfort and advantage. The mechanism of life is so wonderful that I shrink from stopping its action. To tread on a black-beetle would be to me like crushing a watch of complex and exquisite workmanship.'[41]

Gilbert's concern for animals was matched by his affection for children. Although the Gilberts had no children of their own, and there is no way of knowing beyond conjecture why this should have been, other people's children were always happy to be at Grim's Dyke, because they were given such an exciting time. Gilbert delighted in thinking up games for them, and he was especially fond of dressing up.

Offical recognition came to Gilbert on 15 July 1907, when he was knighted by Edward VII at Buckingham Palace. He took the birthday honour lightly; it was a 'tin-pot, twopenny-halfpenny sort of distinction',[42] but one he felt he could not refuse, although it had come a little late in the day. 'This indiscriminate flinging about of knighthoods is making me very nervous; it's quite possible they may give one to my butler. He's a very good fellow, and I'm afraid it will upset him.'[43]

He was amused to find he had been entered on the list as 'Mr William Gilbert, playwright', and said it suggested that his work was

analogical to that of a wheelwright, or a millwright, or a wainwright, or a shipwright, as regards the mechanical character of the process by which our respective results are achieved. There is an excellent word 'dramatist' which seems to fit the situation, but it is not applied until we are dead, and then we become dramatists as oxen, sheep and pigs are transfigured into beef, mutton and pork after their demise. You never hear of a novelwright, or a picturewright or a poemwright, and why a playwright.[44]

He was aware he had not received the honour for his literary work alone, 'as no dramatic author as such ever had it for dramatic authorship alone'.[45] The Restoration dramatist, Sir John Vanbrugh, had been knighted, but then he had been also the architect who designed Blenheim Palace. No, it must be remembered Sir William Gilbert was also Deputy Lord Lieutenant for Middlesex, and secretary of the Bushey Heath Cottage Hospital! If anything Gilbert considered it the greater honour that he was soon to be elected a member of the Garrick Club.

Reporting the investiture *The Times* said Gilbert's works had become classical and the object of such fervent affection as classics seldom enjoy, and then went on to ask: 'Is the knighthood compensation for the temporary ban which was placed on *The Mikado*, or a reward for the sublime mockery of the Peers in *Iolanthe*?'[46]

The Mikado had indeed been banned that year because Prince

Fushimi of Japan was making a state visit and it was thought the opera might have been seen as an insult. Helen D'Oyly Carte had let the theatre soon after her husband's death, but she had returned to present a revival of *The Yeomen of the Guard* on 8 December 1906. Productions of *The Gondoliers* and *Patience* followed, which, Mrs Carte intended, would be succeeded by *The Mikado*, until she received notice from the Lord Chamberlain prohibiting the performance. Suddenly an opera the English had enjoyed for twenty years was seen as 'purposely offensive to Japan'. Neither was the ban restricted to the Savoy, for the Lord Chamberlain also prohibited a performance by the Middlesbrough Amateur Operatic Society 'owing to buffoonery in certain parts'. This drew a letter from Gilbert, published in the *Daily Telegraph*, in which he pointed out that if any buffooonery had crept into the piece during its long career in the provinces, which he had no reason to believe was the case, the Lord Chamberlain's obvious course was 'to suppress the buffoonery, instead of slaughtering the play outright, and by so doing deprive the public of a very popular entertainment'.[47] This was to say nothing of the loss of revenue to the representatives of the late Sir Arthur Sullivan and himself.

It was not until 28 April 1908 that *The Mikado* was able to reappear unashamed and unabashed. Gilbert, attending his first rehearsal since his knighthood, was noticed by Rutland Barrington. 'It was soon evident that his master-mind was as alert and as keen as ever, and those of us who were uncertain as to what was gag and what original in our part were feeling slightly nervous.'[48] There had been no need for alarm: Sir William was full of courtesy, and 'there was a geniality about the proceedings that brought back happy memories.'

On the opening night François Cellier, on taking his seat to conduct, was received almost as if he were the composer, and ironically there was a very large contingent of Japanese in the audience who found 'bright music, much fun and no insults', as Rutland Barrington began his last run of 142 performances as Pooh-Bah.

In March 1909 Helen D'Oyly Carte relinquished her management of the Savoy, which was taken over by Charles Herbert Workman, a member of the company who had first appeared at the theatre in *The Grand Duke*, so it was with Workman as manager that Gilbert's last opera, *Fallen Fairies*, opened at the Savoy on 15 December. The music was by Edward German, the composer of *Merrie England*, who had also completed the score of Sullivan's *The Emerald Isle*. The libretto was adapted from Gilbert's play *The Wicked World*, which had played in 1873 at the Haymarket with the Kendals in the cast, though Gilbert himself had burlesqued it under the title *The Happy Land* for the Court Theatre two months after the opening. In fact, the burlesque had received more attention than the play, and was far more successful, as it was a satire on the politicians of the day. It was banned by the Lord Chamberlain for a while, but then released again, which swelled the audience considerably, so that the theatre was crowded for months.

Now that Gilbert had complete control over the production, and neither Sullivan nor Carte was there to object, there was no reason why Nancy should not play the important part of Selene, the Fairy Queen, who abuses her royal powers by falling in love with a mortal and only keeps the throne by renouncing her love. 'It is a deadly snare – beware of it! Such love is for mankind and not for us.'[49]

It was a very full part with many songs, which required Nancy to be on the stage for most of the time. She spent many hours practising with German, who was said to have been impressed by her ability; however, there had been an altercation in the early stages of the production, because Workman had the singer Elsie Spain, who had sung Josephine in the recent revival of HMS *Pinafore*, in mind for the leading part. This prompted the following from Gilbert:

> I do not press Miss McIntosh on you. Only I say that German and I are completely satisfied with her – that I wrote the part for her and German the soprano music. If you can find a better at her salary (£25 a week) we will accept her – but Miss Spain, an excellent soubrette, would be quite out of place in a stately part calling for scenes of passion and denunciation. Miss McIntosh is an admirable singer and accomplished Shakespearean actress, with an individuality and appearance which are exactly what the part calls for.[50]

Gilbert had his own way, but the opera had not been running for more than a few nights before one of the backers was calling for Nancy to be dropped from the cast. In order to keep her in the part Gilbert threatened to withdraw his permission for the piece to be played at all. On 27 December he informed Workman: 'This is to give you notice that I intend to apply today to a Judge in Chambers for an ex parte injunction restraining you from playing *Fallen Fairies* this evening except with Miss McIntosh or her accredited understudy

Miss Venning in the part of Selene; I give you this notice that you may be in a position to face the contingency.'[51]

In spite of all the effort to keep it alive the opera only survived through the Christmas season, and was taken off on 10 January 1910 after fifty-one performances.

Gilbert saw Workman as another 'slippery character' , and when some months later Workman tried to purchase the performing rights of the Savoy operas the answer was swift and to the point: 'I do not intend to waste any epithets upon you – you can easily supply them yourself. It is enough to say that no consideration of any kind would induce me to have dealings with a man of your stamp.'[52]

In May 1910, the month King Edward VII died, Gilbert took Kitty and Nancy on a cruise to the Azores, and in the autumn, this time journeying alone, he visited Constantinople. From each port of call he posted affectionate letters to Kitty from her 'devoted Old Boy'. The food was not conducive to happiness: 'The fish is poor, the eggs twangy, and the meat tough', he wrote, though the service was excellent, and there were several passengers one could talk to, 'but none of them much above the average'. Little of note was recorded in Gilbert's diary which he wrote in French, and he was glad to reach home again.

The last theatrical piece Gilbert wrote was *The Hooligan* performed at the Coliseum on 27 February 1911. It was little more than a sketch in which the action takes place in the condemned cell where a prisoner is waiting for the moment of execution, but he dies of heart failure just before his reprieve has been announced. Although Kitty attended the theatre on the opening night Gilbert dined at the Beefsteak Club and joined her afterwards. *The Hooligan* was a distinct success and Gilbert was particularly pleased since he had always longed to be noticed for a piece of serious dramatic work!

During the early days of May 1911, Gilbert suffered from rheumatism and he found it was eased by frequent dips in the lake. On 28 May it was hot; besides playing croquet with Nancy on the lawn before and after luncheon, and later listening to her singing, he bathed three times in the course of the day and spent some time attending to his pet lemurs. He also wrote a letter to Winifred Emery inviting her to come to Grim's Dyke the following afternoon for a swim. She could if she wished bring one of her pupils, Ruby Preece, with her. He had to be in town in the morning, he told her, but he would return to Harrow-on-the-Hill by the Grand Central at 3.38. If the ladies could be at the station he would drive them to Grim's Dyke in his motor.

All went according to plan. In the morning of 29 May Gilbert carried out his various engagements: at Chelsea he attended the annual Oak-apple Day Parade at the Royal Hospital, where his friend Sir Charles Crutchley was Lieutenant-Governor; the inspection that year was taken by Lord Roberts. Next he went on to the Junior Carlton Club for luncheon, where he astonished William Kendal, with whom he had recently healed a rift lasting many years, by his affability; then he left to visit May Fortescue, the original Celia in *Iolanthe*, who had later turned to management and put on many of Gilbert's plays. May was in bed after a riding accident in the park. Falling on the back of her head had damaged her optic nerves so that she had to rest in complete darkness. Her mother said to Gilbert: 'I won't ask what you think of her appearance, for you can scarcely see her.' 'Her appearance matters nothing,' Gilbert replied. 'It's her disappearance we could not stand.'[53]

The island in the lake was aflame with red azaleas, along the shore there were flags of golden irises and at their feet a mass of little blue forget-me-nots. The girls were not good swimmers, but it was just possible to touch the bottom. Suddenly Ruby panicked and called out to Winifred for help. Gilbert, who was standing at the side, saw the difficulty the girl was in, and called out that the lake was not very deep and that she should not splash so much. Realising she was not calming herself, he plunged in and swam out towards her. 'Put your hands on my shoulders and don't struggle,' he said breathlessly for he had had to strike out to reach her quickly. She did as he asked, but immediately he seemed to sink beneath her. She struggled on towards the shore alone, soon discovering she could feel the bottom. There was no sign of Gilbert. Presently the gardener came and got out the boat, but it seemed to the girls a long time before they recovered his body.

There was no water in Gilbert's lungs: he had died of heart failure in his attempt to rescue a young girl from drowning. Strangely it was the fulfilment of a wish he had once expressed, when he said quite suddenly: 'I should like to die upon a summer day in my own garden.'[54]

'But Iolanthe didn't die!'[55]

The Dramatic Works of W.S.Gilbert

1866   *Dulcamara*. Extravaganza (St James's Theatre).
1867   *Harlequin Cock-Robin*. Pantomime (Lyceum).
1868   *Robert the Devil*. Operatic extravaganza (Gaiety).
1869   *An Old Score*. Play (Gaiety).
       Ages Ago (Royal Gallery of Illustration).
1870   *Our Island Home*. Opera (Royal Gallery of Illustration).
       The Princess. A whimsical allegory. Being a respectful
       perversion of Mr Tennyson's poem.
       The Palace of Truth. A fairy comedy in three acts
       (Haymarket).
       The Gentleman in Black. An original musical legend in two
       acts.
1871   *Thespis*.
       Great Expectations (after Dickens) (Court).
       Pygmalion and Galatea. Play (Haymarket).
1872   *Randall's Thumb*. An original comedy in three acts.
       Creatures of Impulse. A musical fairy-tale in one act.
1873   *The Wicked World*. Play (Haymarket).
       The Happy Land. Play (Court).
1874   *On Guard*. An entirely original comedy in three acts.
       Ought We to Visit Her? Play (Royalty).
       Charity. Play (Haymarket).
1875   *Trial by Jury*.
       Broken Hearts (Court).
1876   *Dan'l Druce*. Play (Court).
1877   *The Sorcerer*.
       Engaged (Haymarket).

1878   *Sweethearts*. An original dramatic comedy in two acs.
      The Wedding March (Le Chapeau de Paille d'Italie, by E. M.
      Labiche). An eccentricity in three acts.
      The Ne'er Do Well (Olympic).
      HMS *Pinafore.*

1879   *Gretchen* (Olympic).

1880   *Tom Cobb; or Fortune's Toy*. An entirely original farcical
      comedy in three acts.
      The Pirates of Penzance.
      The Martyr of Antioch. Cantata (music by Sullivan) (Leeds
      Festival).

1881   *On Bail*. A farcical comedy in three acts. Adapted from *Le
      Reveillon.*
      Patience.
      Foggert's Fairy. Play (Criterion).

1882   *Iolanthe.*

1884   *Princess Ida.*

1885   *The Mikado.*

1887   *Ruddigore.*

1888   *The Yeomen of the Guard.*
      Brantinghame Hall (St James's).

1889   *The Gondoliers.*

1892   *The Mountebanks*. An entirely original comic opera.
      Haste to the Wedding. Opera (music by Grossmith).

1893   *Rosencrantz and Guildenstern*. A tragic episode in three
      tableaux, founded on an old German legend.
      Utopia, Limited.

1894   *His Excellency*. An entirely original comic opera in two acts
      (music by Osmond Carr) (Lyric).

1895   *Comedy and Tragedy*. An original comedy in one act.

1896   *The Grand Duke.*

1897   *The Fortune Hunter* (Theatre Royal, Birmingham).

1904   *The Fairy's Dilemma* (Garrick).

1909   *Fallen Fairies*. Opera (music by Edward German) (Savoy).

1911   *The Hooligan* (Coliseum).

Notes

Abbreviations

Works of W. S. Gilbert

GBB: *The Bab Ballads* (Macmillan, 1904)

GSO: *The Savoy Operas* (Macmillan, 1926)

GOP: *Original Plays* (Chatto & Windus, 1911–17). Four Vols.

DG: *W. S. Gilbert. His Life and Letters*, Sidney Dark and Rowland Grey (Methuen, 1923)

LB: *The Gilbert and Sullivan Book*, Leslie Baily (Cassell, 1952; revised edition, 1956).

SF: *Sir Arthur Sullivan*, Herbert Sullivan and Newman Flower (Cassell, 1927).

AL: *Sir Arthur Sullivan. Life Story, Letters and Reminiscences*, Arthur Lawrence (James Bowden, 1899).

AJ: *Arthur Sullivan*, Arthur Jacobs (OUP, 1986).

CB: *Gilbert, Sullivan and D'Oyly Carte*, François Cellier and Cunningham Bridgeman (Pitman, 1927).

HP: *Gilbert. His Life and Strife*, Hesketh Pearson (Methuen, 1957).

1 An Unequal Beginning

1. LB p. 30.
2. HP p. 15.
3. LB p. 29.
4. Ibid. p. 41.
5. Lawrence James, *Crimea* (Hayes Kennedy, 1981).
6. SF p. 4.
7. Ibid. p. 5.
8. LB p. 32.
9. Ibid. p. 33.
10. Isaac Goldberg, *The Story of Gilbert and Sullivan* (John Murray, 1929), p. 29.
11. Ibid. p. 31.
12. SF p. 9.
13. Ibid. p. 10.
14. Ibid. p. 12.
15. DG p. 5.
16. Ibid.

17. Ibid.
18. HP p. 19.
19. DG p. 5.
20. HP pp. 19–20.
21. GSO p. 7.
22. GBB p. 2.
23. Ibid. pp. 3–4.
24. Ibid.
25. Ibid.
26. W. S. Gilbert; *The Bab Ballads* 1869, First Edition, Preface.
27. Ibid, sub-title.
28. SF p. 16.
29. Ibid.
30. Ibid. p. 38.
31. H. Saxe Wyndham, *Arthur Sullivan* (Bell, 1903), p. 9.
32. SF p. 39.
33. Ibid. p. 42.
34. Ibid. pp. 38–9.
35. Ibid. pp. 37–8.
36. Ibid. p. 41.
37. Ibid. p. 42.
38. Ibid. pp. 45–6.
39. Goldberg, op. cit., p. 67.
40. LB p. 86.
41. Ibid. p. 84.
42. Ibid. p. 80.
43. SF p. 47.
44. AL pp. 64–5.
45. HP p. 128.
46. DG p. 41.
47. Ibid.
48. SF p. 64.
49. Leslie Baily, *Gilbert and Sullivan and their World* (Thames & Hudson, 1973), p. 29.
50. LB p. 90.
51. SF p. 65.
52. Ibid. p. 54.
53. Ibid. pp. 55–6.
54. AJ p. 44.
55. SF p. 57.
56. Ibid.

2 The Gods Grown Old

1. Charles Dickens, 'Private Theatres' from *Sketches by Boz*.
2. *Oxford Companion to the Theatre*, article on Menken.
3. Townley Searle, *Sir W. S. Gilbert* (Alexander-Ousley 1931), p. 11.
4. W. MacQueen Pope, *Gaiety. Theatre of Enchantment* (W. H. Allen, 1949), p. 43.
5. Ibid.
6. Isaac Goldberg, *The Story of Gilbert and Sullivan* (John Murray, 1929), p. 106.
7. SF p. 39.
8. LB p. 98.
9. SF p. 68.
10. Ibid.
11. GOP p. 447.
12. SF p. 68.
13. GOP p. 459.
14. Ibid. p. 448.
15. Ibid. pp. 455–6.
16. SF pp. 68–9.
17. HP p. 85.
18. LB p. 93.
19. Ibid. p. 94.
20. SF p. 74.
21. LB p. 126.
22. GSO p. 6.
23. Ibid. p. 7.
24. Ibid. pp. 12–13.
25. Ibid. p. 15.
26. Ibid. p. 16.
27. Ibid. p. 17.
28. CB p. 31.
29. *Daily Telegraph*, 26 March 1875.
30. GSO p. 11.
31. *The Times*, 26 March 1875.

3 A Dealer in Magic and Spells

1. HP p. 86.
2. Ibid.

3. HP p. 88.
4. Ibid. p. 90.
5. Townley Searle, *Sir W. S. Gilbert* (Alexander-Ousley, 1931), p. 38.
6. AL p. 114.
7. Ibid.
8. Ibid. p. 116.
9. SF p. 78.
10. Ibid. p. 80.
11. Ibid.
12. Isaac Goldberg, *The Story of Gilbert and Sullivan* (John Murray, 1925), p. 185.
13. Ibid. p. 186.
14. GOS pp. 25–6.
15. Ibid. p. 27.
16. Ibid. p. 37.
17. Ibid.
18. Ibid.
19. Ibid. p. 49.
20. Ibid. p. 59.
21. Ibid. p. 60.
22. LB pp. 134–5.
23. Goldberg, op. cit., p. 189.
24. LB p. 142.
25. Ibid. p. 143.

4   *The Ruler of the Queen's Navee!*

1. Rudyard Kipling, *Verse*, Inclusive Edition 1885–1926, 'The White Man's Burden' (Hodder & Stoughton, 1927), p. 320.
2. HP p. 95.
3. GBB pp. 226–7.
4. DG pp. 75–6.
5. HP p. 95.
6. GSO p. 67.
7. Ibid. p. 72.
8. Ibid. p. 73.
9. Ibid. p. 74.
10. Ibid. pp. 74–5.
11. Ibid. p. 74.
12. Ibid. p. 80.
13. Ibid. p. 81.
14. Ibid. p. 83.
15. Ibid. p. 84.
16. Ibid. p. 86.
17. Ibid. p. 89.
18. Ibid. pp. 92–3.
19. Ibid. p. 95.
20. Ibid. p. 96.
21. Ibid. p. 99.
22. Ibid. p. 100.
23. SF p. 91.
24. HP p. 98.
25. *The Times*, 27 May 1878.
26. CB p. 47.
27. LB p. 98.
28. Leslie Baily, *Gilbert and Sullivan and their World* (Thames & Hudson, 1973), p. 53.
29. Percy M. Young, *Sir Arthur Sullivan* (J. M. Dent, 1971), p. 114.
30. Jessie Bond, *Life and Reminiscences* (John Land, The Bodley Head, 1930), p. 68.
31. AL pp. 134–5.
32. SF p. 96.
33. DG p. 81.
34. GSO p. 107.
35. Ibid. p. 108.
36. Ibid. p. 110.
37. Ibid. p. 112.
38. Ibid. p. 115.
39. Ibid. p. 116.
40. Ibid. p. 119.
41. Ibid. p. 120.
42. Ibid. p. 128.
43. Ibid.
44. GOS p. 139.
45. GOS p. 140.
46. Ibid. p. 145.
47. Ibid. p. 146.

5   *I'm an Aesthetic Sham*

1. DG p. 83.
2. Ibid.
3. Ibid.

4. Vyvyan Holland, *Oscar Wilde* (Thames & Hudson, 1960), p. 29.
5. Ibid.
6. W.A. Darlington, *The World of Gilbert and Sullivan* (Peter Nevill, 1950), pp. 75–6.
7. GSO p. 153.
8. Ibid. p. 154.
9. Ibid. pp. 162–3.
10. Ibid. p. 165.
11. Ibid.
12. Ibid. p. 171.
13. Ibid. p. 174.
14. Ibid. p. 179.
15. Ibid. pp. 181–2.
16. Ibid.
17. Ibid. p. 190.
18. Ibid. p. 197.
19. Ibid. p. 198.
20. Ibid. p. 199.
21. Ibid. p. 200.
22. LB p. 211.
23. GSO p. 196.
24. Jessie Bond, *Life and Reminiscences* (John Land, The Bodley Head, 1930), p. 92.
25. LB pp. 213–14.
26. CB p. 98.
27. Ibid.
28. Ibid. p. 97.
29. Bond, op. cit., p. 102.
30. GOP, Third Series, p. 31.
31. Ibid.
32. Ibid. p. 22.
33. Ibid. p. 34.
34. Ibid. p. 37.
35. Ibid. p. 73.
36. Jeremy Maas, *Victorian Painters* (Harrison House, 1988), p. 148.
37. SF p. 123.

6 *The Peer and the Peri*

1. SF p. 129.
2. GSO p. 204.
3. Ibid. p. 207.
4. Ibid. p. 209.
5. Ibid. p. 211.
6. Ibid. p. 212.
7. Ibid. p. 213.
8. Ibid. pp. 213–14.
9. Ibid. p. 214.
10. Ibid. p. 216.
11. Ibid. p. 219.
12. Ibid.
13. Ibid. p. 221.
14. Ibid. p. 228.
15. Ibid. p. 229.
16. Ibid. pp. 229–30.
17. Ibid. p. 230.
18. Ibid. p. 231.
19. Ibid.
20. Ibid. p. 237.
21. Ibid. p. 239.
22. Ibid. p. 240.
23. Ibid. p. 244.
24. Ibid. p. 246.
25. Ibid. p. 250.
26. Ibid.
27. Ibid. p. 253.
28. Ibid.
29. Ibid.
30. Ibid.
31. Ibid. p. 254.
32. Jessie Bond, *Life and Reminiscences* (John Land, The Bodley Head, 1930), p. 109.
33. *Echo*, 27 November 1882. Quoted in Alan James, *Gilbert and Sullivan* (Omnibus Press, 1989), p. 95.
34. Ibid. p. 97
35. G.K. Chesterton, *Orthodoxy* (Bodley Head, 1909), p. 66.
36. G.K. Chesterton, Introduction to A.H. Goodwin, *Gilbert and Sullivan* (J.M. Dent, 1926), p. xiii.
37. Ibid. p. xiv.
38. LB p. 238.
39. GOS p. 237.
40. Ibid. p. 234.
41. LB p. 238.
42. GSO p. 240.

43. Isaac Goldberg, *The Story of Gilbert and Sullivan* (John Murray, 1925), p. 280.
44. LB p. 238.
45. Ibid.

7 *Castle Adamant*
1. SF p. 137.
2. GSO p. 261.
3. LB p. 255.
4. GSO p. 264.
5. Ibid. p. 269.
6. Ibid. p. 273.
7. Ibid. p. 275.
8. Ibid. p. 284.
9. Ibid. pp. 284–5.
10. Ibid. p. 293.
11. Ibid. p. 296.
12. Ibid. p. 297.
13. Ibid.
14. Ibid. p. 300.
15. Ibid.
16. Ibid. p. 303.
17. Ibid.
18. Ibid. p. 304.
19. Ibid. p. 310.
20. Ibid. p. 311.
21. Ibid. pp. 311–12.
22. Alfred, Lord Tennyson, *The Princess* (Library Edition, Macmillan, 1892), p. 138.
23. SF p. 139.
24. Ibid.
25. Ibid. p. 140.
26. Ibid.
27. Ibid. p. 141.
28. Ibid.
29. Ibid. p. 145.

8 *The Mikado*
1. SF p. 145.
2. GSO p. 319.
3. Ibid. p. 320.
4. Ibid.
5. Ibid.
6. Ibid. p. 326.
7. Ibid. p. 327.

8. Ibid.
9. Ibid. p. 328.
10. Ibid. p. 329.
11. Ibid. p. 330.
12. Ibid. p. 331.
13. Ibid. p. 333.
14. Ibid. p. 335.
15. Ibid. p. 338.
16. Ibid. p. 340.
17. Ibid. p. 341.
18. Ibid. p. 343
19. Ibid. p. 345.
20. Ibid. p. 347.
21. Ibid. p. 353.
22. Ibid. p. 355.
23. Ibid. p. 361.
24. Ibid. p. 362.
25. Ibid. p. 364.
26. Ibid. p. 367.
27. Ibid. p. 369.
28. Ibid. p. 370.
29. Ibid. p. 371.
30. Ibid. p. 372.
31. *Punch*, 28 March 1885.
32. Ibid.
33. Ibid.
34. HP p. 122.

9 *The Witch's Curse*
1. Percy M. Young, *Sir Arthur Sullivan* (J. M. Dent, 1971), p. 138.
2. Ibid. p. 139.
3. Ibid. p. 140.
4. Ibid.
5. Ibid. p. 142.
6. Ibid.
7. AJ p. 215.
8. Ibid. p. 226.
9. S. T. Adair Fitzgerald, *The Story of the Savoy Operas* (Stanley Paul, 1924), p. 126.
10. Ibid. p. 127.
11. Ibid. p. 128.
12. GSO p. 376.
13. Ibid.

14. Ibid. p. 377.
15. Ibid. p. 378.
16. Ibid.
17. Ibid. p. 380.
18. Ibid. p. 385.
19. Ibid. p. 395.
20. Ibid. p. 399.
21. Ibid. p. 401–2.
22. Ibid. p. 405.
23. Ibid. p. 407.
24. Ibid. p. 413.
25. Ibid.
26. Ibid. p. 415.
27. Ibid. p. 419.
28. Ibid. p. 421.
29. Ibid. p. 424.
30. Ibid. p. 426.
31. Ibid. p. 429.
32. Ibid. p. 431.
33. Jessie Bond, *Life and Reminiscences* (John Land, The Bodley Head, 1930), p. 142.

10   *The Merryman and his Maid*
1. LB p. 299.
2. Ibid.
3. Ibid. p. 306.
4. SF p. 174.
5. *Punch*, 13 October 1888.
6. DG p. 106.
7. Ibid. p. 107.
8. GSO p. 437.
9. Ibid. p. 439.
10. Ibid.
11. Ibid.
12. Ibid. p. 440.
13. Ibid. p. 444.
14. Ibid. p. 445.
15. Ibid. pp. 445–6.
16. Ibid. p. 446.
17. Ibid. p. 447.
18. Ibid. p. 452.
19. Ibid. p. 459.
20. Ibid. p. 462.
21. Ibid. p. 464.
22. Ibid. p. 466.

23. Ibid.
24. Ibid. p. 469.
25. Ibid. p. 473.
26. Ibid. p. 475.
27. Ibid. p. 477.
28. Ibid. p. 479.
29. Ibid.
30. Ibid.
31. Ibid. p. 483.
32. Ibid. p. 488.
33. *Punch*, 13 October 1888.
34. Ibid.
35. Ibid.
36. *The Times*, 6 October 1888.
37. Bond, pp. 148–9.
38. Townley Searle, *W. S. Gilbert* (Alexander-Ousley, 1931), p. 56.
39. Ibid.

11   *I am a Cypher in the Theatre*
1. SF p. 185.
2. Ibid. p. 186.
3. Ibid.
4. Ibid. p. 187.
5. Ibid. p. 188.
6. Ibid.
7. Ibid.
8. LB p. 329.
9. SF p. 189.
10. Ibid.
11. Ibid.
12. Ibid. p. 190.
13. Ibid.
14. Ibid. p. 191.
15. Ibid.
16. Ibid. p. 192.
17. GSO p. 500.
18. Ibid. p. 503.
19. Ibid. p. 506.
20. Ibid. p. 508.
21. Ibid. p. 509.
22. Ibid.
23. Ibid. pp 510–11.
24. Ibid. p. 515.
25. Ibid. p. 516.

26. Ibid. p. 521.
27. Ibid. p. 526.
28. Ibid. p. 528.
29. Ibid. p. 532.
30. Ibid. p. 536.
31. Ibid. p. 540.
32. Ibid. p. 557.
33. Ibid. p. 559.
34. Ibid. p. 560.
35. SF p. 197.
36. Ibid.

12   The Flowers of Progress
1. Jessie Bond, *Life and Reminiscences* (John Land, The Bodley Head, 1930), p. 159.
2. SF pp. 199–200.
3. LB p. 350.
4. SF p. 201.
5. HP p.   .
6. SF p. 202.
7. HP p. 142.
8. Ibid.
9. Gilbert Draft.
10. LB p. 35.
11. Ibid.
12. Ibid. p. 357.
13. HP p. 147.
14. LB p. 359.
15. Ibid. p. 360. Quoted from Charles L. Graves, *Hubert Parry* (Macmillan, 1926).
16. GOP p. 381.
17. Ibid. pp. 400–1.
18. Ibid.
19. SF p. 215.
20. AJ p. 342.
21. SF p. 211.
22. Ibid.
23. Goldberg p. 404.

13   Utopia, Limited
1. HP p. 172.
2. John Wolfson, *The Final Curtain. The Last Gilbert and Sullivan Operas* (Chappell and André Deutsch, 1976), p. 26.

3. Ibid. p. 32.
4. Ibid.
5. S.J. Adair Fitzgerald, *The Story of the Savoy Operas* (Stanley Paul, 1924), p. 171.
6. GSO p. 564.
7. Ibid. p. 565.
8. Ibid. pp. 565–6.
9. Ibid. p. 566.
10. Ibid. p. 567.
11. Ibid. pp. 567–8.
12. Ibid. p. 569.
13. Ibid. p. 570.
14. Ibid. p. 572.
15. Ibid. p. 574.
16. Ibid. p. 573.
17. Ibid. p. 578.
18. Ibid. p. 585.
19. Ibid. p. 590.
20. Ibid.
21. Ibid. p. 596.
22. Ibid. p. 597.
23. Ibid. p. 598.
24. Ibid.
25. Ibid. p. 599.
26. Ibid. pp. 601–2.
27. Ibid. p. 602.
28. Ibid. p. 606.
29. Ibid. p. 609.
30. Ibid. p. 610.
31. Ibid. p. 611.
32. Ibid. p. 614.
33. Ibid. p. 619.
34. Ibid. p. 620.
35. Ibid. p. 621.
36. Ibid. p. 626.
37. Ibid.
38. Wolfson , op. cit., p. 54.

14   The Grand Duke
1. John Wolfson, *The Final Curtain, The Last Gilbert and Sullivan Operas* (Chappell and André Deutsch, 1976), p. 54.
2. GOP p. 101.
3. Ibid. p. 112.
4. Ibid. p. 107.

5. Ibid. p. 108.
6. Ibid.
7. Ibid. p. 125.
8. Ibid. p. 144.
9. Ibid. p. 134.
10. GSO p. 634.
11. Ibid. p. 635.
12. Ibid.
13. Ibid. p. 640.
14. Ibid. p. 641.
15. Ibid. p. 645.
16. Ibid. p. 649.
17. Ibid. p. 650.
18. Ibid. p. 653.
19. Ibid. p. 658.
20. Ibid. p. 661.
21. Ibid. p. 663.
22. Ibid. p. 668.
23. Ibid. p. 671.
24. Ibid. pp. 674–5.
25. Ibid. p. 683.
26. Ibid. p. 688.
27. Ibid. p. 691.
28. Wolfson, op. cit., p. 98.
29. Ibid. p. 101.

15 Fallen Fairies
1. S. J. Adair Fitzgerald, *The Story of the Savoy Operas* (Stanley Paul, 1924), p. 181.
2. LB p. 388.
3. Henry A. Lytton, *The Secrets of a Savoyard* (Jarrolds, *c.* 1922), p. 53.
4. DG p. 206.
5. Ibid.
6. HP p. 192.
7. Ibid. p. 193.
8. Ibid.
9. Ibid. p. 194.
10. Ibid. p. 195.
11. Ibid.
12. Ibid.
13. Ibid. p. 197.
14. Ibid. pp. 200–1.
15. Ibid. p. 202.
16. Ibid.

17. Percy M. Young, *Sir Arthur Sullivan* (J. M. Dent, 1971), p. 250.
18. SF p. 238.
19. Ibid. p. 240.
20. Ibid. p. 243.
21. Ibid.
22. Ibid.
23. Young, op. cit., p. 256.
24. LB p. 392.
25. SF p. 249.
26. AJ p. 391.
27. Ibid. p. 392.
28. SF p. 252.
29. Ibid.
30. Rudyard Kipling, *Verse*, Inclusive Edition 1885–1926, 'The Absent–Minded Beggar' (Hodder & Stoughton, 1927), p. 451.
31. SF p. 260.
32. Ibid. p. 261.
33. Ibid.
34. Ibid.
35. Ibid. p. 262.
36. Ibid. p. 265.
37. LB p. 402.
38. DG p. 207.
39. Ibid. p. 208.
40. HP p. 212.
41. DG p. 213.
42. HP p. 244.
43. Ibid.
44. Ibid.
45. DG p. 196.
46. Ibid.
47. Adair Fitzgerald, op. cit., p. 211.
48. Ibid. p. 213.
49. GOP p. 234.
50. HP p. 251.
51. Ibid. pp. 253–4.
52. Ibid. p. 255.
53. DG p. 222.
54. Ibid.
55. GSO p. 204.

Index

Index